"Though much excellent work has been done on understanding utilitarianism itself, and on both the attractions of and problems with it, the fundamental debate remains as intractable as ever. The state-of-the-art essays that follow bring out clearly how much progress has been made since... the early utilitarians, as well how careful and imaginative reflection can take us yet further in understanding the issues at stake and possible resolutions of them."

Roger Crisp, *from the Foreword*

Should We Maximize Utility?

Utilitarianism directs us to act in ways that impartially maximize welfare or utility or at least aim to do that. Some find this view highly compelling. Others object that it has intuitively repugnant results, that it condones evildoing and injustice, that it is excessively imposing and controlling, that it is alienating, and that it fails to offer meaningful, practical guidance.

In this 'Little Debates' volume, James Lenman argues that utilitarianism's directive to improve the whole universe on a cosmic time scale is apt to lead it down a path of imperious moral overreach. The project, he further maintains, ultimately shipwrecks on an extreme lack of epistemic humility in framing the determinants of what is morally right and wrong beyond the limits of what we can ever hope to know. Utilitarianism thus leaves us morally clueless. In contrast, Ben Bramble seeks to develop and defend an original form of utilitarianism, less vulnerable than other, more familiar versions to a number of important objections, including those raised by Lenman. He aims to avoid such unappealing results by presenting it as a claim about what we have the most reason to do and not as a theory of right action, which Bramble urges we should understand quite differently by reference to what would motivate virtuous people.

Ben Bramble is a Lecturer in Philosophy at the Australian National University and a Mission Specialist at ANU's Institute for Space. He is the author of *The Passing of Momentary Well-Being* (Routledge, 2018), *Pandemic Ethics* (2020), and numerous articles, including "The Defective Character Solution to the Non-Identity Problem" (2021).

James Lenman is Professor of Philosophy at the University of Sheffield. He has published many articles, mostly on metaethics and normative ethics, and a book, *The Possibility of Moral Community* (2024).

Roger Crisp is Professor of Moral Philosophy at Oxford University.

Little Debates About Big Questions
Tyron Goldschmidt
Fellow of the Rutgers Center for Philosophy of Religion, USA
Dustin Crummett
University of Washington, Tacoma, USA

About the series:

Philosophy asks questions about the fundamental nature of reality, our place in the world, and what we should do. Some of these questions are perennial: for example, *Do we have free will? What is morality?* Some are much newer: for example, *How far should free speech on campus extend? Are race, sex and gender social constructs?* But all of these are among the big questions in philosophy and they remain controversial.

Each book in the *Little Debates About Big Questions* series features two professors on opposite sides of a big question. Each author presents their own side, and the authors then exchange objections and replies. Short, lively, and accessible, these debates showcase diverse and deep answers. Pedagogical features include standard form arguments, section summaries, bolded key terms and principles, glossaries, and annotated reading lists.

The debate format is an ideal way to learn about controversial topics. Whereas the usual essay or book risks overlooking objections against its own proposition or misrepresenting the opposite side, in a debate each side can make their case at equal length, and then present objections the other side must consider. Debates have a more conversational and fun style too, and we selected particularly talented philosophers—in substance and style—for these kinds of encounters.

Debates can be combative—sometimes even descending into anger and animosity. But debates can also be cooperative. While our authors disagree strongly, they work together to help each other and the reader get clearer on the ideas, arguments, and objections. This is intellectual progress, and a much-needed model for civil and constructive disagreement.

The substance and style of the debates will captivate interested readers new to the questions. But there's enough to interest experts too. The debates will be especially useful for courses in philosophy and related subjects—whether as primary or secondary readings—and a few debates can be combined to make up the reading for an entire course.

We thank the authors for their help in constructing this series. We are honored to showcase their work. They are all preeminent scholars or rising-stars in their fields, and through these debates they share what's been discovered with a wider audience. This is a paradigm for public philosophy, and will impress upon students, scholars, and other interested readers the enduring importance of debating the big questions.

Published Titles:

Should You Choose to Live Forever?
A Debate
By Stephen Cave and John Martin Fischer

Is it Wrong to Buy Sex?
A Debate
By Holly Lawford-Smith and Angie Pepper

Should We Maximize Utility?
A Debate about Utilitarianism
By Ben Bramble and James Lenman

For more information about this series, please visit: https://www.routledge.com/Little-Debates-about-Big-Questions/book-series/LDABQ

Should We Maximize Utility?

A Debate about Utilitarianism

Ben Bramble and James Lenman

Routledge
Taylor & Francis Group
NEW YORK AND LONDON

Designed cover image: Getty Images / Apostrophes

First published 2025
by Routledge
605 Third Avenue, New York, NY 10158

and by Routledge
4 Park Square, Milton Park, Abingdon, Oxon, OX14 4RN

Routledge is an imprint of the Taylor & Francis Group, an informa business

© 2025 Ben Bramble and James Lenman

The right of Ben Bramble and James Lenman to be identified as authors of this work has been asserted in accordance with sections 77 and 78 of the Copyright, Designs and Patents Act 1988.

All rights reserved. No part of this book may be reprinted or reproduced or utilised in any form or by any electronic, mechanical, or other means, now known or hereafter invented, including photocopying and recording, or in any information storage or retrieval system, without permission in writing from the publishers.

Trademark notice: Product or corporate names may be trademarks or registered trademarks, and are used only for identification and explanation without intent to infringe.

ISBN: 978-1-032-29105-5 (hbk)
ISBN: 978-1-032-29104-8 (pbk)
ISBN: 978-1-003-30004-5 (ebk)

DOI: 10.4324/9781003300045

Typeset in Sabon
by SPi Technologies India Pvt Ltd (Straive)

For our students, past, present and future.

Contents

Foreword   xiii
BY ROGER CRISP

I   Against Utilitarianism   1

1   Utilitarianism and Its Discontents   5

2   Goodness   16

3   Welfare   28

4   Repugnant Conclusions   38

5   Intuitions   51

6   Cluelessness   60

7   Cluelessness and the Climate   74

8   Beyond Utilitarianism   84

II   For Utilitarianism   95

9   Introduction   99

10	Total or Person-Affecting Utilitarianism?	103
11	Philosophy of Swine	112
12	Cluelessness	127
13	Reasons or Requirements?	135
14	Demandingness	138
15	The Alienation Objection	146
16	The 'Harming to Help' Objection	156
17	Conclusion	159
III	**Reply to Bramble**	**161**
IV	**Response to Lenman**	**181**
	Glossary	195
	Further Reading	210
	References	213
	Index	222

Foreword

Bernard Williams closed his influential 'Critique of Utilitarianism' (1973) with the following: 'The important issues that utilitarianism raises should be discussed in contexts more rewarding than that of utilitarianism itself. The day cannot be too far off in which we hear no more of it.' The wide-ranging, profound, and engaging discussion between Ben Bramble and James Lenman in this book is enough to disprove both of Williams's claims, even if we leave aside the huge progress made in philosophical ethics over the last fifty years on utilitarianism, its nature, advantages, and disadvantages.

When utilitarianism emerged is itself a difficult question, exacerbated by the lack of agreement on exactly what it is. One key moment was the publication in 1672 of *De legibus naturae* by the philosopher Richard Cumberland. Cumberland became the bishop of Peterborough, and his book provides good evidence of the theological origins of utilitarianism. According to the theological utilitarian, God created the world for us so that we could be happy within it. Since God cares equally for each of us, and is rational, he will create a world containing the greatest overall happiness. God is, of course, perfectly virtuous, and so we should follow him, ourselves seeking to promote that same goal. The related conceptions of equality and of rationality in this brief argument are revealing: strictly speaking, God loves not each of us equally but each element of the happiness of each of us (i.e., he does not distinguish between each us as persons, or care how happiness is distributed between us), and the divine attitude to happiness is to maximize it. Those ideas – now usually shorn of their religious origins – still remain as attractive to some as they do rebarbative.

The name 'utilitarianism' was coined in the nineteenth-century. Even then it brought with it connotations of well-made furniture rather than fundamental evaluation of worlds, persons, actions, or whatever, and the term 'the greatest happiness principle' would have been much better, but it is probably now too late to change it. The word 'consequentialism', invented by Elizabeth Anscombe to describe the difference between utilitarianism (which she understands as the view requiring us to bring about the best overall consequences rather than avoid certain actions such as killing the innocent, or lying) is even more misleading. For any utilitarian can badge themselves as non-consequentialist by claiming that the only action we must perform is that of maximizing overall happiness, regardless of the consequences (which might include one's killing, or having killed, the innocent, say, or lying, or having lied). Approaching utilitarianism with pre-prepared distinctions is likely to mislead. Those with a serious interest should try carefully to work out what it says, and why people continue to be attracted or repelled by it.

So, what does it say? At its most general, utilitarianism is a theory of evaluation that can be applied to anything. The best possible cosmos, or history of the cosmos, the best possible universe, world, life, week, day, experience, or moment is that containing the greatest overall happiness. What is 'happiness'? Again we should take care so as not to be misled. 'Happiness' is here best taken as a 'technical' (or 'jargon') term for 'well-being' or 'welfare' – that is, what is 'good *for*' anything. This notion of 'goodness for' is somewhat basic, and best understood with reference to paradigm cases – 'this severe pain is bad for me, making my life go worse for me, in a way that the scratch on this chest of drawers is not bad for it' – and to contrasting types of value, such as aesthetic (what is beautiful, for example), or moral (what is right or wrong, say, or kind or cruel). All these types of 'ultimate' or 'final' or 'intrinsic' value should be distinguished from 'instrumental' value (as possessed by the pill I take to stop the pain in my head – which is, of course, 'utility', in its usual sense).

Note again the emphasis on maximization in utilitarianism. The *best* cosmos or experience is that which contains the *most* happiness – that is, the greatest balance of what is good for the possessors of well-being in that cosmos or the subject of that experience. (As Lenman notes, this notion of overall 'goodness' has been questioned by some philosophers in recent years, who have argued that a world, say, cannot be *just better* than another, only better in a certain respect. But utilitarians give us such a respect: that of degrees of overall happiness. Most English speakers will not find it difficult to answer the question, 'Is a world that contains nothing but entirely innocent individuals suffering horribly better than one containing only entirely innocent individuals enjoying their lives, with no pain?') On the utilitarian view of 'goodness' or 'bestness', then, it does not matter how happiness is distributed, and this is what lies behind many of the objections to utilitarianism discussed by Bramble and Lenman, in which innocent people are sacrificed for the overall good, as well as the problem of evil raised against the claim of God's existence: it may be that this is the overall happiest world God could have brought about, but does that justify the suffering or the fawn caught in the forest fire?

The globally evaluative conception of utilitarianism is also found in the arguments of Cumberland and later utilitarians, but the view that developed over the centuries was narrower and concerned morality in particular. The right action is that which maximizes overall happiness, or 'utility', and actions are wrong to the extent that they fail to do this (so an action which almost produces the maximum is not as objectionable as one which produces a world much more distant). In ordinary life, though less so in philosophy, it is standard for people to see a possible conflict between their moral reasons (to return a lost wallet, say) and their self-interest (to take a holiday using the contents of the wallet). Most philosophy textbooks will tell you that utilitarianism is extremely demanding, but it need not be if it is seen as explaining one source of our reasons. In other words, it would be entirely coherent to claim that, overall, my self-interested reason to take the holiday outweighs my (utilitarian) moral reason to return the wallet (the contents of which I might know will be donated to some effective charity). As Bramble notes, a utilitarian may prefer to express their view with reference to *reasons* rather than *rightness* alone. But once self-interest is out of the picture, a reasons-based view will be the same as the standard version of utilitarianism, expressed in terms of rightness and wrongness.

Utilitarianism is a highly contested view, and it would be natural to see the debate as between those who accept and those who deny the utilitarian principle. In one sense, this is clearly right. But it is important to note that, if we take the utilitarian principle as just one principle among others, it is all but undeniable: other things equal, one should bring about the greatest happiness. Imagine you can buy two possible toys as a gift for a young relative and have narrowed down the decision to A and B, both of which are identical except B will make the child happier. Buying A rather than B would be, literally, pointless. Since at least the time of Plato and Aristotle, morality has been understood as a set of principles, requiring us to perform certain actions, and not to perform others. The utilitarian principle could be said to be present in any plausible set. But utilitarianism emerged as a self-standing position when its proponents saw its potential in two respects: its intrinsic plausibility as a single principle (how can it be rational to bring about less than the best possible world?), and its capacity to serve as an underpinning for all other principles (we should aim to be just, generous, courageous, even-tempered, and so on *because* that is the most effective way to promote happiness).

Utilitarianism, as we have seen, is extremely impartial: one unit of happiness is worth the same, whether it occurs in the life of an already very well-off individual, or someone much worse-off, perhaps someone whose life is of negative value. This lies behind some of the most serious difficulties it faces: distributive justice (many will say that a unit of happiness given to a worse-off individual has greater moral value than it would if given to a better-off individual), rights (individuals are not to be treated as mere means to the happiness of others, as in the 'footbridge' case discussed by both Bramble and Lenman), or special obligations (I have stronger reason to provide a unit of happiness to my child on their birthday than to some child unrelated to me). Here, alongside the power of the idea of the greatest happiness, utilitarians can seek to undermine common-sense morality as a self-standing system of justification, not only by bringing out its instrumental value in promoting happiness but also by pointing out its contingent, evolutionary sources (imagine that we find that Martians are impartial, utility-maximizing utilitarians, and how puzzled they would be to find that we are ready to sacrifice happiness on the ground of biological relatedness, or the avoiding of involvement in certain causal relations, such as pushing someone over a bridge).

The contingency of our moral beliefs (note also the dramatic differences between human moral systems across both space and time) raises the question of moral epistemology – that is, of what epistemic justification a utilitarian should seek for their view. On one view, defended by Lenman, we should seek coherence in our overall moral views so that it counts strongly against utilitarianism that it conflicts with so many of our deeply held moral beliefs. But a utilitarian might argue that the utility of common-sense morality itself provides some form of coherence between it and utilitarianism, even if the common-sense principles are downgraded to the status of means to overall happiness. Or they might point to the 'philosophical intuitionist' approach recommended in the work many utilitarians have seen as the greatest expression of utilitarian ethics, Henry Sidgwick's *The Methods of Ethics*, first published 150 years ago: "[W]e should expect that the history of Moral Philosophy ... would be a history of attempts to enunciate, in full breadth and clearness, those primary intuitions of Reason, by the scientific application of which the common moral thought of mankind may be at once systematised and corrected" (7th ed., 373–4). Sidgwick himself deduces utilitarianism from a plurality of such allegedly-self-evident principles, but many utilitarians will claim that, after careful reflection, they can see that the only justification for any action is its maximizing overall happiness.

Here we can grasp two ways in which a view might be described as 'historically utilitarian' (i.e., stated by some utilitarians) or 'essentially utilitarian' (i.e., a necessary component of any utilitarian position). As Bramble and Lenman explain, many utilitarians – most, in fact – have been hedonists about well-being or welfare: an individual's life is made good for them by nothing other than pleasure, and bad by nothing other than pain or suffering, the value of a life for the individual living it consisting in the overall balance between pleasure and pain. Over the centuries, many have objected that there is more to life than pleasure and pain, one of the most famous expressions of the position being Robert Nozick's 'experience machine', which makes an appearance in the essays of both Bramble and Lenman. It is important to remember that an objection to a particular theory of happiness (or 'utility') propounded by utilitarians is not an objection to utilitarianism. Utilitarianism is the view that worlds, actions, or whatever are to be evaluated purely in terms of how effectively they promote happiness (that is, 'goodness for'), whatever happiness might be.

The main focus of the debate between utilitarians and their opponents, as this volume well illustrates, is the question of right action. But this question must be understood not just as concerning which actions are right, but *why* they are right. Over the last few centuries, utilitarians have repeatedly been charged with advocating many forms of immorality, including the killing of the innocent, in order to prevent a riot, perhaps, or to save the maximum number of lives. And it has often been pointed out how the impartiality of utilitarianism leads to alienation, to its failing to recognize the significance of human bonds and relationships. The standard utilitarian response has been to claim that the theory is in fact less revisionist than it seems: it will maximize utility overall if sheriffs are taught never to frame innocent people, if doctors are taught never to kill people for their organs, and if people are encouraged to act out of love and concern for those close to them. These are good responses to the charges as they have standardly been made. But they also bring out how those charges *should* be made. Perhaps utilitarianism does tell us not to punish the innocent and to take special care of our own children. But – the objection should go – it fails to provide the full account of why we should do these things. We might agree that *one* reason we should do these things is that it will increase happiness overall (recall how the utilitarian principle will be found in any plausible non-utilitarian morality). But, the opponent should say, there are other reasons, which utilitarians entirely fail to recognize: it is unjust to kill the innocent, and we have directed duties to our children quite independent of any non-directed duty to improve the world.

This debate between utilitarianism and a pluralistic ethics which goes beyond utilitarianism is central to contemporary moral philosophy, and, because it is about how all of us should live our lives, to all of us. Though much excellent work has been done on understanding utilitarianism itself, and on both the attractions of and problems with it, the fundamental debate remains as intractable as ever. The state-of-the-art chapters that follow bring out clearly how much progress has been made since the work of Cumberland and the early utilitarians, as well as how careful and imaginative reflection can take us yet further in understanding the issues at stake and possible resolutions of them.

– Roger Crisp

1 Against Utilitarianism
James Lenman

生而不有.

What we give birth to we do not own.
Laozi

Acknowledgements

I presented this material in draft over a series of six online lectures at Shandong University, China, in September 2022. I am grateful to Peng Guo, who did me the great honour of inviting me to do this and organized everything; to Jie Tian, Yingying Tang, Jiafeng Zhu, Lun Zhang, and Yong Li, who acted as my respondents for their thoughtful and valuable comments; and to everyone who took part, providing me with such an enjoyable, rewarding, and instructive experience. I am also grateful to Jules Holroyd, Brad Hooker, Anneli Jefferson, Rosanna Keefe, Jonathan Parry, and Valerie Tiberius for their helpful comments. Ben Davies gave me good advice about the literature. Conversations with Eric Olson and Dominic Gregory helped me sharpen stuff up. Ed Matthews helped me make the graphs in Chapter 4 look presentable. I used draft versions of this material as teaching materials in my undergraduate ethics course at Sheffield in the academic years 2021–2 and 2022–3. I am grateful to the students in those courses, and all my students, who help me in more ways than they can know.

I owe a particular debt of gratitude to Ben Bramble. This project was his initiative, and I am very honoured to have had the opportunity to collaborate with such a brilliant and distinguished young philosopher. We disagree about fundamental things—that is the reason this book exists—but disagreeing with Ben has been a very amicable and rewarding experience.

Chapter 1

Utilitarianism and Its Discontents

1.1 Consequentialism, Welfarism, Utilitarianism

My concern in this chapter will be mostly exegetical, aiming to brief readers on what utilitarianism is and what some of the best-known arguments against it are.

Ethics is the study of how we should live. And one of the most popular and apparently attractive answers to the question of how to live is that we should try to do good. And not just *some* good but *as much good as we can*. If you think that and if you think that is, in essence, the *whole* story about what we ought to do then you are a *consequentialist*.

A classic statement of consequentialism is by G. E. Moore:

> Our 'duty'... can only be defined as that action, which will cause more good to exist in the Universe than any possible alternative. And what is 'right' or 'morally permissible' only differs from this, as what will *not* cause *less* good than any possible alternative. When, therefore, Ethics presumes to assert that certain ways of acting are 'duties' it presumes to assert that to act in those ways will always produce the greatest possible sum of good.[1]

For consequentialists, then, the good is prior to the right which is understood by reference to it. We start out by saying what goodness is and then characterize rightness as whatever makes *the world*, as Moore has it, *the Universe*, as good as possible.

The consequentialist, as I am here understanding them, thinks a lot in terms of *worlds*—that is to say, complete possible worlds, ways the world, everything there is, might be. It is such complete possible worlds, what Jack Smart called *total situations*,[2] that we think of as each having a certain value, a certain amount of overall goodness such that we can rank these worlds in order of their goodness. What we ought then to do is seek to bring about, to make actual, a world that is as high up this ranking as possible.

There is not one ranking for me, another for you, or anything like that: Just one single ranking that orders worlds by goodness.[3]

Yes, but what is goodness? And here a natural and popular claim is that goodness is happiness or, as it is often also known, **welfare** or **well-being** or sometimes **utility**. (These words often get used here more or less interchangeably.) If you believe this, you are a **welfarist**.

My welfare, or well-being, roughly speaking, is what I have when my life goes well for me, yours what you have when your life goes well for you. There are different ways of understanding welfare here, and people argue about which is the best way. Some think of it just as having pleasurable experiences and avoiding painful ones. Some think of it as getting what you want. Some think of it as comprising various rather more particular ingredients thought to make for a good human life. These varying understandings of welfare mean welfarism comes in a variety of flavours. I'll say more about this in Chapter 3.

If we combine these two claims, consequentialism and welfarism, we get the claim that what we ought to seek to do is to create as much net welfare as possible, to make as much positive difference as we possibly can to how happy people are. This popular and to many attractive claim is what is usually known as *utilitarianism*.[4]

I say 'people', but most utilitarians think human persons are not the only things that are capable of being happy. Other kinds of things can plausibly also have welfare, notably at least some animals. More speculatively, it is widely supposed likely there may come a day when we can and maybe do make artificial minds that can meaningfully be said to have welfare. If and when this happens, their welfare counts too. Even more speculatively, there may perhaps be sentient creatures living on other planets. It seems very unlikely now that anything we do might have any effect on such vastly distant creatures, but the future is a long time, and who knows what it might hold. Anyway, they count too.

Utilitarianism is a very simple ethical theory and a hugely influential one. Many people think it immensely compelling and find it hard to compute how any thoughtful, morally decent person could deny it. Many people who take themselves to be committed to trying always to think about life in a rational and scientific spirit take that commitment to push them ineluctably to accept some form of utilitarianism. For other people, utilitarianism is a profoundly mistaken way of understanding our ethical lives. As my contribution to this book will make clear, I am one of the latter group of people.

1.2 Some Problems: Hungry Monsters and Barely Happy Multitudes

The utilitarian wants to, as they like to say, *maximize utility*, to bring about as much utility, welfare, as possible, but just what does that mean?

Utilitarians tend not to mind much where happiness is so long as there is as much of it as possible. Lots of people living short, happy lives might be better when everything is weighed up than a small number of people living long and happy lives.

Also, it might turn out that an extremely large number of people living lives that were on balance happy, but only *just*, might be better, with regard to how much happiness there was in total, than a much less massive population all leading blissfully happy lives.

Or there might be a single creature with a massive capacity for happiness which we could fully satisfy only by denying happiness to a very large number whose capacity for happiness was more ordinary.

We here meet already two famous objections to utilitarianism. Like many objections to utilitarianism these take the form of supposed **reductio** arguments. A **reductio** argument, or **reductio ad absurdum** argument to give it its full name, is an argument that shows some falsehood or absurdity to follow from some claim which we might thereby suppose refuted. Such arguments identify things which the utilitarian seems committed to saying are true that are not very plausible and attractive. Utilitarianism, we noted at the outset, is an apparently attractive claim, but if it turns out to have unattractive consequences, we may conclude that its prima facie attractiveness does not survive close scrutiny.

Our first two problems for utilitarianism are as follows:

> ***The Repugnant Conclusion.*** This was the name given by Derek Parfit in his influential book *Reasons and Persons* to the conclusion that a vast population living drab but OK lives is to be preferred to a much smaller population living wonderful lives.[5]

> *The Utility Monster.* This was dreamed up by Robert Nozick in 1974. Utilitarian theory is embarrassed by the possibility of *utility monsters* which get enormously greater gains in utility from any sacrifice of others than those others lose. For, unacceptably, the theory seems to require that we all be sacrificed in the monster's maw in order to increase total utility.[6]

There are no utility monsters among us today that we need to worry about. But perhaps one day we might figure out how to make one. In those circumstances, the utilitarian might be forced to the unpalatable conclusion that we would have a moral duty to do so and proceed to feed ourselves to it if that was the way to generate the most utility. The thought is not wholly fanciful, as we will see.

A utilitarian might aim to mitigate the first of these worries by espousing a version of utilitarianism that seeks to maximize not *total* but *average* utility. But this **average utilitarianism** might seem to have unsatisfactory consequences. Consider Adam and Eve. (The example is also Derek Parfit's.[7]) Adam and Eve are the first humans newly created by God. But God doesn't instruct them to go forth and multiply. He gives them a choice. He has supplied them with birth control pills if they would rather not have any kids. He also tells them a thing. That thing is that if they do have kids, their descendants will go on to people the Earth for a very long time and they will all be very happy indeed. But while they will all be very happy indeed, none of them will attain quite the extraordinary level of happiness enjoyed, whatever they may decide about having kids, by Adam and Eve themselves. All their descendants will be *slightly* less happy than they are. So by having kids Adam and Eve will make average utility less than it would otherwise have been. So even though their kids, grandkids, etc., will be very happy indeed, average utilitarianism seems to say that in these circumstances it is morally wrong for Adam and Eve to procreate. Which seems a little silly.

1.3 Rawls's Problem: Distributive Justice and the Separateness of Persons

John Rawls, right at the start of his great book *A Theory of Justice*, wrote,

> Each person possesses an inviolability founded on justice that even the welfare of society as a whole cannot override. For this reason justice denies that the loss of freedom for some is made

right by a greater good shared by others. It does not allow that the sacrifices imposed on a few are outweighed by the greater sum of advantages enjoyed by many.[8]

This is a conception of justice that seems antithetical to utilitarianism, which, as I already noted, doesn't much mind where happiness is so long as there is a lot of it. Justice, many people, like Rawls, believe, is very concerned with how *fairly* good things are *distributed*. By not taking this to be important except perhaps indirectly, utilitarianism, Rawls thinks, fails to take seriously *the distinction between persons*.[9]

What does Rawls mean? Consider an example. Some people in Scotland, where I am from, work on offshore oil rigs. This is hard work in a bleak environment with long working days. But the pay is good, and the downtime is good. Two weeks on, two weeks off is, I have been told, how it often works. So you have two quite grim weeks working hard on the rig and then two weeks off living an agreeable life with your nice earnings. You might think that is quite an appealing trade-off. The fun downtime compensates you for the grim days of hard labour.

Now consider another scenario. You are my slave. You are to spend *all* your time on the oil rig working long shifts every day without a break. By doing this, you make lots of money, which I use to live a very agreeable life *all the time*. I might think that is also an appealing trade-off. Your grim life of constant labour is compensated by my never-ending fun downtime.

Only of course it is not. The second case is *very* different from the first. *My* fun cannot compensate for *your* hardship *because you are not me*. It matters not just how much fun is being had in total but how the fun is shared. It is not a thing we should welcome that you have less in order for me to have more, even if that way there is more overall.

1.4 More Problems: Harm and the Greater Good

The utilitarian seems committed to tolerating or even requiring things that most of us think are not to be tolerated. For the utilitarian, intentionally harming people in the interest of the greater good looks like it might prove to be OK rather too often. This worry has been the stuff of countless thought experiments of which I recall just three of the most famous.

Bridge (Thomson 1976, 207–8). An out-of-control trolley car is hurtling down the tracks towards where it will hit and certainly kill five people who are trapped on the line ahead. But first it will pass under a bridge. You could leap off yourself to try to stop it with your body—which would kill you—but that will not work. You are too little to stop the trolley. But there is a big person standing by the edge, quite unsuspecting. You could push him in the trolley's path. That would work.

Transplant (Thomson 1976, 205–6). In your hospital in a remote place are five people who are dying from organ failure. They could all be saved with transplants. The organs that are failing are different, so just one fresh, healthy corpse would do the job. As you are alone in the reception area, a healthy young person comes in to make some inquiries. You know who this person is. He has no family and no friends. No one will miss him or notice he has gone. No one will ever find out what you did. You have a gun.

Sheriff (McCloskey 1957, 468–9; Smart, Smart, and Williams, 1973. 69ff). You are the sheriff of a rough town in the Wild West. A popular citizen, Angela, was murdered this morning. You arrested someone, Frank, a guy no one much likes. But since then, you have figured out that the criminal was definitely not Frank. Frank is innocent. You should let him go. But because Angela was so popular, an angry crowd has gathered. They want blood. Frank's blood. If you take Frank out and hang him outside the jail, they will be appeased and go home. If you do anything less, there will be a serious riot. It is certain people will be killed. More than one person.

1.5 Even More Problems: Normative Imposition

Utilitarianism appears to permit or even require things most of us think should not be permitted, let alone required. It also appears to *demand* more of us than many of us will find palatable. Indeed, utilitarianism appears to be an immensely *imposing* view. It appears to tell you that the thing you should be aiming to do is the actions, out of all the actions available, that will generate the most utility in the future. You *must* aim for that, and nothing else is permitted. That seems to leave you no space of freedom in which you can decide what to do with yourself for other, non-moral reasons. This is what we might call an *imperial* conception of morality, where morality seems to fully determine what we should be doing at any time, seeking to take full control of our lives.[10] It imposes heavily on us, and it licenses us to impose heavily on others.

So perhaps you would like to go to the cinema tonight. That will be nice. You enjoy the cinema. But the resources you spend going to the cinema could surely be used to do something that would generate more welfare than you generate by going to the cinema. Donated to a well-chosen charity, they might save a child's life. So it is not morally permissible for you to go to the cinema. We have the following:

> **Cinema.** (The specific example is from Shelly Kagan[11]). Utilitarians are committed to saying it is morally wrong to go to the cinema.

Other understandings of morality are less imposing. One view is that morality *constrains* but does not *determine* what we should do.[12] There are some things you really must not do, like kill people or steal from them or deceive them. And there are things you must do like keeping your promises and caring for your dependent children. But if you stay within these constraints, there is a large space in which you can choose what you do in the light of other, non-moral reasons.

One important way in which people who like the constraint view motivate that preference is to affirm with moral common sense the importance of a distinction between what we *do* and what we merely *allow* or fail to prevent. I have certainly failed to prevent many deaths that I could have prevented by, for example, giving more money to well-chosen charities. That may be grounds for moral criticism of me, but my moral career is far less of a dramatic failure than that of a serial killer who has actively inflicted death on many people. I am prohibited from killing or otherwise seriously harming because to kill or otherwise harm a person is to *impose* on them by causing them harm, but a prohibition against allowing others to be harmed is a *normative imposition*, leaving us so little residual freedom as to be an intolerable assault on our freedom of action.[13] So, it is often objected, by collapsing **the doing-allowing distinction** and making us as responsible for what we fail to prevent as what we do, utilitarianism deprives us of our autonomy.

1.6 Williams's Problem: Integrity

Utilitarianism, its critics contend, limits our freedom and compromises our autonomy. It has also been claimed that it undermines our *integrity* by alienating us from the commitments and concerns that structure and shape our various particular lives. Let me try to explain.

I do my best to do my job well. I worry about this a lot more than I do about you doing your job well. Of course, if I am your boss or we work on a team together, I might worry about the latter quite a lot as part of my job. But if you are a stranger running a hotel in Morocco, I wish you well, but I plan just to leave you to get on with it. My job getting done well is, well, my job. Your job getting done well is, well, not.

Now suppose we have dependent children. It is my very particular responsibility to look after my children. It is your job to look after yours. Why? Well, again, because those are our respective jobs. Talk of jobs is now less literal. But that is how society is arranged. And it may be quite a sensible arrangement providing, e.g., we do what decent societies must and make collective arrangements to ensure that some provision is made for children who fall through the cracks, finding themselves without living parents able to provide for them.

It is the same with many things in our lives. I live in a space of particular projects, relationships, and responsibilities. I am perhaps trying to learn Spanish, succeed as a professional philosopher, be a good dad to Andrew and Sam, be a good friend to David and Lisa, campaign to save the marine environment from plastic pollution. These projects and relationships and others like them matter to me; they are at the centre of my life, and my core concern is to cherish and further them. The problem, then, is that the consequentialist does not allow me to see them in this way. For the consequentialist, these are just projects and relationships among many others, and there is nothing special about them that I should make them the object of my particular concern. And this seems strange and rather alienating.

Imagine a world which is a bit different from the real world. In this world, our moral and emotional energies are wholly focused on gardening. We each have our own garden, and we each focus almost all our energy on cherishing and cultivating our respective gardens. Other people have gardens too, and they are as important to them as ours is to us. Well-disposed to others as we are, we care that their gardens flourish and wish them well. We even sometimes intervene to help when we know such intervention is needed and welcome.

Mostly, though, we look after our own gardens and let others look after theirs. Because, as we see it, looking after their gardens is their job, and looking after our own is our job.

The consequentialists of the garden world, *G-consequentialists*, take a different view. They think it is *everyone's* responsibility to look after *all* the gardens. I shouldn't focus on my own as special.

What is subtle is what difference this difference makes. Because the focus on our own, on what is close to us, makes a fair bit of consequentialist sense. Such a focus engages our main energies on people and things we are best placed to know and understand well, are most emotionally connected to, and have the causal levers to make a difference to most readily to hand.[14] So there is a lot to be said, from a G-consequentialist perspective, for this kind of moral division of labour where we each cherish and cultivate our own patch.

Things get a little complicated here. At the start, I said I would understand utilitarianism as the claim that what we ought to do is aim to create as much net welfare as possible. And consequentialism is the more general claim that what we ought to do is aim to create as much goodness as possible, where utilitarianism is one way of making that more precise. There is a variant form of consequentialism, and hence also utilitarianism, that does not fit that definition, and these variants are often called *rule consequentialism* and *rule utilitarianism*, respectively. Rule consequentialism comprises two claims. First, it claims that what we should do is *obey the ideal moral code*. And secondly, it says that we should understand the ideal moral code as the code general acceptance of which would generate as much goodness as possible. Rule utilitarianism is the same, of course, except, instead of goodness, it says, more precisely, welfare.

Because the moral division of labour where we each cherish and cultivate our own patch makes such obvious sense, *rule* G-consequentialists are going to have little trouble furnishing a rationale for it. The same is true with rule consequentialism and rule utilitarianism for other kinds of moral division of labour. These rule-focused variants on utilitarianism and consequentialism thus seem apt generally to do less violence to moral common sense than the more standard version. However I have been focusing on—and will continue to focus on—*act consequentialism*, as it is usually known, whose focus is on the value of individual acts.[15]

Act consequentialism cannot rescue us in the same way. For act consequentialists, the question, *What should I do?* is answered without reference to questions about what it is best for people *generally* to do. At least it is, let us be careful, answered without *direct* such reference. *Some* people should concern themselves with what the best rules might be, and those are the legislators, the people who make them. And we are all, in our small ways, legislators insofar as the rules are sustained as social realities by us all respecting and observing them. The rules, whatever rules my society has made, whether they are formal codified laws or just shared understandings of what we expect of one another and take to be important, are there, and it is often easier to do whatever it is I am trying to do by working with and not against them. Once there are rules in place, they form part of the social reality in the context of which the question confronts me: *What is the right thing for me to do?* But that question, for the act consequentialist, is just the question, *What can I do that would contribute most to the goodness of the whole world?*, and the rules are just another feature of the background to my decision with no more intrinsic moral clout than the state of the economy or the weather. The moral division of labour, where my particular concerns, projects, and responsibilities are in a very special way *mine* and yours *yours*, has, for the act consequentialist, no real independent normative significance in the proper shaping of our moral agency.

For the act consequentialist, my own projects, commitments, and relationships are just another feature of the situation carrying no more weight than anyone else's. As Bernard Williams puts it, in the classic statement of this concern,

> [H]ow can a man, as a utilitarian agent, come to regard as one satisfaction among others, and a dispensible one, a project or attitude around which he has built his life, just because someone else's projects have so structured the causal scene that that is how the utilitarian sums come out?[16]

This, Williams continues,

> is to alienate him from his actions and the source of his actions in his own convictions. It is to make him into a channel between the input of everyone's projects, including his own, and an output of optimific decision. But this is to neglect the extent to which his actions and his decisions have to be seen as the actions and decisions which flow from the projects and attitudes with which he is most closely identified. It is thus, in the most literal sense, an attack on his integrity.[17]

And so, it is objected, utilitarianism threatens our integrity by alienating us from our projects and commitments.

Notes

1. 1903, 148.
2. Smart 1973, 32–39.
3. I am understanding *consequentialism* as positing a single ranking of worlds which determines the moral duty of every agent. This is sometimes known as **agent-neutral consequentialism**. Sometimes the term 'consequentialism' is used to cover any ethical theory that understands what someone ought to do by reference to some ranking of outcomes that can be different for different persons and, perhaps, for different times. There is much discussion of whether consequentialism in this broad sense is trivial. See Portmore 2009. Here I am only going to discuss agent-neutral consequentialism.
4. In characterising utilitarianism as consequentialism plus welfarism I am following Sen and Williams 1982, 3–4.
5. Parfit 1984, 388.
6. Nozick 1974, 41.
7. Parfit 1984, 401–2.
8. Rawls 1971, 3–4.
9. Rawls 1971, 27.
10. Baier 1958, 203–4.
11. Kagan 1997, 154–5.
12. Nozick 1974, chapter 3.
13. Woollard 2013.
14. Cf. Jackson 1991, 473–5.
15. Hooker 2002 is an excellent defence of a form of rule consequentialism. See especially Section 6.5 on the kind of concerns here under discussion.
16. 1973, 116.
17. 1973, 116–17.

Chapter 2

Goodness*

2.1 The Right and the Good

Ethics can be thought of as concerned fundamentally with three things whose relationships to each other different theories understand in different ways. The first is *goodness* together with *badness* where these concepts, it is widely supposed, can be used to describe almost anything. Things, states of affairs, events, people, government policies, desserts, the weather we tend to think can all be good or bad. This is the realm of *value* or *axiology*.

Then there is the realm of the ***deontic***, which is the realm of what we *ought* to do, what is *right* and *wrong*, what is our duty, and what is morally forbidden. These are concepts that apply particularly to *actions*.

Finally, there is the ***aretaic*** realm of *virtue* and *vice*; here we are evaluating primarily *people*, as when we say someone is virtuous or vicious, brave, cowardly, just, unjust, generous, mean, whatever.

Because the value words like 'good' can be so broad-ranging in application, we count rightness and virtue as themselves kinds of goodness, and these same value words are sometimes used to express thoughts we would think of as deontic or aretaic. As when we say, *You did good* to mean *You did as you ought* or *Henry is a good man* to mean *Henry is virtuous*.

For consequentialists, goodness is fundamental. Right acts are acts which promote goodness. We make reference to the good in characterizing the right but not vice versa. For consequentialists, we say the good is prior to the right.[1] The simplest consequentialist

---

* The discussion of Judith Jarvis Thomson in this chapter uses, with permission, material from Lenman 2018.

DOI: 10.4324/9781003300045-3

theories will likewise just characterize virtues as traits of character that are conducive to bringing about goodness.

Utilitarianism, we said, is welfarism plus consequentialism. Consequentialism is a theory of *right action*. Welfarism is a theory of *value* or *goodness*. It is a theory that says only one thing: *welfare is good*.

More precisely, it says that only one thing has **final goodness**, where we distinguish final goodness from **instrumental goodness**.[2] Instrumentally good things are things that are good as *means* to a good end but may not be good in themselves. An example of a thing that is only instrumentally good might be a painful medical procedure. It is a horrible thing, but we submit to it, hoping it will save us from still greater unpleasantness down the line. An example of a thing that has final goodness might be the delight you experience swimming in a cool mountain pool on a hot day. Some things have both, such as reading poetry you love partly for its delightful own sake but also because it is on a literature curriculum you are preparing for an important exam on that you want to pass to get a good degree.

2.2 Comparing Worlds

Welfarism is a *monistic* theory of value. It tells us that exactly *one* thing, *welfare*, has final value. It can be opposed by *pluralist* theories. W. D. Ross believed that pleasure was good. But, being a pluralist, he also believed three *other* things were good: virtue, knowledge, and justice.[3] He sought to establish this by a practice of *world-comparing*.

Think of two worlds equal in all other evaluatively important dimensions but people in one of them are having much more fun. Everyone, it is urged, will agree in judging the fun world a better one. So pleasure is good.

Likewise, think of two worlds equivalent in all other evaluatively important dimensions, but people in one are all virtuous, in the other all vicious; we cannot but judge the virtuous world better.[4] The value of knowledge is established in the same way.

With justice, a rather more complicated thought experiment is required.

> If we compare two imaginary states of the universe, alike in the total amounts of virtue and vice and of pleasure and pain present in the two, but in one of which the virtuous were all happy

and the vicious miserable, while in the other the virtuous were miserable and the vicious happy, very few people would hesitate to say that the first was a much better state of the universe than the second.[5]

Welfarists will disagree. They do not deny that knowledge, virtue and justice are goods, but they will deny that they are *final* goods independent of welfare. This might be either because they are seen as important *means* to welfare or because they are seen as, in some way, *ingredients* of welfare.

2.3 Getting a Grip on Goodness

Rather than try here to adjudicate this argument, I would like to stand back from it a little. We play this world-comparing game where we imagine two worlds, a happy world and a sad world, and we judge that the happy world is better than the sad world, that it has more goodness or value.

Many philosophers simply take it for granted that we know what we are talking about when we do this. I think this is an assumption it is very important to challenge.

Certainly, our ordinary, everyday talk and thought make extensive use of the concept of goodness, but it is not at all evident that it is safely to be transferred from the familiar contexts where we talk about which beers are good, who would be good in goal for France, to these way more grandiose realms of application. Is there really a thing, goodness, such that we can compare worlds, *whole worlds*, in terms of how much goodness they contain, just as we might the glasses on our table in the pub in terms of how much beer is in them?

Some people think goodness is a property that things have, a real feature of the world, prior to and independent of our evaluative engagement with it.[6] Goodness, so understood, is a very elusive property. Scientists have not devised an instrument for measuring it, and it does not seem to be something we observe by sensory means. Indeed, we often make judgements about the goodness of things we do not observe but merely imagine, as when we read a novel or think about Ross's thought experiments.

This understanding of ethics finds expression in the writings of British **intuitionists** like Moore and Ross. For Moore and Ross, goodness is not a natural property but a non-natural one, a simple non-natural property that can be apprehended but cannot be defined. Ross writes of the ethical claims he defends:

> The moral order expressed in these propositions is just as much part of the fundamental nature of the universe (and, we may add, of any possible universe in which there were moral agents at all) as is the spatial or numerical structure expressed in the axioms of geometry or arithmetic.[7]

This view of goodness as a property, often conceived as non-natural, of things that is constituted prior to and independently of human moral experience, and that it is the business of ethics to investigate is sometimes labelled **robust realism**.

Others balk at this elusive and mysterious property and propose that in calling something *good* I merely express my liking for it and invite you to like it also. This kind of view, often labelled *emotivism*,[8] is consistent with utilitarianism, as indeed, it is consistent with any substantive normative ethical outlook. J. J. C. Smart, in his classic defence of utilitarianism, professes to accept such a view. Smart likes utilitarianism and thinks we can be got to like it too by appealing to "the sentiment of generalized benevolence which is surely present in any group with whom it is profitable to discuss ethical questions" and against a propensity people have "to obey the rules of some traditional moral system into which they have been indoctrinated in youth".[9] Sympathetic and benevolent people such as Smart takes his readers to be will, he reasons, "have a favourable attitude to the general happiness" and consequent readiness "to submit to an ultimate moral principle which does no more than express that attitude".[10]

That seems a bit unsatisfying. For one thing, people, including many sympathetic and benevolent people, may have favourable attitudes to things other than happiness, such as justice, virtue, knowledge, and autonomy.

For another, I doubt it is true that to be worth discussing ethics with you need to have a favourable attitude to the *general* happiness if we take that, as the utilitarian does, to mean the happiness of all sentient beings that will ever exist regarded in a spirit of strict impartiality. A great many ethical questions are very profitably to be discussed with people who are mostly exercised by the welfare *of the people around here*, whatever they may feel about, for example, people in the remote future.

A third concern is as follows. Consider someone who is not emotionally engaged by the happiness of others and so does not deem it good. On this view, we can say of such a person that they are *mistaken* only, if at all, in a very attenuated sense of 'mistaken'. Smart clearly thinks there is nothing to be said for the traditional systems into which we have been indoctrinated, but what can this mean if not a denial that they are *correct* in some way that a mere liking cannot be?

I think we can tame the mystery and avoid the elusive understanding of ethics espoused by Ross and others without having to settle for the very simple emotivism of Smart. There is a middle way. Members of well-functioning human societies live in a space of shared evaluative understandings that enables us to engage in discussions of these matters that are not merely idle comparings of emotional notes.[11] Many things are objectively good in that pretty well all humans tend to regard them favourably in ways that survive reflective scrutiny, such as the delight involved in swimming in a cool mountain pool on a hot day, kindness directed at children, and people who show great courage defending others from harm. Nonetheless, these things' goodness is still ineliminably *perspectival* insofar as it is an expression of a distinctively *human* evaluative sensibility.[12] It is certainly very different from the perspective that might be expressed by conceivable rational creatures of other kinds that may well come to exist in the future or in some possible futures. *Their* good will make a difference to how the various possible worlds get ranked, but it may be a very different difference from their perspective than from ours. Henry Sidgwick aspired to employ rational intuition to determine what was good, as he put it, "from the point of view of the universe"[13] and some contemporary utilitarians continue to defend the intelligibility of that idea.[14] I don't myself suppose the universe is much interested in ethics or in anything else.

2.4 Thomson on Goodness

One of the most interesting and instructive writers on these matters in recent times has been Judith Jarvis Thomson, who rejected both the robustly realist intuitionism of Moore and Ross and the emotivism embraced by Smart. Both, she thinks, rest on a confusion: a proper understanding of goodness frees it of the mystery that seems to adhere to it when we understand it as the intuitionists did without reducing it to an arbitrary-seeming expression of what a given speaker happens to like.[15]

Thomson also considered a proper understanding of goodness to be quite fatal to utilitarianism and, indeed, to consequentialism. Consequentialism supposes there to be a single general property, *goodness*, which good things share, such that the right action for a given person at a given time is the action that maximizes, or aims to maximize, how much of this property the world as a whole has.

Consequentialism wants our actions to promote maximally good *total* states of the world, *total situations*, as Smart calls them. These are very big states of affairs that each compromise a possible total history of the whole world. Each of these states of affairs, we suppose, has some total value, where that is determined by the amount of goodness it contains. In the case of utilitarianism, it is determined by how much welfare all the sentient things in it have between them. In terms of this, the various possible worlds may be compared and ranked. Our aim in action is then to make this value of the whole world through its whole history as large as possible.

This is all, according to Thomson, hopelessly, deeply wrong, and indeed nonsensical. Thomson thinks there is no such general property as goodness. There are various *ways* of being good, but they cannot be measured and compared on some single scale. And there is no such thing, Thomson thinks, as a good state of the world or a good state of affairs.

Thomson thinks there is no such thing as being good full stop, good, as it is sometimes put, *simpliciter*. There is only what she sometimes talks of as being good *in a way* or being good *in some respect*. A thing can be good *at* stuff, good at football or baking or whatever. A thing can be good *for* stuff, good for your health, good for Sheffield Wednesday Football Club, good for carrying your shopping in. *Great Expectations* is a very good book, and the Fox and Hounds does very good food, but it makes no sense to ask which of these things has more goodness because goodness qua book is a quite different thing to goodness qua pub grub. I might be good at making pizza. You might be enjoying a spell of good weather. But it is a silly question which of these things is better, me qua pizza chef or the weather where you are. They are simply good in different ways. Some kinds of things, moreover, are not intelligibly described as good of their kind at all.

'Good book' and 'good food' instance the central *attributive* use of good where we speak of being *a good K*, or good *qua* K, where

K is what Thomson calls a *goodness-fixing kind*. A goodness-fixing kind K is just a kind K such that there is such a property as being good qua K.

A pebble is not a goodness-fixing kind. There is no such thing as a good pebble *qua* pebble. Of course, there are other ways for a pebble to be good. Some pebbles are, while others are not, good for skimming, but that is not being good simply *qua* pebble. There is no such property as being good simply *qua* pebble. And things and states of affairs, like pebbles, are not goodness-fixing kinds.

So we have a further objection to utilitarianism. According to Thomson, we can make no clear sense of the idea of a good state of affairs or a good thing. So consequentialism in general and utilitarianism in particular make no clear sense.

Surely, this cannot be quite right. I'm not comfortable because I think talk of the goodness of states of affairs is not just a figment of consequentialist theorizing but also part of everyday evaluative thought that I would be reluctant to throw out. Suppose George and Joy are very good people. (Thomson is happy with talk of good people or good human beings.) And suppose too that they are very happily married to each other and their marriage brings both of them great joy. Then I want to say that the happiness of their marriage is a good thing and so I think does everyone else and not just consequentialists. That looks to me like a theory-neutral platitude, an appearance we should save if we can. Likewise, I think the Covid-19 pandemic was a bad thing, and that again looks like a platitude everyone would surely endorse not just an obscure theoretical thought only intelligible to consequentialists.

There is a way in which Thomson does not deny that states of affairs can be good. They can be good *in a way*, for example, by being good for somebody—my getting promoted to professor was good for me. So she can often handle what is happening when we greet some item of news, Sheffield Wednesday winning the cup, my winning the lottery, Nelson winning the Battle of Trafalgar, with a cry of, *Now there's a good thing!* Sheffield Wednesday's victory after all is good for Sheffield Wednesday (to whom a speaker might be well disposed), my lottery win is good for me, and the victory at Trafalgar was good for Great Britain (to which again a speaker might be well disposed). And Thomson is quite happy with all these ways of being good, even for things or states of affairs.

Indeed, *everything* is good *in some way* just as everything is bad *in some way*. The fact of George and Joy's happy marriage is good for them but bad perhaps for Algernon, George's embittered rival in love. The Covid pandemic was bad for those it visited with death or bereavement but good in, er, what way exactly? Well, if nothing else, we might think it is a good *example* of something that was quite awful. But that too is a way of being good. Goodness, in some way or other, really does come cheap.[16]

2.5 Goodness and Virtue

I remain unsatisfied. The fact that George and Joy are happily married is good for George and Joy and bad for embittered rival Algernon. But when I say it's good, I don't just mean that it is good for George and Joy. And I don't either mean it is good in some way or other in the near trivial sense in which everything, or at least nearly everything, is good in some way or other. I think it is a good thing in a sense which is neither of those senses. And I think, moreover, that we can make sense of this thought in a way that is pretty friendly to the spirit of Thomson's own thinking.

The presently relevant sense in which I think it a good thing that George and Joy are happily married is roughly, at a first approximation, a matter of my *welcoming* it. The fact of George and Joy's happy marriage is not, as we just saw, good for Algernon. But even Algernon might nevertheless welcome it. In particular, Algernon might welcome it if Algernon is generous and just. In fact, surely a fact like this should be welcome to any virtuous person (even if they are disadvantaged by it, so long as that disadvantage is not itself unjust), just as the fact of some appalling tragedy or crime should be unwelcome to any just and generous person. And I propose that this is a good way to understand such commonplaces of ordinary talk as that happy marriages between nice people are good things and states of affairs involving tragedies and crimes are bad states of affairs. So my proposal, a little less roughly, is that a good state of affairs is a state of affairs that a virtuous person would welcome in a way that proves stable under reflective scrutiny.

The first approximation that opened the previous paragraph—that to think something good is to welcome it—may seem very different from the formulation that closed it—that a good thing is a thing that a virtuous person would welcome. The first looks very like Smart's simple emotivism, the second rather more objective. But we could tie them together by proposing that welcoming of this kind is an attitude that can be taken up correctly or incorrectly and that the facts about what a virtuous person would, stably under reflective scrutiny, welcome help determine the correctness conditions of that attitude. This takes us a long way from simple emotivism without embroiling us in mystery.

To say this is to rehabilitate the idea of a good state of affairs, but does it do so in a way that is helpful to the consequentialist? I am not sure that it does. The idea of a good state of affairs is rehabilitated, but now we understand it in a way that makes essential reference to virtue and thereby dethrone it as the fundamental ethical idea that consequentialism wants to make it.[17]

We can push a little further. *What is a virtue?* The question has been answered in various ways. They include a consequentialist way. Thus Julia Driver has suggested we think of virtues as "character traits that systematically produce more actual good than not".[18] Plugging that into what I just proposed, we can think of a good state of affairs as a state of affairs a virtuous person would welcome and a virtuous person as a person with a character that is good at producing good states of affairs. Which does not look promising.

But surely, someone is sure to object; virtues have to be thought of as states which are beneficial to us, states which do *good*. We may well think like Ross that virtues have final value but they surely have instrumental value also. They conduce to human flourishing, to *eudaimonia*, as people say whose habit of emphasizing virtue takes inspiration from the ancient world and, in particular, from Aristotle, for whom eudaimonia is quite simply the good at which everything we do is aimed.[19] And doesn't that again take us right back to a kind of consequentialism?

No, it does not. In three ways. To see the first, let us go back to Thomson. Thomson has a nice way to characterise the virtues. She thinks they are characteristics of human beings that it is good for us for people to have. She elaborates,

> It is better for us that the people among whom we live be just than that they not be just. Indeed, this is not merely better for us, but essential to us, since we can form a community at all and thereby obtain benefits which are essential to us and which only community can provide—only if a substantial number of those among whom we live are just.[20]

Us here is us. The people round here among whom we live. My community. It's not all the sentient beings that ever get to exist in the history of the universe. Virtuous people are the kind of people we want our neighbours to be. Virtue is what we need to make a good community, not what we need to make a good universe. The latter is above our moral pay grade. Virtue is local.

It is local in another way, the second way in which this does not take us back to consequentialism. The conception of goodness that informs our understanding of goodness in an Aristotelian framework is inescapably shaped by and expressive of *human* nature and *human* experience. And there is, it seems to me, a sense in which this Aristotelian thought is right.

Consider some basic facts about human beings. We are mortal with a natural life span of maybe 80 plus or minus 20 years. We depend on natural resources, many of which are subject to scarcity. We are social animals that live in groups having (at least the overwhelming majority of us) a deep need for companionship and affection. We are medium sized mammals, weaker and slower than many of our fellow creatures who might fancy eating us but compensating for that by being smart and, again, social. We are, like all mammalian species, sexually differentiated, and we reproduce sexually. Again, like all mammalian species and unlike most fish, we are **Ks and not rs**. That is the technical expression for the fact that we have a small number of offspring and take very good care of them till they are old enough to look after themselves, rather than having thousands of offspring, most of which will be eaten in short order but whose sheer weight of numbers ensures a few will get lucky and survive long enough to reproduce in their turn. It is surely wildly implausible that if all or many of these facts about us were different, our ethical consciousness would not also be very different indeed.

Our ethical consciousness is, in this way, anthropocentric;[21] we might say terrestrial.[22] That is not to say only human beings are ethically significant to us. But the perspective we bring to understanding the ethical significance of non-human creatures is inescapably human. There is no point of view of the universe.

Virtue is local in a third way. I have suggested that a good state of affairs is a state of affairs a virtuous person will, stably under reflective scrutiny, welcome. But the states of affairs virtuous people are given to welcoming are things like George and Joy's happy marriage or a war coming to a peaceful conclusion. These are relatively small, manageable states of affairs. They are not complete worlds, Smart's total situations. Complete worlds are not what virtuous people focus on, being as they are way too big meaningfully to be objects of moral thought. Exceptions might be worlds which are very simple. Perhaps by being very small. World A contains only one sentient person. His name is Derek. He is happy. End of story. Or perhaps by being very homogenous. World B contains a trillion people. They are all happy enough. Nice lives. These are not worlds that have much in common with the extreme complexity of human reality. We might call them *toy worlds*. As we saw looking at Ross, philosophers sometimes work such toy worlds very hard, trying to establish very large ethical results. Would virtuous people welcome such toy worlds? I am not quite sure how that would work. I don't really understand how one might welcome a world from outside, from some perspective external to it. And I'm not sure one can welcome a whole world from somewhere within it. Where?

Indeed, toy worlds like these, where everyone is happy and everything is lovely, likely do not contain any people you or I would recognize as virtuous. Much of what we think of as virtue is about responding decently and intelligently to all the things that often make human life difficult and challenging. Such difficulties and challenges—what we might call *the circumstances of virtue*—are presumably largely absent from the Everybody Is Happy world we meet in such thought experiments. And these circumstances are another of those very basic facts about human life that shape our ethical thinking and from which that thinking cannot credibly abstract away.

Notes

1 Cf Rawls 1971, 24–25.
2 The distinction is found in Plato's *Republic*, 357.
3 2002, chapter 5.
4 This might seem dubiously conceivable. Surely life in the vicious world will be horrible and people will be less happy. Ross anticipates this concern and notes in response that our happiness is affected by natural as well as moral evils. So in the Everybody Is Nice World people are happier because everybody is so nice, but there are a lot more earthquakes, horrible viruses, and so on than in the Everybody Is Horrid World. So what the Everybody Is Nice people make on the swings of moral goodness they lose on the roundabout of natural evil.
5 2002, 138.
6 Moore 1903, Ross 2002.
7 2002, 29–30.
8 Stevenson 1944.
9 1973, 7.

10 1973, 31.
11 Cf. Gibbard 1990, Part 3, Lenman 2024, chapter 7.
12 As even the more modest 'moral realists' acknowledge, Cf., e.g, Taylor 1989, 68 Lenman 2024.
13 Sidgwick 1981, 382, 420.
14 de Lazari-Radek and Singer 2014.
15 For Thomson's understanding of goodness, see Thomson in Harman and Thomson 1996, Thomson 1997, 2003, 2008.
16 Thomson 2008, 10.
17 Compare Foot 1983, 282.
18 2001, 68.
19 *Nicomachean Ethics*, 1094a, 1095a.
20 1997, 282.
21 Again cf.Taylor 1989, 68, Lenman 2024.
22 Cf. Arpaly 2023.

Chapter 3

Welfare

3.1 What Are We Asking When We Ask *What Is Welfare?*

Utilitarianism is consequentialism about rightness plus welfarism about goodness. Welfarism about goodness says the only thing that has final goodness is welfare or well-being. (To save words, I'm just going to say *welfare* from now on.) But utilitarians disagree about what welfare is. Some think it is pleasure. The classical English utilitarians, Bentham and Mill, thought this. Some think it is the extent to which our desires or preferences are satisfied. Some think of it as something rather more complex and plural, identifying it with certain core goods that make for a good human life, pleasure, to be sure, but also perhaps love, friendship, achievement, autonomy, and aesthetic experience.

Things can get confusing here. Thus when we are told some philosopher is a hedonist, that might mean they are a hedonist *about value*, about the good. They think what is good is just pleasure. Or it might mean they are a hedonist *about welfare*. They think the best understanding of welfare is that it is pleasure. Someone might be a hedonist about welfare but not a hedonist about value because they do not think welfare is all there is to value. (This was Ross's position.)

What is welfare? That is now a central question in moral philosophy taking up a large literature, by no means all of it written by welfarists. But it may make a difference to how we understand it whether we are welfarists or not. That is because before we understand it, we need to have some pre-theoretical purchase on what we mean by 'welfare' if we are to even understand what it is we are asking.

DOI: 10.4324/9781003300045-4

There is an old paradox made much of by Plato, who has the character Meno raise it in the dialogue named after him.[1] There can never, the paradox suggests, be a meaningful research project to answer a question of the form, *What is X?* For if we know what X is, we know what X is, and we are done: there is nothing left to investigate. Suppose, on the other hand, we do not know what X is. In that case, we cannot understand the question at all and so do not know where to start our investigation.

The paradox, sometimes called the **Paradox of Inquiry** or the **Meno Paradox**, is a good example of a *false dichotomy*—where we are presented with two often alarming eventualities which purport to be mutually exclusive and exhaustive of the relevant space of possibilities, but it turns out they are not.

If we know *everything* about X, there is nothing left for us to investigate. If we know *nothing* about X, we cannot understand what we are even asking. But there are obviously many intermediate possibilities. Inquiry gets off the ground when we have *some*, as I will say, *cognitive purchase* on X, enough to pick it out as an object of inquiry, but have still to discover certain important things about it. So the detective can ask *Who killed Mr Smith?* because he knows something about that person to give him the needed cognitive purchase: that that person killed Mr Smith. (The German philosopher Gottlob Frege taught us this lesson. What I call *cognitive purchase* is effectively what he called *sense*.)

Some *What is X?* questions are, of course, satisfactorily answered by consulting a dictionary. Someone asking what chiromancy is will probably be happy if we tell them it is "divination by the hand; the art of telling the characters and fortunes of persons by inspection of their hands; palmistry".[2] Here our prior cognitive purchase is just that the object of our interest is a word of English, which we can say and spell, but whose semantic value, whose meaning, we don't know. But most interesting *What is X* questions are not about lexicography. In the history classroom, someone asking what a Lollard is will not be happy with "a name of contempt given in the 14th cent. to certain heretics, who were either followers of Wyclif or held opinions similar to his".[3] I want to know what opinions those were, and for that, I need a history book, not a dictionary. And in the science classroom, *What is water?* or *What is heat?* are almost certainly requests for something deeper and more substantial than a dictionary can supply. Cognitive purchase is not a problem. We know what these things are. They are extremely familiar constituents of our everyday experience. But we want to know what their nature is.

A lot of *What is X?* questions crop up in philosophy that are about something deeper than lexicography. Or we hope they are. *What are numbers? What is justice?* In such cases, we need to be clear what question that is not merely lexicographical we are asking without building a substantive answer into our prior understanding of the question. Philosophers who argue about such questions are not, we hope, simply discussing English usage. In the case of *What are numbers?*, somewhat as with water and heat, the question gets its sense from our everyday experience. The everyday practices of counting and adding up. How are we to make sense of these activities? Are the numerical expressions we use in these activities *referring* to things? If so, what kind of things? If not, what are they doing? Or when we ask about justice, at least in contexts where we are concerned with distributive justice, we are asking the question, *How can we best share out the various things we want in life that are scarce?* That is the question we are asking when we ask what justice is, and we can ask it without using the word 'justice' at all.

OK, so what about *What is welfare?* And right now, I am concerned not so much with *answering* this question as finding a way of *understanding* it that is neutral among the various possible ways we might answer it. I do think this is quite hard to do. We can perhaps point to the way we often talk about a person's *interests*. There is stuff that is in my interest and stuff that is in your interest, and my interest may sometimes conflict with your interest.

We might well want to get a clearer sense of what that means. A first stab might be what is in my interest is just what I want. But that will need some finessing. I might want things that are not in my interest, as when I want to smoke a cigarette. Or fail to want things that are, as when a child feels no enthusiasm for going to school and studying. And it also might need limiting. I want the war in Ukraine to end. I want that nice young person on her way to a job interview whom I was chatting to on the train the other day to succeed in her job interview and flourish in her new career.[4] These things we maybe don't want to include in my interests because they are not sufficiently *about me*. But nothing of real philosophical moment seems at stake here. We can just acknowledge that some of the things I care about are all about what happens to me, and some are not.

Of course, I care about more than my interests. That is just what it means not to be wholly selfish. So how should we understand this reference to my interests, that subdomain of the sphere of my concern? What is *good for me*? That is one of the ways of being good that Thomson thought nice and clear. I am not so sure. Perhaps what is good for me is not what I care about but what I rationally *should* care about—that will take care of smoking. And perhaps not everything I should care about—not the welfare of Ukrainians and strangers on trains but what I should care about *insofar as I am concerned with my self-interest*. But that is too like saying *insofar as I am concerned about my welfare* and gets us no further on. And by now, it should be apparent just why getting a clear handle on what we are asking here can be so tricky.

Perhaps a better way to get a handle on the question would be to say, following Stephen Darwall and Valerie Tiberius, that what is good for me is what you should want for me if you love me.[5] But that still might not do. Imagine some circumstance arises where there is a course of action that is clearly, as we might say, *the right thing*, but it is a thing that will *cost* me. Perhaps I should stick up for someone who is being bullied or harassed at my place of work, say, but doing that means I will be bullied and harassed in my turn. It seems natural to say the right thing to do is not what it is in my interest to do. What would you want me to do if you were someone who loves me? I think it would often make perfect sense for you to want me to do the right thing despite the cost. Indeed we might intelligibly think this was truly in my interest. Plato in the *Gorgias* has Socrates urge that to do an injustice is to submit to an injury to one's soul far more serious than any injury to the body that might be suffered by a victim of injustice.[6]

Tiberius has urged that we think of welfare, what you should want for me if you love me, in terms of *living well according to our values*.[7] Here again, we get the odd consequence that people who make great sacrifices to do the right thing are not really making sacrifices at all.[8]

Perhaps we can tame that worry. Compare the young athlete who sacrifices a lot to train really hard, who for years is out running in the rain while her friends are out partying and enjoying themselves, so in the end, it all pays off, and she wins an Olympic gold medal. This young athlete is making a very real sacrifice, one that we may admire her for; the good-for-her things she sacrifices she is sacrificing for other things that are also good for her but in a different way.

Suppose we are utilitarians (or any kind of welfarists). *Then* it seems clearer what we are asking when we ask, *What is welfare?* For a utilitarian thinks that welfare is the only thing that has final value. So we want to know what conception of welfare looks most promising with a view to that being plausibly true. So when we ask, *Is welfare pleasure, or desire satisfaction or whatever?*, we are asking which of these things is most plausibly supposed to be the thing that is uniquely finally valuable. Which of them is best suited to play the role welfare plays in our theory?

We can understand the question like that if we are utilitarians or welfarists of any kind. For people with other views, the question might still be one that can be brought into focus. So if you are a Ross-style pluralist who thinks there are four basic goods—welfare, knowledge, justice, and virtue—you have the job of clarifying what is best understood by each of those to make your theory plausible.

But with no such prior theoretical commitments, it is not very clear what to make of the question, *What is welfare?* I can certainly say pleasure is a thing and a very nice thing, and so perhaps is having things work out as I desire, and so is being healthy, wealthy, and wise. But which of these things *is welfare?* It is obscure what we are even asking here.

I like Tiberius's view that welfare[9] is living well in accordance with our values. But the more I reflect on it, the more I come to suspect that I like her view not so much because it is necessarily my favourite answer to the question, *What is welfare*, but more because I think, *How can we live well in accordance with our values?* is just a more interesting question to put in the centre of ethical inquiry than the question, *What is welfare?* Once I have figured out how to live well in accordance with my values, I don't know what residual difficulty there might be for *What is welfare?* to engage with. Of course, some ways of living well in accordance with my values might be a lot easier than others. And of course there are always more particular questions. *What might be fun to do this weekend?* But such questions, while they can be very important, are going to lack the sweeping generality of a question like *What is welfare?*

3.2 Understanding Welfare: Some Bad Ways

For the utilitarian, however, our question is central, so let's try to come at it from a utilitarian standpoint. We have persuaded ourselves that welfare is the only thing with final value. So now let us figure out what it might be. Here the menu of options, in some ways, repeats what we saw when we looked at the question, *What is goodness?* Just as with goodness, we can be pluralists, or we can be monists. A popular monistic view is that welfare is just pleasure. Another is that it is whatever satisfies your desires or preferences, whereas pluralist accounts might include these things and others on a list.

The simplest, most familiar monistic views look unpromising. If pleasure is all you want, we can supply you with lots of it by directly stimulating the appropriate part of your brain.[10] We could just do that, your whole life, while you lay there passively. Or we could put you into a blissful drug-induced stupor. Perhaps we could even construct some digital synthetic sentience that would just sit there on the mantlepiece having a lovely time.

More popular in the 20th century was the understanding of welfare as the satisfaction of desire. Sometimes this is expressed in terms of the maximization of *utility*.

The terminology can be confusing here. 'Utility' is sometimes used, alongside 'well-being' and 'welfare' and 'happiness', as a general term for the thing welfarists think is valuable, the thing some people think is pleasure, some others think is desire satisfaction, and so on. But sometimes it is used in a narrower sense, as a technical term for, roughly speaking, desire satisfaction, where that is defined mathematically in terms of a ranking of states of the world with respect to the extent to which they satisfy a given person's preferences. Such a ranking can get mathematical expression in something called a **utility function** when a person's preferences among alternatives satisfy certain formal properties. So we can understand welfare as maximizing utility in this sense, though really that is just a fancy way of saying we are to understand it as your desires, whatever they may be, being satisfied to the greatest extent possible.

While we are with the slipperiness of language, be careful with **satisfaction**. Sometimes 'satisfaction' is used to describe a way someone might *feel*. *The critical reception of Mary's first novel filled her with satisfaction.* But the satisfaction of a desire is just for the proposition you desire to come true. Often, we feel satisfied when our desires are satisfied. You want an ice cream; you get an ice cream; now you are happy. But we might not be. Sometimes yearned-for experiences disappoint. And sometimes we never know when our desires are satisfied or frustrated and so feel nothing about it. You want the young person from the train to flourish even though if she does you will never know. You want your lover not to be unfaithful and your desire is unsatisfied when he is unfaithful. For hedonists who think welfare is pleasure, such an unknown disappointment makes you no worse off. For hedonists, *what you don't know can't harm you*. For desire-satisfaction theorists, it can.

The desire-satisfaction conception of welfare is a good place to stand to see why a certain kind of utilitarianism is so easily found attractive. You see, *everything I want is something I want*. All my desires aim at things that will satisfy them. So, really, you see, all I ever do is pursue the satisfaction of my desires. All *anyone* ever does is pursue the satisfaction of their desires. So it can be tempting to suppose maybe the satisfaction of our desires is somehow what life is all about, a kind of overarching end to which all our more particular ends are somehow subordinate.

But this, too, looks decidedly unpromising and in fact it is a horrible moral fallacy. It is true enough that all we ever want to do is satisfy our desires. But that is not to say I am all that interested in satisfying my desires *as such* or, as we sometimes say, **under that description**.

Suppose I want to marry Daisy Melrose. And suppose Daisy is the second youngest granddaughter of the Reverend Arthur Melrose. Then it can truly be said of me that I want to marry the second youngest granddaughter of the Reverend Arthur Melrose. But it is not, we say, *under that description* that I want to marry her. (At least it is not unless I am very odd.) Likewise, when I want to visit Paris, I am having a desire that a desire of mine be satisfied. But being a thing desired by me is not the thing about visiting Paris that appeals to me. Paris is an object of desire to me not because I desire it—that would be very weird- but because it is, well, Paris, with all that is so substantively appealing about Paris—the food, the galleries, the parks.

We might try to imagine a situation where I do not know what my desires are because I have been put behind a **veil of ignorance** that strips me of that information. I have no idea which person in society I am, but I know I have an equal chance of being any one of them. Then we might think I am just going to try to maximize my utility because my affective psychology has been so impoverished there is nothing else I can do. John Harsanyi famously constructed an imaginary scenario like this to motivate utilitarianism.[11]

R. M. Hare does something similar in his famous argument for utilitarianism. He urges that it is a conceptual truth about normative concepts that they are **universalizable**, i.e., that they must be applied consistently across different circumstances, and then argues that this **universalizability** demands I put myself in the shoes of everyone concerned in any moral decision and give each of their profiles of desires the same weight as my own. Again, by abstracting away from the substance of what I care about in all its rich particularity, I am left with nothing to guide me except the formal imperative to go after utility as such.[12]

It is a tempting line of thought. We start with the **Golden Rule**. Do unto others as you would want them to do unto you. But we have to apply it carefully. As George Bernard Shaw says, "Do not do unto others as you would that they should do unto you. Their tastes may not be the same".[13] I like hot, spicy food. You can't stand it. So if you come over to my place for a meal, I should not offer you a fiery vindaloo curry however much I myself like that. But that does not mean we must abstract away from all our particularities to collapse the Golden Rule into an injunction to simply satisfy people's desires, whatever they are.

It is true enough of me that I might very naturally have a general hope and desire that my life not be one of constantly having my will thwarted and my desires frustrated. What is false is that this operates as a kind of *master desire*. Satisfying my desires, maximizing my utility, *as such*, is really not what gets me out of bed in the morning. If it was, a smart thing to do would be to try to bring it about that my desires were so fabulously modest that it was extremely easy for me to satisfy them. All I care about is that the sun be hot, the snow be cold, and the rain be wet, and, hey, they are, so my felicity is perfect. If I am unable to reengineer myself to be extremely *easily pleased* in this way, perhaps some clever technicians can make some AI that is just like this. Maybe they can make LOTS of it. That will be good. Or perhaps not.

3.3 Understanding Welfare: A Better Way

I think we should turn away from these very thin and formal theories of well-being and think instead, in the spirit of Tiberius, of living well in accordance with our values. Or, as she, like me, is given to saying, echoing David Hume, living a life that will bear our survey.[14]

Tiberius favours a relatively neutral reading of living in accordance with our values. For her, that is a matter of me living in accord with my values, you with your values, Uncle Fred with Uncle

Fred's values. I am prepared to be more perfectionist in spirit and speak in terms of *us*, me and you and Uncle Fred each living in accord with *our* values where that is a matter of realizing well the possibilities of human life: a life that is fun, for sure, and not overfull of disappointment and frustration, for sure, but also rich in activity, creativity, love, friendship, exploration, curiosity, learning, understanding, adventure, achievement, experience and appreciation of beauty, rich engagement with the natural world. It is not necessary to tick all the boxes. Intellectual activity is splendid, but as philosophers who do it for a living, we should be careful not to overrate it as Aristotle perhaps did. Many people, of course, live wonderful, worthwhile lives who are not remotely intellectual.

3.4 Comparing Welfare

I stress again, as when we concluded the last chapter, that this is a pretty anthropocentric picture. It is a story about what a good life is like *for a human being*. We have perhaps an idea of what a good life might be like for a tiger or a panda insofar as we have studied these creatures and formed a sense of what it is for them to flourish. But there is no clear metric for comparing these things to say if my life is better or worse and by how much than that of a certain tiger or a certain panda. Never mind the extraterrestrial or the piece of sentient AI that may sit on my shelf one day. And so, of course, no clear metric by which to sum them as we need to if the utilitarian is to do their sums.

Interpersonal comparisons are notoriously a headache for utilitarians even before we start to concern ourselves with creatures other than human beings. Even when we deal in preference satisfaction as represented by utility functions.

While, as we noted above, certain formal assumptions allow us to represent a given person's utility on a scale, that scale is an **interval scale**, which yields a whole family of functions unique only up to **positive linear transformation**, i.e., transformations that scale our function up or down and/or change which point in the scale we count as the 'zero' point while preserving the order and proportion of utility values. So given enough data, we might represent your utility function as showing that you prefer hot baths to cream donuts twice as much as you prefer cream teas to cryptic crosswords and mine as showing that I prefer hot baths to cream donuts only half as much as I prefer cryptic crosswords to cream teas but we are still in no position to know if I like cream teas more than you do. It is as if we know how to value things in the currency of your utility scale and in the currency of mine but we have no idea of the exchange rate.[15] And you and I are both human beings. If we were more different, the headache here would grow. Such headaches are highly consequential for consequentialists, as will become again apparent in Chapter 7.

Notes

1. Meno, 80.
2. Oxford English Dictionary, apud 'chiromancy'.
3. Oxford English Dictionary, apud 'Lollard'.
4. Parfit 1984, 151.
5. Darwall 2002, 8–9, Tiberius 2018, 8–10.
6. Gorgias 474–81.
7. Tiberius 2018.
8. For a nice discussion of this problem, see Heathwood 2011.
9. I'm sticking with welfare for terminological consistency, but Tiberius prefers to talk of well-being.
10. Nozick 1974, 42–45, Smart 1973, 18–22.
11. Harsanyi 1955.
12. Hare 1981.
13. The words open his "Maxims for Revolutionists".
14. Treatise, III, iii, 6, 6. Tiberius, 2008, 12–13.
15. Sen 1970, chapter 7, Narens and Skyrms 2020, chapter 7.

Chapter 4

Repugnant Conclusions*

In 1943, C. S. Lewis published *That Hideous Strength*, a strange but very entertaining combination of science fiction, popular theology, and supernatural horror in which the peace of a leafy old English university town is shattered when it is taken over by a coterie of academics and activists of roughly the sort we would now call **transhumanists**. One day, over dinner, Filostrato, one of their leaders, unfolds his vision.

> In us organic life has produced Mind. It has done its work. After that we want no more of it. We do not want the world any longer furred over with organic life, like what you call the blue mould—all sprouting and budding and breeding and decaying. We must get rid of it. By little and little, of course. Slowly we learn how. Learn how to make our brains live with less and less body: learn to build our bodies directly with chemicals, no longer have to stuff them full of dead brutes and weeds. Learn how to reproduce ourselves without copulation.
>
> I don't think that would be much fun, said Winter.[1]

Reading this years ago, as a teenager, I thought it all a bit far-fetched. I am not so sure now.

4.1 Animals, Nature and Control

Let's think about the welfare of animals. A lot of thinking has, of course, gone on in recent decades about the welfare of domestic animals, especially those we rear for their meat, hides, milk, and

---

* Section 1 of this chapter incorporates material from Lenman 2022.

DOI: 10.4324/9781003300045-5

eggs. But I don't want to talk about them now. I want to talk about *wild* animals. Wild animals lead hard lives. Many of them live by killing and eating many others. And to be a prey animal, as most animals are, means not only an unpleasant and violent death but a life of stress and anxiety living in close quarters with terrifying creatures who are constantly looking for a chance to kill you.[2]

Shouldn't we *do* something? If we want to make the world a better place, surely here is a bit of it that stands in great need of improvement. Maybe we could kill off the predator species and find another way to control the numbers of the prey. Perhaps we can do what we do with domestic pets and neuter many of them by surgery under suitable anaesthetic. More radically, we might perhaps genetically reengineer them to have fewer offspring. Or, now that I think, why not reengineer the predators so they are gentle and friendly and live on plant-based diets? We can reengineer the whole natural world, sanitize it, make it a kinder, gentler place.

This line of thinking got a first outing by Bernard Williams and Alison Hills who intended it to be a *reductio* of utilitarianism.[3] But it has suffered the fate of many arguments that were first cooked up as *reductios* of utilitarianism and been embraced by many utilitarians as correctly identifying a thing we really need to do. Perhaps not now. It would be a fantastically difficult and challenging project with huge scope for things to go horribly wrong, but if a time comes when the relevant technologies are more advanced than they are now, then yes, this is what we should do.

One might well go further. Why would we be content to reengineer the domain of wild animal nature by turning the animals who live difficult lives into new animals who live happier lives? Might it not just be more efficient to *eradicate* it altogether? We don't really need animals. Why not replace them with synthetic sentient creatures that have a more potent capacity for whatever we think welfare is? If we get good enough at science, we won't even need plants. We can synthesize food in laboratories from raw chemicals. Of course, we rely on plants to convert carbon dioxide into oxygen, but surely, one day, we can build some kit that does that job for us too.

Come to think, why not replace *ourselves* with synthetic sentient things that have a more potent capacity for whatever we think welfare is? And now we *really* don't need plants. Synthetic sentience doesn't need oxygen to breathe and doesn't care if climate change has made everything a bit hot. And it doesn't need organic matter to eat and convert into energy. It can run on solar-powered batteries. Yay! Let's do that. Let us make a brave new *postbiological* world where technology liberates us (I use the word 'us' extremely loosely) from nature. Our synthetically sentient successors will go on to colonize space, harvesting the energy of the stars to make a vast utopian utilitarian future, albeit one devoid of organic living things, to be sure. Such organic living things are the product of the blind, purposeless process that is evolution by natural selection. Technology will someday, perhaps someday very soon, get smarter than evolution at making psychological systems and physical systems to realize them. That is what will save us. Or at least save something. Filostrato's dream will come true.

I am not making this up. People really do say these things in a spirit of immense seriousness.[4]

They respond to people like me who find these ideas entirely repellent and chilling that we are just muddled, blinded most likely by a kind of *nature worship*, a superstitious hang-up from days when we saw the natural world as something special and sacred and not just the slow upshot of a blind and cruel evolutionary process.

This utilitarian scepticism about the valorization of nature goes back to Mill's great, neglected 1874 essay "On Nature", which is splendidly eloquent on nature's shortcomings.

> Nature impales men, breaks them as if on the wheel, casts them to be devoured by wild beasts, burns them to death, crushes them with stones like the first Christian martyr, starves them with hunger, freezes them with cold, poisons them by the quick or slow venom of her exhalations, and has hundreds of other hideous deaths in reserve, such as the ingenious cruelty of a Nabis or a Domitian never surpassed. All this Nature does with the most supercilious disregard both of mercy and of justice, emptying her shafts upon the best and noblest indifferently with the meanest and worst; upon those who are engaged in the highest and worthiest enterprises, and often as the direct consequence of the noblest acts; and it might almost be imagined as a punishment for them. She mows down those on whose existence hangs the well-being of a whole people, perhaps the prospect of the human race for generations to come, with as little compunction as those whose death is a relief to themselves, or a blessing to those under their noxious influence.[5]

Mill's essay concludes,

> The scheme of Nature, regarded in its whole extent, cannot have had, for its sole or even principal object, the good of human or other sentient beings. What good it brings to them is mostly the result of their own exertions. Whatsoever, in nature, gives indication of beneficent design proves this beneficence to be armed only with limited power; and the duty of man is to cooperate with the beneficent powers, not by imitating, but by perpetually striving to amend, the course of nature - and bringing that part of it over which we can exercise control more nearly into conformity with a high standard of justice and goodness.[6]

Nature, for Mill, is something we should *amend*, something we should *control*, certainly not something we should *follow* or *respect*.

He has a point; of course he does. Think, for example, of the successes of modern medicine in enabling us to fight back often highly effectively against the terrible suffering and shortening of life with which we are perpetually threatened by the countless diseases to which our organic constitution makes us vulnerable. Nobody wants to respect smallpox. Everyone rejoices at its eradication.

But I think we can overdo this. Nature provides the diseases that carry too many of us too early from the living world. But nature, evolved organic nature, also makes the healthy, living world we are so unwilling to leave, the living world of humanity, where that is who we are, our lives, our bodies, our culture, and our values. We are ourselves nature and cannot stand back from it and turn a critical 'rational' gaze on it, as it were, from the outside with any meaningful expectation that we will find anywhere to place our feet when we do so. In Chapter 2, I argued that we cannot step away from our humanity when we engage in ethical thought. That we might step away altogether from *nature* is still more unthinkable, contemplating a still deeper excursion into nothingness.

William MacAskill, one of the leading lights of such contemporary transhumanism, has suggested that he is happy enough if we get replaced by digital sentience providing it has the right values.[7] But I don't really know what right values would look like for digital sentience, and neither does he. Digital Dickie hanging out around Alpha Centauri in a postbiological world a few million years hence is not, we might suppose, a social animal like you and me. He has no need for love and affection and a sense of community. Did I say 'He'? Of course, I should not. He, she—it has no sex in both obvious disambiguations of that phrase. It doesn't have children it loves and cherishes. There is no reason to suppose it is troubled at the prospect of its own death if it even has enough recognisably in the way of personal identity for concepts of survival and death even to apply to it. For something so remote from fleshy organic human experience, anything recognizable as human values would likely be of little relevance and make little sense. Will such a creature ever replace us and fill the universe? Maybe. I don't really care.

We ourselves, and everything we value about ourselves, are part of the evolved natural order. But then there is the other part. The part that is not us but that we are rapidly destroying. The world of Spix's macaw, the northern white rhino, the Pyrenean ibex, the Chinese river dolphin, the Bramble Cay melomys, the splendid poison frog, the ivy-billed woodpecker, the South Island kōkako, the Hawaiian crow, the slender-billed curlew, the robust burrowing mayfly, the Santa Cruz pupfish, the Lake Lanao freshwater fish, the smooth handfish, etc., etc., the vast number of living species that are rapidly disappearing before our eyes in a catastrophic mass extinction that is wholly the result of human activity, most notably our degradation and destruction of the often fragile, ever shrinking habitats of our fellow-creatures.[8] To me and to many others this seems clearly to be one of the grimmest and most urgent problems facing human beings.

But perhaps we should not think it is a problem at all. Thus MacAskill writes,

> It's very natural and intuitive to think of humans' impact on wild animal life as a great moral loss. But if we assess the lives of wild animals as being worse than nothing on average, which I think is plausible (though uncertain), then we arrive at the dizzying conclusion that from the perspective of wild animals themselves, the enormous growth and expansion of human beings has been a good thing.[9]

This breezy complacency in the face of ongoing anthropogenic ecocide horrifies some people. It certainly horrifies me. For utilitarian—or utilitarian-adjacent—true believers, such horror is just to be dismissed as we have seen, as giving way to a sentimental and romantic nature worship, an irrational hang-up from the days when we thought of the natural world as something sacred. Rather more of us, I am hoping and guessing, will want to say a moral theory that cannot even compute the ongoing devastation of the natural world as a loss cannot be a moral theory fit for purpose.

We should not destroy the natural world. We should protect and cherish it. Nor should we reengineer it to make it nice. I guess the thing to say here is that sometimes the best response to something we care for and love is not to seek to control it and improve it but simply to protect and cherish it where that means, in many, many ways, to *let it be*, *to leave it alone*. As Clare Palmer writes,

> Ultimately, then, defenders of the intrinsic value of wildness in the sense I've described seek a kind of human humility (Hill, 1983) where humans step back from their drive to manage and to control the world around them, even when this control takes a beneficent form.[10]

The world of wild nature is not *ours to improve*. To think otherwise is to succumb to a dangerous kind of moral hubris or, maybe more aptly, to a kind of imperial instinct—a sense that we have a mission of improvement that extends to *everything*. And what we would *improve* we must first, of course, *control*. So while beneficence is often a very fine thing, you can find yourself carried away by it to the point where you finish up gripped by megalomania.

Indeed, much of the justificatory narrative for very literal British imperialism in the 19th century is provided just by the great utilitarian voices who did so much to shape that era, as when we find Mill in *On Liberty* writing (not his finest moment):

> Despotism is a legitimate mode of government in dealing with barbarians, provided the end be their improvement, and the means justified by actually effecting that end.[11]

David McPherson's excellent recent book, *The Virtues of Limits*, makes an illuminating contrast between what he calls the accepting appreciating stance and the choosing controlling stance, arguing for the primacy, as he calls it, of the former. The choosing controlling stance is, as he puts it, Promethean in its aspiration to dominate and improve the whole world. McPherson is wary of this hubristic impulse, fearing that a drive to realize some ideal of perfection not rooted in loyalty to what is given to us by way of "what is of value in the given world and in the human condition" can only ever issue in a chilling nihilism.[12] He echoes and affirms the words of Jerry Cohen:

> [The] attitude of universal mastery over everything is repugnant, and, at the limit, insane.[13]

4.2 Total Utilitarianism and the Repugnant Conclusion

Many creatures are going extinct all around us, as I just noted, something many people, including myself, deplore. Humans, not so much.

We might. We are not so clever and might get ourselves into a massive nuclear war, or properly poison our planet, or just get clobbered by a massive meteor or a new ultra-lethal and contagious infectious pathogen. It would take rather a lot to wipe us out completely, and many of the likelier-looking potential cataclysms on the road ahead would take out maybe a great many of us, but most likely not *all* of us. Still, it would be nice to avoid them if we can so contrive. Something that kills off 99.9% of us would be better than something that did for us all but still be pretty awful.

Something that kills 99.9% of us sounds pretty unfortunate. Almost as bad, perhaps, as something that kills us all. But actually, many utilitarian (and utilitarian-adjacent) philosophers do not agree. Derek Parfit famously urged that total wipeout is not somewhat worse but actually *much, much, much worse* than near total wipeout.[14] The difference in awfulness between 99.9% and 100% indeed, according to Parfit, is *much, much, much greater* than the difference between nothing bad happening at all and 99.9% wipeout.

You might think if there are at the time, say, 10 billion humans and 0.1% survive, that is a saving of 10 million human lives. But not all utilitarians see it that way. For that is to neglect the vast number of future lives that we would rescue from oblivion by averting complete extinction. Nick Bostrom has estimated the number of lives that could potentially people the future at around something equivalent to 10^{58} human lives. Though they will not actually be human lives, as we have seen, the idea seems to be that they will be synthetic sentient things scattered through space plugged into virtual reality.[15]

It is very hard to take the numbers that get bandied around in this context seriously. Let us just say lots. Or maybe even say LOTS, where that is a number astronomically larger than the number of human beings who have ever lived so far—which I believe is estimated to be a number of the order of 100 billion or 10^{11}.[16] So if the death toll from the cataclysm is 100% rather than 99.9%, that is very, very bad. So bad we might think it is worth incurring vast costs to stop it from happening or even to make it a bit less likely.

This is just the remote future operating as an effective utility monster I sketched in Chapter 1. I told you then the thought was not entirely fanciful.

All this makes an important assumption. Utilitarianism comes in a variety of flavours, as we briefly already saw, again in Chapter 1. Relatively bland versions think what morality asks of us is that we make such humans and other welfare-attributable creatures as there are as happy as possible. Other versions, like that in play here, are not so bland and say it is not just important to increase utility by making people more happy; it is also important to *make more* happy people. What is sometimes called *total* **utilitarianism** then says simply that we must aim to produce as much total utility as possible, be that by making people more happy or by making more happy people.

This is not a very credible view. The first thing wrong with it is just the obvious thought that people who do not exist have no moral claim on us to make them exist, however nice their potential lives might be. That is because people who do not exist have no moral claims on us of any kind. And that is because people who do not exist do not exist. As Karin Kuhlemann writes,

> I consider that the lives of actual people matter, and so does the fair apportionment of harms and benefits within a society; but merely hypothetical persons are not persons at all. "They" are merely abstractions, linguistically useful in considering future scenarios, but not actual entities of any kind. Hypothetical persons have no interests, no preferences and cannot be harmed or benefitted by whatever we do.[17]

I should be clear that by people who do not exist, I do not here mean people who do not exist *now*. In the year 2160, I think it is highly likely that there will be people living in Jinan and Sheffield who do not exist *now*. We can wrong those people by, for example, bequeathing a planet to them that excess warming has made hostile

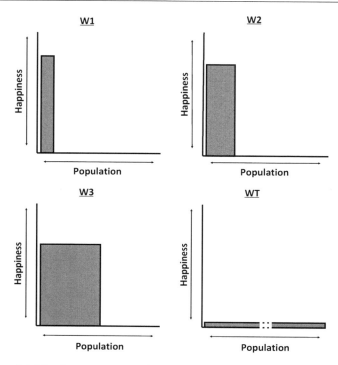

Figure 4.1 The Repugnant Conclusion.

to human life, and we should not do that if we can possibly avoid it. But a person who lives a life of perfect celibacy cannot meaningfully be said to wrong the children she never has by never having them because they do not exist now, and they never will exist. We do not have a duty to the universe to see that it contains as much value as possible, nor do we have a duty to non-existent people to bring them into being.

A more particular problem for total utilitarianism is that it leads to what Derek Parfit famously labelled the Repugnant Conclusion.[18] We met this before but again only briefly. Here is how it works (Figure 4.1). We suppose there is some threshold below which the value of a life is overall negative, and it is not worth living. (MacAskill, remember, thinks animals have lives like this.) Lives *just* above this threshold then are worth living but only barely. So we shall suppose they are, on balance, pretty low quality, if not quite no quality lives.

Now imagine a world W1 with a population of some size or other where everyone is blissfully happy. As happy as can be imagined. I don't know who the happiest person was who ever lived, but these people are happier than that.

But now compare a different world W2 where the people are all happy but a bit less happy than in the first world, maybe 95% as happy, which is still very happy indeed. That means we still have less happiness if we keep the population constant but let's not. If everyone in W2 is 95% as happy as in W1, there will be some increase we can make to the population that will be enough for W2 to be better than W1. Remember, we are assuming for argument that total utilitarianism is true. Maybe doubling it will do the trick. So W2 has twice as many people as W1 and they are all 95% as happy, but the bigger population makes up for the lower per capita welfare, so W2 is better.

Now compare W3. In W3, people are 95% as happy as in W2, but again, there are twice as many of them, and we are supposing again that is enough to compensate for the loss of per capita happiness and then some, so W3 is again better.

Now you have the idea. We are just going to keep doing this, making the graph ever shorter and ever fatter, and, eventually we end up with a world WT which has happiness per capita just barely above the threshold level and a population much, much larger than W1 had. And that world is better, according to total utilitarianism, than W1, blissful, heavenly, uncrowded W1. And that, says Parfit, is repugnant.

Many utilitarians reject total utilitarianism, taking the Repugnant Conclusion to be just what Parfit named it as being. But there are now some who confidently proclaim its truth. The commonest defences of it involve numerous variations on another famous piece of reasoning devised by Parfit. It is called the **Mere Addition Paradox**. It is intended to show that if we do not allow numbers to count in the way that threatens to lead to the paradox, we end up with a ranking of worlds that is not transitive.

A relation is **transitive** if when A has it to B and B to C, A must have it to C. I am taller than you. You are taller than Brian. So I am taller than Brian because "taller than" is transitive. I love you, and you love Brian, but maybe I do not love Brian. That is quite possible, as "loves" is not transitive. "Is better than", those who play these world-comparing games like to insist, is transitive.

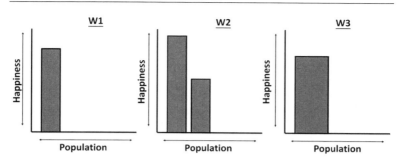

Figure 4.2 Mere Addition.

MacAskill offers a version of the argument based on premises he thinks are "close to indisputable".[19] (See Figure 4.2.) The first is just the transitivity of betterness.

The second is called **Dominance Addition**. It says this. Take a world with some people in it and make all those people better off. Also, add some other people with positive welfare. The result is better. After all, people being made happier can only be good, and even if we doubt that adding happy people makes things better, we surely do not suppose it makes things worse.

Dominance addition tells us that if we can contrive to move from W1 to W2, we make the world better. We have made the people who were there before better off, and we have added some more people who are not as happy as the others but still very happy. Great.

The third premise is called **Non-anti-egalitarianism**. It says this: suppose one world has greater average welfare than another. The first world also has greater total welfare. And it is more equal. In that case, non-anti-egalitarianism says the first world is better.

Now consider world 3. In W3, we have made the following changes to W2. We have raised the happiness of the new, less happy people and lowered the happiness of the old, happier people so as to make everyone equal. But we raised more than we lowered, so we have made people both on average and in aggregate better off. Non-anti-egalitarianism says this is better.

So W3 is better than W2, and W2 is better than W1, so by transitivity, W3 is better than W1. But hang on. The two-step move from W1 to W3 is equivalent to one of the steps that make up the sequence of changes that led us down the grim staircase from bliss to barely worth living that was the Repugnant Conclusion. But instead of appealing to total utilitarianism as a premise, we appealed to these "close to indisputable" principles, Which I will now dispute.

At least I will dispute one of them. For argument's sake—and only for argument's sake—you can have Non-anti-egalitarianism and transitivity—I will here only dispute Dominance Addition.[20] The argument might surprise us, as it may seem intuitive that W1 to W2 is an improvement and that W2 to W3 is an improvement, but W1 to W3 does not look much like an improvement. People are less happy in W3 than in W1, which looks like a loss, and there are more people, which, at this stage, the total utilitarian had better not assume is a gain if no questions are to get begged. But if we think W1 to W3 is plausibly a loss, we should, simply for that reason, no longer regard Dominance Addition as anywhere near indisputable.

Why? Well, because when we move from W1 to W2, what we do is not stable. It is a move which exposes us to *normative pressure* to move to W3, which is not somewhere where, *from the vantage point of W1*, we want to be. Suppose I do not have enough money to go on holiday. So I borrow some money from Lenny the Loan Shark. Hooray! I have money now! Off I go on my holiday! But now I am under normative pressure that I was not under before. I have a contractual obligation to pay Lennie back at his sky-high interest rate. And when I do that, I will no longer be able to afford a holiday. I also will not be able to afford to eat. So while borrowing the money looked like a good idea, it created a new obligation for me, a new normative pressure, and meeting that obligation makes me worse off than I was before. So borrowing the money was not a good idea after all.

Moving from W1 to W2 is like that. It seemed like a good idea. But that was before we looked at the new obligations it would engender. By making more people, people we would not have harmed had we chosen not to make them, we burden the people who were there before with an obligation to sacrifice some of their happiness in the name of equality. But equality was fine at the start in W1. And average welfare was even better in W1 than in W3. The only thing that has got better in W3 from the standpoint of W1 is total welfare, and that is just the thing whose value MacAskill is supposed to be convincing us of. So we should not agree to move from W1 to W2 because it would be a position where we would be obliged to agree to move to W3, and, from the standpoint of W1, we have good reason not to want that.

More generally, in cases like the above, where we have a clear sense that C is worse than A combined with a clear sense that for some B, B is better than A and C better than B, we can always resist the sense that B is better than A by appealing back to C's worseness than A: if C is better than B there is normative pressure for the consequentialist to go there from B and that, if we do indeed have a clear sense that C is worse than A, then it looks like a good reason not to think the move from A to B an improvement after all. Something as thin and formal as the supposed transitivity of better than is never going to tell us anything substantive and interesting about values unless we load the argument with values from the start in even diagnosing its violation.[21] And when we do that, the confident certainty of MacAskill's reasoning is apt to disintegrate.

I don't think the mere addition paradox constitutes a compelling argument for total utilitarianism or a reason to suppose the Repugnant Conclusion is anything other than what its name implies.

Notes

1. 1996, 173. © copyright 1945 C. S. Lewis Pte Ltd. Extract used with permission.
2. Johanssen 2020. See Browning and Veit for a rather different picture.
3. Williams, "The Human Prejudice" in his 2006, Hills 2010.
4. This footnote could be quite long. But see, e.g., Bostrom 2009, Shiller 2017, Tomasik 2017, Ćirković 2022.
5. 1904, 17–18.
6. 1904, 32–33.
7. MacAskill 2022, 88.
8. IPBES 2019, WWF 2022.
9. 2022, 213.
10. 2022, 860–1. Palmer is referencing Hill's 1983.
11. 1975, 16. On Mill on Empire, see Sullivan 1983, Bell, 2016, chapter 9.
12. McPherson 2022. Especially chapter 1.
13. Cohen 2013, 149, quoted McPherson 2022, 16.
14. 1984, 453–4.
15. 2014, 103.
16. Give or take. Kaneda and Haub 2022 guesstimate 117 billion people.
17. Kuhlemann 2019, 39–40.
18. 1984, chapter 17.
19. 2022, 181.
20. Astute readers will note that if we reject non-anti-egalitarianism, my argument against dominance addition won't work. Either way we are left without a useful argument.
21. Essentially, this point was made compellingly by John Broome in his "Can a Humean Be Moderate?" 1999. See further Hurley 1989.

Chapter 5

Intuitions*

5.1 Theory and Common Sense

Something must be clear by now. Utilitarianism appears, when we think through its consequences, to be constantly coming into conflict with moral common sense. It seems to forbid us to do some very innocent things like going to the cinema while failing to prohibit anywhere near as strictly enough quite terrible things like killing people to harvest their organs.

Some, as we have seen, look with equanimity on the eradication of the natural, biological world and urge us to give overriding priority to enabling squillions of synthetic sentient thingummies to rock around the galaxy having fake experiences. There seems to be no reductio argument against utilitarianism whose conclusion at least some are not prepared happily to embrace.

Faced with such cases, utilitarians will defend themselves in one of two ways. Sometimes they will try to argue that, in fact, their view is not committed to these conclusions that seem so repellent to common sense. Or they can and very often do seek to *outsmart* us where 'outsmart' is a word coined by Daniel Dennett in honour of Jack Smart.

> Outsmart v. To embrace the conclusion of one's opponent's reductio ad absurdum argument. "They thought they had me, but I outsmarted them. I agreed that it was sometimes just to hang an innocent man".[1]

---

* I say a lot more about the issues discussed in this chapter in Lenman 2024, especially Chapter 7.

One person's *modus ponens*, they say, is another's *modus tollens*. You know the story.

Person A: If P, then Q! P! So Q!
Person B: If P, then Q! Not Q! So not P!

We meet this all the time thinking about utilitarianism.

Utilitarian: If utilitarianism is true, you can push the big man off the bridge! Utilitarianism is true! So you can push the big man off the bridge!

Non-utilitarian: If utilitarianism is true, you can push the big man off the bridge! You can't push the big man off the bridge! So utilitarianism is not true!

This is an unfortunate impasse. Some people are very confident utilitarianism is true, confident enough to be OK with pushing people off bridges when the stakes are high enough.[2] Some people are confident it is not OK to push people off bridges in circumstances like these, so if utilitarianism says it is, so much the worse for utilitarianism. Can it be resolved?

5.2 Theory and Prejudice

Where do these confidences come from? Well, we might say they express *moral intuitions*. Though that is, so far, unhelpful, as all we can uncontroversially say about a moral intuition is that it is a state of mind of being more or less confident about some moral matter. We have these all the time. Just think of simple, uncontroversial cases. When we hear about or witness acts of clear cruelty or injustice, we just find ourselves thinking, *That is wrong*. Other, very different kinds of actions may impress us with their goodness, as when people show great courage in resisting cruelty or injustice, people like Sophie Scholl, her brother, Hans, and their friend, Christoph Probst, who were murdered by the Nazi authorities in Germany in 1943 for distributing leaflets denouncing that regime. I am morally impressed by these courageous people and what they did, morally appalled by their murderers.

Some intuitions are like these: intuitive judgements about particular people and particular things they do. Others are about general principles that we find attractive. For example, you may remember in Chapter 1, my quoting Rawls:

> Each person possesses an inviolability founded on justice that even the welfare of society as a whole cannot override.

I like the sound of that, and many others agree. It has, we might say, intuitive appeal.

It seems wise to me in thinking these things through to give a certain authority to particular cases over general principles. Very abstract, very general principles can be difficult things to know what to make of until we plug them into reality and see what they do there. So, for example, if there was some abstract principle, however attractive on the face of it, that turned out, when we carefully worked through its implications, to condone the judicial murder by the Nazis of the Scholls and of Probst, I don't think I would see much mileage in giving that principle further time.

Intuitions are the inputs to the pursuit of *reflective equilibrium* on the picture of moral epistemology given classical expression in the writings of John Rawls and now very widely accepted in the literature on ethics. On the understanding of this picture I would wish to defend, it is about the pursuit of coherence, seeking to articulate and clarify through reflection the values and moral understandings we embrace so we are better able to affirm them stably through our lives and share them as widely as possible across and among the communities we live in. When we seek reflective equilibrium, we start from where we are, with the intuitions, what Rawls calls *considered judgements*, on which we most confidently and stably agree and seek to regiment this often inchoate material into something systematically coherent and attractive.

The word 'attractive' is important. Coherence is not enough. Many repellent ethical outlooks can be made coherent. It is a mistake to see coherentism in moral epistemology as making of coherence a kind of master value.[3] We are looking to articulate a moral outlook that is coherent, yes, but also just, compassionate, decent, etc. To have such requirements is again just to trust our stable and widely shared intuitive sense that these things are important.

This reliance on intuition, sensibly carried out, might seem innocuous enough. Surely no one can take seriously the possibility that perhaps we are mistaken about justice and compassion, and maybe an ethic of cruelty and injustice is really, in some sense, true? That kind of moral scepticism seems barely intelligible. But the method of reflective equilibrium has its critics. Richard Hare spoke in this context of "the argument from received opinion"[4], while Richard Brandt dismissed it as a mere "reshuffling of moral prejudices".[5]

The philosophical rhetoric is strong here, but not all 'prejudices' are disreputable. Here is Bernard Williams:

> "Prejudice" is a powerful and ambiguous word, and its relations to theory are equally ambiguous. It has played a large role in the Cartesian tradition, in which any belief counts as a prejudice that has not yet been given a foundation. In this sense, it is certainly contrasted with theory, but in this sense, as I have already said, everything is a prejudice, in science as in ethics.[6]

And here, famously, is Edmund Burke:

> You see, Sir, that in this enlightened age I am bold enough to confess that we are generally men of untaught feelings, that, instead of casting away all our old prejudices, we cherish them to a very consider-able degree, and, to take more shame to ourselves, we cherish them because they are prejudices; and the longer they have lasted and the more generally they have prevailed, the more we cherish them. We are afraid to put men to live and trade each on his own private stock of reason, because we suspect that this stock in each man is small, and that the individuals would do better to avail themselves of the general bank and capital of nations and of ages.[7]

The word 'prejudice' is nowadays widely associated with contexts where we use it to deplore noxious and bigoted prejudices respecting (for example) sex or race. But that is not what Burke means here. He is rather using the word to involve the moral attitudes we absorb—we might here follow Hare and say 'receive'—from the moral culture that is our shared inheritance.

Shared is the important word. It is only insofar as the moral utterance I address to you connects with and is able to express, albeit in an idealizing spirit, the moral culture that we share that shapes our moral conceptual environment, making a space of shared reasons in which relations of moral accountability are possible, that human moral community can work. Prejudices, in this sense, are not so very terrible and that is just as well. We have precious little else to go by. When we try to see past them to some supposed rational foundation for ethics, there is not much to be found there except more prejudices. Though perhaps that word has too many negative associations. It is best to use different language and speak of emotions and shared commitments, such as our aspiration to live together in a just society where we treat each other with decency and compassion. Such an aspiration is not a thing we are compelled to by pure reason, but it is widely shared and endorsed and has proven highly stable under reflective scrutiny.

Human beings, moved by such desires as this one, converse and have conversed for many millennia about what moral concepts, understandings, codes, and rules should govern our lives together. That conversation is still going on. We disagree but there is actually a large space of very widespread agreement to be found even among people of diverse cultural backgrounds and political outlooks. We all admire kindness and deplore cruelty, admire generosity and deplore meanness, admire fairness and deplore injustice, even as we may experience sometimes deep disagreements about how we are to understand these things.

When I say that Sophie Scholl was a morally exemplary person or that it is wrong to push people off bridges I am, I think, doing something quite complex. I am certainly to be sure expressing an emotion, an aspiration to live in a society where people are expected to behave in this or that way and forbidden to behave in this or that way and perhaps honoured for behaving in certain ways. But I am here purporting to express not a private sentiment but something I take to be held in common, a shared aspiration incorporated in a shared moral culture. I have to take what I say to connect up with and be defensible from the perspective of such a shared moral culture if I am to expect other members of my moral community to take me seriously and find what I say interesting at all.

These things we find ourselves intuitively finding plausible or not plausible are, we already had occasion to propose, to a great extent, a reflection of our biological nature. The thought is an old one. Darwin famously wrote in *The Descent of Man*,

> If,... to take an extreme case, men were reared under precisely the same conditions as hive-bees, there can hardly be a doubt that our unmarried females would, like the worker-bees, think it a sacred duty to kill their brothers, and mothers would strive to kill their fertile daughters; and no one would think of interfering.[8]

Likewise, we invest immense love and energy in rearing our children, and whether others do likewise is a major factor in how well we regard them morally. Plausibly, this has a lot to do with the fact that we are mammals and not fish, Ks and not rs, when it comes to the reproductive strategy our species follows.

Our shared moral outlook is shaped by our biology and the history of our culture. It is natural to suppose that any recognition of this biological and historical contingency should have a debunking effect. But it should not. Morality is not a body of truths about the universe independent of humanity, but a body of truth humanity has shaped, deeply woven into our culture and our practice, expressive of our own very human moral understandings and concerns. It is at the heart of who we are, and without it, we would be altogether lost.

This was part of the great debate that was had at the time of the French Revolution, where we find on one side, in a British context, ardent revolutionaries like Tom Paine and Mary Wollstonecraft aspiring to make the world anew on a foundation of pure reason and, on the other hand, Burke, that great liberal conservative, who cautioned,

> When ancient opinions and rules of life are taken away, the loss cannot possibly be estimated. From that moment we have no compass to govern us, nor can we know distinctly to what port we steer.[9]

Pure reason, what Burke likes to call abstract metaphysical speculation, tells us nothing about morality. Rather, we inherit our moral sensibilities from our forebears. Fired up with revolutionary zeal, we can reject it and seek to make the moral world anew, but this is a project that can only fail and can only lead not to a beautiful new moral order but to a murderous nihilism. We strip away traditional, inherited forms of moral understanding, hoping to find behind it the light of pure reason, but what we actually find is…nothing.

5.3 Debunking

Fast-forward to a more recent moral philosophy and we find the same debate between rationalists such as Richard Hare, Derek Parfit, Katarzyna de Larazi Radek, and Peter Singer on the one hand, and other more communitarian moral philosophers such as John Rawls, Susan Hurley, Michael Walzer and Charles Taylor on the other.

Lazari Radek and Singer defend Henry Sidgwick's approach, which relies on axioms supposed to be self-evident truths of reason. Axioms such as the axiom of universal benevolence:

> [T]he good of any one individual is of no more importance, from the point of view (if I may say so) of the Universe, than the good of any other; unless, that is, there are special grounds for believing that more good is likely to be realised in the one case than in the other. And it is evident to me that as a rational being I am bound to aim at good generally—so far as it is attainable by my efforts,—not merely at a particular part of it.[10]

There is what we might call a **foundationalist** picture of moral epistemology where we start out with axioms such as these which we take to have a special certainty as self-evident findings of reason. Confident of their truth, we go out and build our theory on that foundation. Perhaps when we build it, we find it keeps coming into conflict with basic features of moral common sense, widely shared intuitions about, e.g., autonomy, justice, and the wrongness of pushing people off bridges. And when this happens we say, *So much the worse for moral common sense. It is doubtful and insecure. Our axioms cannot be wrong.*

This foundationalism seems in stark contrast with the method of reflective equilibrium. Singer and Lazari Radek urge that it really is not if we insist that reflective equilibrium be *wide*, where **wide reflective equilibrium** is what we get when our theorizing is responsible not just to moral intuitions but to everything else we know from the various sciences. And the sciences, Singer and Lazari Radek go on to urge, include biology, which offers evolutionary explanations of many aspects of moral common sense. Evolutionary explanations of moral beliefs, Singer and Lazari Radek claim, *debunk* those beliefs. However there is, they contend, no evolutionary explanation of the appeal of the principle of universal benevolence. So it, almost alone, remains undebunked, a truth of reason, not just something (like the incest taboo) it enhanced reproductive fitness for our ancestors to embrace.[11]

Utilitarian philosophers do have a habit of deploring appeals to intuition, to the considered judgements that comprise so much of moral common sense, while at the same time finding reasons to exempt from this scepticism the intuitions they like, the core intuitions that ground utilitarianism. Everything else is superstition and folly, these and these alone are truths of reason. The argument made by Singer and Lazari Radek does not greatly impress me, as it rests on a supposition I think false: that evolutionary explanations of moral beliefs always debunk. Whether it is true will depend on our **metaethical** view. For a robust realist like Sidgwick, Ross, or Singer and Lazari Radek, there may be a problem. For a more modest terrestrial view like my own, I think there is not.

For the robust realist, I think it may credibly be claimed that evolution debunks *everything*. The realist's independent moral reality was constituted independently of our moral sensibilities as shaped by contingent particularities of our biology and culture. That we have pro-social, altruistic impulses at all, caring for and looking out for each other, undoubtedly reflects the way we have evolved as social animals like baboons and not as solitary loners like the desert tortoise. The shaping of human nature was not a process that tracked any truths.[12]

Intuitions are not credibly seen on the model of a kind of perception where, by means of a faculty we understand nothing about, we somehow detect some independent body of moral truths out there in the world. There is no credible picture of how this supposed faculty came into being and how it might be supposed to work that allows the moral truth to shape and explain our moral beliefs.

But for the terrestrial understanding of intuition I adopt here, evolutionary explanation does not debunk. Our moral sensibilities express what we are, biologically and culturally, and as such, they are shaped by all the forces that have shaped us. Morality is a human, terrestrial thing, a part of who we are, and not some external authority to which our evolved nature might match up only as a matter of good luck. Romeo only thinks Juliet is beautiful because evolution made him that way. But Romeo is not making a mistake. From the evolved human perspective, which is all we have got, she really is.

Notes

1 Dennett 1987.
2 See, e.g., Greene 2013, 251. The whole book is an attack on moral common sense.
3 Hurley 1989, 261–2, 318–9, Lenman 2024.
4 1971.
5 1979, 22.

6 1985, 130.
7 1790/1982, 183.
8 1871, chapter 4.
9 1790/1982, 172–3.
10 Sidgwick 1981, 382.
11 de Lazari-Radek and Singer, 2014, chapter 7.
12 Street 2006 argues this case brilliantly.

Chapter 6

Cluelessness

6.1 Epistemic Humility: From Moderate Utilitarianism to Cluelessness

I have been misleading you. Forgive me. I put it to you that utilitarianism would have us push the man off the bridge in the bridge example and that it would have us kill the friendless man in the transplant example and harvest his organs. And that it tells us we can never go to the cinema when we might, as we always might, be doing more good some other way. And none of these things are true.

This chapter will concern itself with a reason why none of these things are true, which I think is devastating to utilitarianism. But before we get to that, we might note that not all utilitarians themselves believe these unpalatable claims. Some utilitarians, we have seen, favour the outsmarting response here, which embraces the conclusion of the putative *reductio*. But it is important to note that not all do.

J. L. Mackie, who was not a utilitarian, offered six reasons why he thought the most credible form of utilitarianism would recommend a close adherence to moral common sense. Sticking to the latter would be, Mackie urged, a far better strategy for utilitarians than trying to calculate and compare the expected utility of every prospective action that confronts us. The six reasons were as follows:

1. We don't have the time and energy we need to perform the appropriate utilitarian calculations.
2. We don't have the information to perform the appropriate utilitarian calculations.

DOI: 10.4324/9781003300045-7

3. Our judgement is too easily swayed by our interests and affections.
4. Even when we figure out correctly what to do, weakness will often stop us from doing it.
5. Even our right decisions will be misused as precedents in circumstances where it would be wrong so to use them.
6. It would be counterproductive for us to try to live by a highly demanding morality that we have little chance of living up to.[1]

"Considerations of these sorts," Mackie continues,

> entail that a reasonable utilitarian critical thinker would recommend the adoption of fairly strict principles and the development of fairly firm dispositions in favour of honesty, veracity, agreement-keeping, justice, fairness, respect for various rights of individuals, gratitude to benefactors, special concern for some individual connected in certain ways with the agent, and so on, as being more likely in general to produce behaviour approximating to that which would be required by the utilitarian ideal than any other humanly viable morality.[2]

There is much that might appeal in this, as we might call it, **moderate utilitarian** view in contrast with the bolder, more extreme contemporary outsmarters.

The contrast made here between moderate and extreme is, of course, a spectrum, not a simple binary affair. Most utilitarian philosophers manage to be at least somewhat accommodating to moral common sense, though some much more than others.

We should not confuse moderate utilitarianism with rule utilitarianism. Rule utilitarianism, remember, says follow the rules general acceptance of which would generate as much goodness as possible. Moderate utilitarianism is a form of act utilitarianism that just says do the thing with the best prospect of generating as much welfare as possible, but supposes the best strategy for doing that is to follow the familiar rules of common sense morality.

We then have to address the question of how we are supposed to be in a position to know that this strategy is more likely to produce behaviour approximating to the utilitarian ideal.

Mill (a utilitarian very much on the moderate end of the spectrum) has an answer:

> Again, defenders of utility often find themselves called upon to reply to such objections as this—that there is not time, previous to action, for calculating and weighing the effects of any line of conduct on the general happiness. This is exactly as if any one were to say that it is impossible to guide our conduct by Christianity, because there is not time, on every occasion on which anything has to be done, to read through the Old and New Testaments. The answer to the objection is, that there has been ample time, namely, the whole past duration of the human species. During all that time, mankind have been learning by experience the tendencies of actions; on which experience all the prudence, as well as all the morality of life, are dependent. People talk as if the commencement of this course of experience had hitherto been put off, and as if, at the moment when some man feels tempted to meddle with the property or life of another, he had to begin considering for the first time whether murder and theft are injurious to human happiness. Even then I do not think that he would find the question very puzzling; but, at all events, the matter is now done to his hand.[3]

So here is one story. Mankind has been learning empirically what actions have what tendencies and shaping our common sense moral outlook in the light of that knowledge to best serve the promotion of overall utility.

Only, I'm sorry to say, we have been doing no such thing.

The heart of Mackie's rationale for moderate utilitarianism is a measure of epistemic humility about our ability to know the consequences of what we do. But in fact, the degree of humility that is warranted on this score is considerably greater than is often appreciated. This is because we are simply *clueless* about the overall consequences of anything we do, clueless in a way that goes far beyond the ordinary uncertainties attendant upon all our practical reasoning.

In a nice discussion of these issues, Richard Boyd puts the problem eloquently:

> We lack both the information gathering and the information processing capacity to anticipate with any reliability the

consequence for human flourishing of particular action choices or even to retrospectively assess the overall consequences for flourishing of particular actions.[4]

The important word here is 'overall'. When the utilitarian tells us to look to the consequences of our actions, they do not mean the relatively immediate, proximate consequences that we can see coming and that inform all our decisions. They mean *all* the consequences of our actions for human flourishing, all of them forever.

That is what we are supposed to be concerned with promoting, but we do not know how to promote it. And we do not have any meaningful empirical data on how to promote it. The empirical data we have deals with relatively short-term consequences. If you have sex, you are liable to have children. If you smoke tobacco, you are liable to have poor respiratory health. If you push the big man off the bridge, you will stop the trolley, and he will die. But we do not know what *any* action anyone *ever* did has had by way of total consequences for so long as it had—and will have—any consequences.[5]

We don't know this because the world is very intricate and the future very long. In fact, except for the most recent actions, we don't even know the score *so far*. Think about it. From a utilitarian point of view, was, say, the Peloponnesian War in 5th century BCE Greece a good or a bad thing overall? Of course, it was pretty awful at the time but we can be certain its long-term effects will have been colossal and continue to this day. We cannot compute or start to compute their effect on, as it were, the total net value of the universe as a whole for the whole of time. In fact we can't even compute it *up to now*. How could we? In the maelstrom of subsequent history, there can be no tracing that thread.

So we cannot learn from experience which kinds of actions score well or badly from a utilitarian standpoint in any way where that experience might feed back to shape the ideals and principles that make up our moral common sense. Those are scores that never come in.

6.2 Cluelessness

And this is the consideration I consider devastating for utilitarianism. We push the big man off the bridge, and he stops the trolley and is killed while the five people who would otherwise have died are saved. Which is better. Yes? So the utilitarian thinks we should do it. Well maybe. But maybe not. Maybe one of the people who survive will go on to have a family, children, grandchildren, and one of their grandchildren will be a terrible criminal who causes terrible suffering to many. Maybe the man we push would have gone on to live a life of great generosity and kindness, making many people happy. What about all this stuff? What about all the stuff that is *off the page* in this and all such examples? All the *other* stuff *causally downstream of* the immediate effects of what we do. Does that not matter?

Thinking about examples like *Bridge*, what we ordinarily do with such more distant consequences of our action is ignore them completely, screen them off as irrelevant. We go in for a form of what I understand is sometimes called **sandboxing**, a term from computing which in this context means we pretend in effect that the consequences spelled out in the examples are all the consequences there are.[6] It is almost as if the example is asking us to imagine a fantastically simple universe where you, the big man, and the five imperilled people are all the people there are, and the world will end in a day or two, leaving no time for causal chains to snowball on, as they are liable to, for a very long time. We forget that these are toy examples that are really only very telling if we frame them in toy worlds.

Looking at the toy examples, we got concerned. Utilitarianism, it seems, tells us we cannot go to the cinema. It tells us to kill innocent people to prevent riots, harvest their organs, or stop lethally directed runaway trolleys. Intuitively, that looks like bad news for utilitarianism. But many utilitarians care little for intuitions.

But in fact, the real news is *much worse* for the utilitarian. What does utilitarianism tell us to do in these situations when we do *not* frame them in toy worlds? The answer is very simple and very clear. It tells us *nothing*. Nothing at all.

The causal chains we set in motion by our actions last a long time. Terrible things can be found down them. And reliably so. And here, if you will indulge me, I want to talk about sex. I want to talk about *a lot* of sex. Come with me to Germany, or what is now Germany, 500 years ago. Here are Hans and Marthe on their wedding night happily making love. This is joyful consensual sexual intercourse between two married people who love each other and are lawfully married. There can be no possible moral objection to what is happening here. Only perhaps there can.

For as it happens, Hans and Marthe are, through the child that will be conceived as a result of what they are now doing, distant ancestors of Adolf Hitler. What Hans and Marthe are doing is *causing the Holocaust*. We think they are doing nothing wrong, but if they are causing the Holocaust, surely they are, at least from the standpoint of a consequentialist.

If they had murdered their child, we would naturally think that was awful. And yet, at least from a consequentialist standpoint, perhaps it would not have been. For them to have done that would have been *preventing the Holocaust*.

The example is not at all extravagant or fanciful. I made Hans and Marthe up, but Hitler really did have ancestors. Like us all, he had two parents, four grandparents, eight great-grandparents, 16 great-great-grandparents, and so on in increasing powers of 2. By the time we are 400 years before Hitler's day he has a LOT of ancestors. Let's say a century is four generations, and we are talking 2^{16}. That gives Hitler 65,536 great-great-great-great-great-great-great-great-great-great-great-great-great-grandparents happily conceiving his great-great-great-great-great-great-great-great-great-great-great-great-great-grandparents. Now a little reflection will satisfy you that some of those 65,536 people were in fact the same people occupying different slots in a very big family tree. Still, we are talking, as I warned you we would, about *a lot* of sex. If we allow 300,000 years as the time homo sapiens have been around, that is 12,000 generations by my (obviously very rough) rule of thumb, giving Hitler 2^{12000} ancestors—or slots for ancestors—of that order. That is a huge number, far, far bigger than the roughly 100 billion human people that intelligent guesswork says ever lived.[7] So multiple slot occupancy goes up an awful lot as we go back in time. But still, we really are now talking about *an awful lot* of sex. *All* that sex was causing the Holocaust. And so was everything causally upstream from it, acts of courtship, of introduction, choices made, to turn down the cowherd and marry the potmaker, to join the army and see the world, to start a cheese business, to conquer Lydia, to plant a tree, just there by the inner walkway. There is no limit really to the things that can and do lead, by whatever causal chain, subtle or obvious, to the making of children.

Acts of procreation are apt, we might say, to be ***identity-affecting***. They make a difference to the identities of people who will subsequently come to exist. Acts which lie causally upstream from such acts, we might say, are indirectly identity-affecting. Both of these make a difference to which people come into existence in the next generation, a difference that can be relied on to make a difference to what identity-affecting actions get to be done in that generation and so is apt to ramify endlessly down the generation. So rather than petering out like the ripples on a pond when a stone hits it (as some have supposed[8]), the causal ramifications, at least of very many of our actions, are massive and grow larger, snowball-like, as they progress.

An awful lot of people all through human history did, quite innocently, an awful lot of stuff that was causing the Holocaust and failed to do a lot of stuff that was preventing it. Little did they know. And little do *we* know what huge and tiny terrible and wonderful things we are certainly every day causing or failing to prevent. Actions that cause death or births are especially liable to have huge downstream consequences that soon overwhelm their more immediate consequences in magnitude. Given this, we can simply never know, from a consequentialist standpoint, of an act of killing, say, if it is right or wrong. Such a consequential thing as a killing will have consequences too vast and incalculable for anybody to compute. If that is true of an act of killing a single person, it must also be true of an act of killing a large number of people, something like the Holocaust itself. Indeed, I fear it turns out that, from a consequentialist perspective, we do not know the Holocaust was wrong.

But of course we *do* know the Holocaust was wrong. This utilitarian *ponens* must be any decent person's *tollens*. There is an intuition in play here, but I am happy with it: if we do not know the Holocaust was wrong, we do not know anything.

Is our complex endowment of emotions and concerns that disposes us to deplore the Holocaust a consequence of our evolutionary history? Very likely, yes. But that should not, even for a moment, diminish our confidence that the Holocaust was an appalling and inhuman thing.

If utilitarianism is true, we do not know the Holocaust was wrong. We do know the Holocaust was wrong. So utilitarianism is false. QED.

If that is still too dependent on intuition, it suffices to note that these considerations, the *Cluelessness Considerations* we might call them, teach us that utilitarianism tells us nothing about what to do in the kinds of difficult circumstances the examples engage with and, indeed, in all circumstances we are realistically likely to encounter, and we can see that much without appealing to any ethical intuitions at all.

For an ethical theory that is fatal. For what we should do is the subject matter of ethics, and a theory with *nothing*, or as good as nothing, to say about that has failed as completely as any theory can.

6.3 Cancelling Out and Large Numbers

A distinction is often made between *objective* consequentialism, which says the right thing to do is the thing that will *actually* produce the most value, and *subjective* consequentialism, which says the right thing is the thing with the highest *expected value* given the agent's information. Where the expected value of a choice is what you get by summing all the numbers obtained when the value of each possible outcome is multiplied by its probability. The distinction is important in examples like this one of Frank Jackson's:[9] you are a doctor and can give patient pill A, pill B, or pill C. Pill A will not completely cure them but make them much better so their condition impacts only a little on their quality of life. Of pill B and C, you know one will completely cure them, the other will kill them, but you do not know which. Objective consequentialism says give them whichever of B and C will cure them. Subjective consequentialism says give them A. Or so it is supposed.

But of course, this is another toy example. When we sandbox in the more foreseeable, proximate consequences of action, it makes a big difference whether we take our consequentialism as objective or subjective. When we take the sandbox away and have to consider *all* the consequences of what we do in perpetuity, this makes no meaningful difference to our cluelessness. In reality, in this case and any other, consequentialism tells you nothing about what you should do: there are just way too many conceivable outcomes, and your information about their probabilities is too impoverished to leave you anything other than clueless.

We might still think it is OK to focus on the immediate effects, like the trolley killing the people now, today that it is going to kill now, today and ignore the far greater unknown consequences further down the line. We might think this because we reasonably imagine the expected good and bad in the unknown consequences will somehow probabilistically *cancel out* leaving the difference made by the consequences we can readily foresee to tip the balance.

In supposing this, however, we are appealing to an *a priori* **indifference postulate** of a kind that is not very reputable. The idea is that when we are confronted with a range of possible future outcomes about whose respective probabilities we have no information, we reasonably assign them equal probabilities.

It doesn't work.[10] It doesn't work because there are too many different ways of carving up the space of possible futures into distinct possible outcomes and, without relevant empirical information, no non-arbitrary way of choosing between them. So we can reasonably do nothing of the sort.

Consider an action whose consequences ramify far into the future, as we can be certain those of many actions do. Pretend, for argument's sake, that we have some meaningful way of identifying and individuating discrete consequences of that action. So if we suppose, just for simplicity, we are hedonistic utilitarians for whom all value attaches to sentient experience, we might then decide a minute of sentient experience of a sentient creature is a 'unit' consequence. And pretend, again for argument's sake, we have some meaningful metric for the goodness of these consequences. We have perhaps a goodness scale where everything zero or above we think of as good and everything below zero as bad.

Two possible kinds of consequence, then, we might say good and bad, zero or above and below zero. So by invoking a principle of indifference, we might suppose these, good and bad consequences, to be equally likely with zero as the axis of some nice symmetrical probability distribution. So in the long-term future, when there will be a huge number of unforeseen consequences, they cancel each other out, conveniently giving everything we don't know about an expected value of zero. The consequences we know about then make a decisive impact on expected value.

But then we ask the fatal question. *What is so special about zero?* Why not divide this possibility space up some other way? Take another point, say 15 of whatever fanciful units we are using above zero. Call it Y15. (I am thinking of a point on the y-axis of some fanciful graph.) Now we can say there are two possible kinds of consequence, Y15 or above and below Y15. By invoking a principle of indifference, we take these to be equally likely. So in the long run, they cancel each other out.

Now take another point, say 20 units below 0. Call it Y-20. There will be two possible kinds of consequences then: Y-20 or above and below Y-20. By invoking a principle of indifference, we take these to be equally likely. So in the long run, they cancel each other out. To say nothing of *three* possible kinds of consequence answering to the ranges up to Y20, between Y20 and Y15, and from Y15 on up. By invoking a principle of indifference...

The problem, of course, is that there are too many ways of carving up the probability space, and it is an *empirical* question which way gives the right results. It is an empirical question where the axis of symmetry is if there even is one, a question that can only be answered with empirical data that will shed light on the mean value of the unforeseen consequences of an action in the very, very long term. And about that, we are clueless.

Joanna Burch-Brown, in an interesting paper on this topic, suggests it might help to invoke **the law of large numbers**.[11] The law of large numbers is a statistical law that says that if we grow the size of our sample of whatever it may be that we are interested in, we will find that the actual distribution of whatever variable may concern us will approach ever more closely to the **underlying probability distribution**. That is why if, say, you toss a coin ten times, it would be no very great surprise if you got eight or more heads. But if you tossed a coin a million times and got 800,000 or more heads, you would be very rightly very astonished. The underlying probability distribution with coin tossing is just 50/50, and that is what we will expect to approximate ever more closely as the numbers get bigger and bigger. (This is why in gambling, the House always wins in the long run.)

OK. But surely this is only any help to us *if we know what the underlying probability distribution is*. And we don't. We can't know this *a priori* by appealing to some indifference principle, and we can't know it *a posteriori* because the questions we confront if we are serious consequentialists, questions about the total effects of the things we do between now and the end of the universe, are not questions for which we have any meaningful prospect of obtaining any meaningful data.

There is more to Burch-Brown's argument: there may still be a rescue strategy in the offing for the utilitarian. Even if we do not know what the underlying probability distribution is, it might seem significant if we just know or have good reason to believe *that there is one*. As would be the case if the distribution had some kind of stable, overall *pattern*. And we know, Birch-Brown reminds us, from a thing in statistics called the **Central Limit Theorem** and related results, that features of things that result from the interaction of large numbers of disconnected causal influences tend to end up distributed in patterned ways, such as those represented in familiar bell curves, as *normal distributions* which are symmetrical around the mean with probability getting lower in symmetrical ways the further from the mean we get. Patterns emerge out of chaos, possibly offering consequentialism hope.

As Burch-Brown puts it, with reference to that notoriously **chaotic** thing that is the weather,

> It is notoriously difficult to predict weather more than a short while in advance. Weather systems are chaotic, which means their behaviour is extremely sensitive to initial starting conditions. Minute differences in initial conditions can lead to dramatic differences in the resulting weather. But the *climate* does not share the weather's level of unpredictability.[12]

The now proverbial butterfly flaps its wings in China, and by so doing, it changes the weather; a bit later on, there is a storm in Oregon on what would otherwise have been a sunny day. But while the weather is affected, the *climate* does not change. The relative overall prevalence over time of stormy and sunny days stays what it is unperturbed by the activities of butterflies.

Suppose the value of consequences is like that. Then even if we do not know where on our imaginary value scale to put a fixed axis of symmetry, we might think we *have reason to believe there is one*. Suppose the average value of a given unit consequence is some number N on our imaginary metric of value. So the way we were imagining things, N is the average value of a minute of sentient experience of a sentient creature considering all the minutes and all the creatures. So N will provide our axis of symmetry.

We don't know what N is, but maybe *we don't need to*. We then take these, N-or-above and below N, to be equally likely with N, whatever it is, as the centre of some symmetrical probability distribution. So in the long-term future, when there will be a huge number of unforeseen consequences, they will, in the long run, cancel each other out, conveniently giving everything we don't know about an expected value of N, whatever that is. And whatever that is, the consequences we know about can now make a decisive impact on expected value. So consequentialism works just fine. Yes?

Well, no. No. I talked earlier about stable, overall patterns and a fixed axis of symmetry; the words *stable* and *fixed* do a lot of work here. Are we talking about loads of local patterns or about one huge, uniform, overall global pattern?

N is defined as the average value of stuff *globally*. But we can also think about the more *local* mean value of stuff (experienced minutes) in a given region of space and time which we might represent by the letter L. So is L, the more local mean value of stuff around here—say, on planet Earth in the 21st century the same as it was in the Jurassic Era and the same as it will be in the 31st century when the circumstances of life—if there is any life—will surely be very different from what they are now? Is L highly variable, taking different values at different historical periods? Or is L stable and fixed, effectively a constant, so that L, the mean value of stuff, at least in any given relatively large region, is always just the same as N, the global mean?

If we think of L as fixed, constant, unchanging then human activity is not changing it. Were it not a constant but instead changing and fluctuating through history as the circumstances of life change, those fluctuations might prove to be *dependent* on the choices people make or do. But if it is fixed, nothing is changing or influencing it and so, a fortiori, we are not. It doesn't care about us, just as the climate doesn't care about butterflies.

If L is a fixed constant equal to N, we live in a universe whose value we can readily state: it is just L (or N) times however much stuff (understood in terms of the number of experienced minutes) there is.

In these circumstances, N will most likely be either positive or negative.[13] This has interesting consequences. If N is negative, if we are *total* utilitarians, we should be **anti-natalists**: we should try to bring it about that there is as little evaluatively significant stuff as possible so that sentient life is extinguished as fast as possible. Because life is bad, and it is going to go on being bad as long as life goes on, and, hey, we can do nothing about it because L is a constant.

If L is a positive constant and we are *total* utilitarians, we should devote all our efforts to make sure life goes on as long as possible seeing as, whatever happens, it is sure to be good. So we need to maximize how much stuff there is. And so long as we do that, it doesn't much matter what else we do as L is a positive constant, so everything is bound to be, on average, good and good to degree N.

Suppose L is constant, and we are *average* utilitarians. Well, then it just doesn't matter what we do. Because in the long run the average value of the stuff that happens, all of it, foreseen and otherwise, is just going to be L. The utilitarian mission of making the world (on average) a better place is doomed to fail. So do what you like; it makes no moral difference. So we may escape from cluelessness but are still left with a moral theory that gives us no guidance at all.

But that is surely idle talk. We have no reason at all to suppose L is a stable constant, and we can surely be extremely confident that it is *not* a fixed constant, the same on planet Earth in the early 21st century as it was in the Jurassic Era and the same as it will be in the 31st or 301st century. Because if we know anything, we know that the conditions of life change and change a great deal over time. So we can be sure that L is not constant but it fluctuates, and we can be very sure, given how large we now know the impact of human action is, that L is not independent of the choices people make. And if L is not independent of the choices we make, then neither is N, the global average. In which case the pattern, if there is a pattern, is not stable, and the axis of symmetry is not fixed. The rescue strategy crashes, and we are clueless again.

The Central Limit Theorem and related results may give us reason to suppose there are going to be patterns to whatever emerges from the chaos that ensues when we trouble the causal order by our agency. But it doesn't tell us what these patterns will be, how stable or variable they are, or how they themselves are affected by our own activity as the sometimes vast effects of our actions continue to ramify across the immensity of future time. Both metaphorically and literally, what we do affects not only the weather but also the climate. Let's turn to the climate.

Notes

1 1985, 190.
2 Mackie 1985, 190.
3 1861, 69–70. "Done to his hand" means already prepared for him in advance.
4 Boyd 2003, 513.
5 It is famously said of the late Chinese Prime Minister Zhou Enlai that, asked by Henry Kissinger about the impact of the French Revolution, he replied that it was "too early to say". It's funny because Zhou is so cautious but in fact he is nowhere near cautious enough. It will *always* be too early to say. (A point which stands even when we learn that in fact Zhou was referring to the French upheavals of 1968 and not 1789. See Ratcliffe, 2016.).
6 I learned about this talking to Philip Mallaband.
7 Kaneda and Haub, 2022.

8 Moore 1903, 153, Smart, 1973, 33.
9 Jackson 1991.
10 See Shakel 2007, North 2010.
11 Burch-Brown 2014.
12 Burch-Brown 2014, 113.
13 I'll leave considering the case where N is zero as an exercise for the reader.

Chapter 7

Cluelessness and the Climate

7.1 A Question About Climate Change

Earth is about four and a half billion years—or four and a half aeons—old. Sometime upward of three and a half aeons ago, the first living things came into being in a world very different from our own in fundamental ways. The atmosphere at the time life first appeared would seem to have contained a good measure of carbon dioxide but no free oxygen. ('Free' oxygen as opposed to oxygen tied up in carbon dioxide—CO_2—molecules.) That state of affairs didn't last as some early life-forms developed that went in for photosynthesis, absorbing carbon dioxide from the atmosphere and releasing free oxygen back into it. At first, the consequences do not seem to have been very dramatic, as the oxygen generated was chemically captured by iron and other such materials that reacted with and absorbed it. But this brake on atmospheric oxygen did not last forever, and in due course, maybe around two and a half aeons ago, a great catastrophe occurred, the so-called **Great Oxygenation Event (GOE)**, whereby free oxygen first became abundant in the atmosphere, as indeed it has continued to be.[1] I say *catastrophe* advisedly, for oxygen was toxic to the anaerobic organisms that were then abundant. Such organisms were not wholly wiped out. There are still anaerobic creatures to be found, notably the bacteria in our guts. But the GOE was nonetheless a catastrophic mass extinction event. From the point of view of the living creatures that preceded it, what it amounted to was the disastrous contamination of Earth's atmosphere by a deadly poisonous gas, oxygen, a quite tremendous and disastrous environmental catastrophe. Of course, from our point of view, it might appear, with hindsight, a rather good thing. We humans are aerobic beasts. No oxygen, no humans.

DOI: 10.4324/9781003300045-8

A bad thing, then, perhaps, for the anaerobic life-forms that were around at the time but a jolly good thing for us humans who are around now. But let us rise above such parochial, localised perspectives and ask what might seem a fundamental question. Did the GOE make the world a better place? Was it, as we might say, *a good thing*? Not a good thing for us, not a good thing for whatever was around at the time, but just a good thing.

7.2 Humean Cost-Benefit Analysis

The curious question of whether the world—the whole of it—is a good thing crops up in Hume's *Dialogues Concerning Natural Religion* in a very different context, where the discussion turns to the Problem of Evil, the famous problem of how a good God could have created a world so full of evil.

Under pressure to address the awfulness of so much of the world, Cleanthes urges we should simply insist that the good in the world, considered as a whole, outweighs the bad:

> The only method of supporting Divine benevolence, and it is what I willingly embrace, is to deny absolutely the misery and wickedness of man. Your representations are exaggerated; your melancholy views mostly fictitious; your inferences contrary to fact and experience. Health is more common than sickness; pleasure than pain; happiness than misery. And for one vexation which we meet with, we attain, upon computation, a hundred enjoyments.

At which point Philo jumps on him:

> What! no method of fixing a just foundation for religion, unless we allow the happiness of human life, and maintain a continued existence even in this world, with all our present pains, infirmities, vexations, and follies, to be eligible and desireable! But this is contrary to every one's feeling and experience: It is contrary to an authority so established as nothing can subvert: No decisive proofs can ever be produced against this authority; *nor is it possible for you to compute, estimate, and compare all the pains and all the pleasures in the lives of all men and of all animals*: And thus by your resting the whole system of religion on a point, which, from its very nature, must for ever be uncertain, you tacitly confess, that that system is equally uncertain.[2]

That, then, is Cleanthes's project if you want to know if the world, all of it, is a good thing. You need to "compute, estimate, and compare all the pains and all the pleasures in the lives of all men and of all animals". At least that is the project if you follow Hume here in adopting a hedonistic conception of value whereby it consists in pleasure and freedom from pain. If it is more complicated than that, then, well, it is more complicated than that. Even if it isn't, that's quite a computation, an enormous cost-benefit analysis for the whole of creation.

Let a *Humean cost-benefit analysis* be an imagined exercise of this kind where we compute, estimate, and compare, well, everything that has a value to arrive at a valuation that applies to an entire world. So we might say that the GOE was a good thing if the world, as it has turned out is, in the light of a Humean cost-benefit analysis, a better world than the world we would have had—or the world *someone* would have had, a world where there would be no *us*—had it never happened.

And we might say that any action I perform, such as the action of begetting a child or planting a tree, will count as making the world a better place if the world where I perform it is a better world, in the light of a Humean cost-benefit analysis, than the world would otherwise have been.

7.3 Compared to What?

If we wish, like Cleanthes, somehow to determine whether the *actual* world is on the whole good, it might be unclear what we should *compare* it to: to the various other worlds that there might have been? Or to the case where there is no world at all if we think that represents a genuine possibility? Or, if we think, as utilitarians do, that sentient life, or at least sentient something, is a condition for there being anything of value, perhaps compared to a dead world where sentience is everywhere and always absent? And do we think of that empty world, or dead world, case as somehow representing a baseline of neutrality, neither good nor bad? Or does the question of how good an empty or dead world would have been fail to make any clear sense?

Attempting to put an axiological estimate onto an empty or dead world is at best a difficult and at worst, as I myself am disposed to believe, a thoroughly meaningless exercise. But we get a different kind of difficulty when we turn to the question I raised at the outset, *Was the GOE a good thing?* Here the obvious and natural term of comparison is not to compare it with nothing happening ever or nothing ever being sentient or with how things were before it but with *it*, the GOE, not happening at all. What we presumably need to do is to compare how things have gone in the actual world, causally conditioned as it has been by the GOE, with the way things would have gone in the counterfactual possible world in which the GOE did not occur. Had the GOE somehow not happened, other stuff would, of course, have happened instead. Life on Earth would have had a very different history, no doubt, one in which human beings never evolved but perhaps one in which different, perhaps unimaginably different, creatures emerged instead and got up to who knows what wonderful or terrible adventures.

One thing that is obviously true about this vast counterfactual history, stretching forward from the actual date of the GOE in our own world, is that, if there is a fact of the matter about how it goes, that—very big—fact is *utterly, comprehensively inscrutable*. Of course, we can have a stab at the early stages. The stuff that got poisoned by oxygen soon after the GOE would not have been poisoned by oxygen at that time if the GOE had not occurred. But imagining how that history would have unfolded in the very long term, all the way up to the present and beyond to the death throes of the universe, forget it, we have no idea; the fact in question here is simply epistemically out of our reach.

Perhaps it is worse than that. Perhaps there simply is no such fact. Of course, there are familiar stories about how to understand **counterfactuals** in terms of possible worlds. Thus a follower of David Lewis will say that when we think about the counterfactual circumstances where the GOE never happened, we are thinking about the nearest possible worlds where it never happened.[3] An account like this brings with it a significant philosophical headache in the form of the difficulty of making sense of talk of possible worlds, assuming we do not follow Lewis himself in taking it literally and realistically and embracing a **modal realism** that most would consider a cure for which there is no adequate disease.[4] If we balk at this, we are left searching the *actual* world, the only world many of us think there is—for facts that might somehow ground the truth of counterfactuals. And sometimes they can readily enough be found. Here is Stalnaker:

> Is there an informative way to say what the fact about the actual world is in virtue of which a true counterfactual is true? In particular cases, there surely is. Sly Pete would have lost if he

had called in virtue of his losing hand; Heath would have won if Wilson hadn't in virtue of the dispositions of the voters; the match would have lit if struck in virtue of its chemical composition and the presence of oxygen in the environment.[5]

These are nice, tame counterfactuals. Little counterfactuals of the kind we know and love. If kangaroos had no tails, they would fall over.[6] If Charlie's parachute had not failed, she would not have been killed. Here we just apply our knowledge of the laws of nature to the known facts of kangaroo anatomy or of the circumstances of Charlie's fall. But might it also be a fact that if Charlie's parachute had not failed, she would have gone on to raise a family and, in due course, she would have had a great-great-grandson who was frightfully good at the clarinet? Deep metaphysical waters loom here but it is hard to see how this could ever be straightforward in anything like the same way. Perhaps we can make sense of such clarinet counterfactuals having a truth value fixed by plugging the laws of nature into the circumstances specified by their antecedents on the assumption that **determinism** is true. Then the laws of nature perhaps would settle the question of her counterfactual great-grandson's prowess or lack of it on the clarinet given a suitably precise specification of how exactly we are to imagine things differing from how they actually are. But even then, we are in some trouble as a suitably precise specification to determine something as remote as that is surely going to be *very precise indeed*, far more so than, "If Charlie's parachute had not failed...," or "If the Great Oxgenation Event had not occurred..." or anything like the antecedents to counterfactuals we employ in ordinary thought and deliberation. Events like Charlie's parachute not failing or the GOE not happening are multiply realizable. They can happen in many ways, and unless we are to specify these with a fabulous precision very far beyond what is realistically possible in practice, they are unlikely to settle a truth value for such facts about their very remote consequences.[7] All this assuming the truth of determinism, which is quite an assumption. So there is perhaps much to be said for the kind of scepticism well expressed by Elizabeth Anscombe when she recollects her youthful encounter with

> the doctrine of *scientia media*, according to which God knew what anybody would have done if e.g. he hadn't died when he did. ... I found I could not believe this doctrine: it appeared to me that there was not, quite generally, any such thing as what

would have happened if what did happen had not happened, and that in particular there was no such thing, generally speaking, as what someone would have done if… and certainly there was no such thing as how someone would have spent his life if he had not died as a child.[8]

7.4 Humean Cost-Benefit Analysis Again

Someone might persist in saying what we need is to do a cost-benefit analysis of the GOE. But it should now be clear, and was maybe always clear, that this could only be a sort of a joke. Some people of course struggle to take more ordinary forms of **cost-benefit analysis** seriously as a measure of value, where we identify value with prices fixed by people's behaviour in markets or, where markets can't help us, bother citizens with questionnaires asking how much they would be willing to pay for the Amazon Rain Forest or whatever and then pretend the numbers coming out the other end are meaningful except as meeting the pragmatic demand to satisfy government decision-makers constitutionally unwilling to taking seriously any cost or benefit not represented as a number.[9]

With Humean cost-benefit analysis, the difficulties are different and deeper. For one thing, the value assignments we obtain by observing the behaviour of people in markets or by the kind of contingent valuation just alluded to might, at best, give some extremely loose indication of how good things are from the perspective of rational creatures of the sort we are familiar with in the 21st century: modern human beings. But the question we are trying to ask is bigger than humanity. Much bigger. Not a good thing for us. Not a good thing for whatever was around at the time. But a good thing. Simpliciter. From the point of view of the universe.

For that, we need to compute, estimate, and compare all the interests of all the creatures, human beings, dogs, wolves, rats, possible future sentient androids, possible future distant evolutionary descendants of humans, dogs, wolves, rats, possible future sentient AI, possible extraterrestrial creatures with whom we may possibly some day interact that have existed or that will exist, or that might have existed had things been otherwise. Good luck with that.

It's not just a matter of the sheer massive epistemic infeasibility of determining all the relevant facts. Rather, for us to make sense of the idea that there is a fact of the matter here at all, we also would need to make sense of the idea of some meaningful metric of valuation that achieves a form of objectivity that transcends even human moral sensibility to make neutral comparisons of things that might have different evaluative significance to ourselves and to other creatures, perhaps to other, very different rational creatures to be found in counterfactual history or the actual future of our own world.

Cost-benefit analysis, or something like it, is maybe good, if it is good for anything, for evaluating choices for human populations over the short to medium term. For the seriously long term, its Humean version is just a fantasy. We have no idea how to do a huge Humean cost-benefit analysis of the last two and a half billion years of life on Earth. And that is the past, which is epistemically at least easier to access than the remote future. Humean cost-benefit analysis is strictly for the birds.

7.5 Global Warming

This chapter is all about climate change. I began with a question about an episode of catastrophic climate change in the very distant past. But of course, climate change is also a matter of urgent concern to us now, conscious as we are of how our own activity is changing the global climate in ways that have us on course for a significant rise in global temperature that will leave us and our children with a hotter world, higher sea levels, and a refugee problem from Hell as what are currently populous places disappear under water or become in other ways inhospitable to human life.[10]

When we think of these more current changes to the atmosphere, we rightly worry that some given rise in average temperature would be catastrophically bad for human beings over the next century and perhaps the next few centuries. But how will the still-ramifying consequences be panning out in, say, ten million years' time? Even if we do enough damage to wipe ourselves out, life will almost certainly, unless the temperature rises so high the oceans boil, go on without us quite happily, or otherwise, much as it did before we were around. And who on Earth is to say that, from the point of view of the universe, in the very long term, that is a bad thing, or at least a worse thing than all the other extinctions we have relentlessly helped along in recent years? Something else will have a go at the top of the food chain and may well make a better job of stewarding its environment than we have done. Perhaps in time, if Earth remains inhabitable, that, or something, will evolve into something as clever and interesting as we take ourselves to be.

In fact, the present climate change emergency will certainly lead to the extinction of many things, but most likely, humans will survive it. There will surely be some liveable space left above water somewhere, and some humans, being the resilient creatures we are, will surely hang on there. Nonetheless, global warming, especially if we do not swiftly take strong measures to contain it, will almost certainly be awful and will likely cause immense disruption, suffering, and death for large numbers of people over a number of generations. From a natural human perspective, ours, now, that is a terrible thing which we should be at great pains to avert.

But utilitarianism does not occupy such a perspective. It occupies the perspective of eternity. And from the perspective of eternity catastrophes that fall short of making us extinct are not, in the greater scheme of things, a great deal.

> What distinguishes extinction and other existential catastrophes is that a comeback is impossible. A non-existential disaster causing the breakdown of global civilization is, from the perspective of humanity as a whole, a potentially recoverable setback: a giant massacre for man, a small misstep for mankind.[11]

MacAskill, in the early parts of his book, *What We Owe the Future*, tries to soften his readers up to the ideas comprising his **longtermist** outlook by singing the praises of the Iroquois people whose folk wisdom embraces looking at decisions they made with a view to seven generations into the future, comparing that favourably with the much shorter term perspective of too much human decision-making.[12]

Nobody should disagree with that much. Thinking seven generations ahead is an excellent way for a society to approach important decisions. Using the generational metric of the last chapter, that is about 175 years, perhaps around the limit of how far in the future we can meaningfully expect to predict and shape what will happen. But this **moderate longtermist** thinking that looks seven generations ahead is radically different from the **strong longtermism** writers like MacAskill advocate. That is an ideology that would have us focus on the next 70, the next 7,000, the next 7 million generations. That we can hope to predict and shape what will happen in the future on that scale is quixotic folly.

What is right is that when we ascend not to the perspective of seven generations but to this dizzying, Godlike perspective of all of time, the issue of whether a measure of global warming in the 21st and 22nd centuries CE, however locally disruptive, will be a good thing or a bad thing is going to come out looking exactly like the same issue as applied to the GOE: an entirely idle, empty thing to concern ourselves with. If, as I very much doubt, there is a fact of the matter at all, it is abundantly possible, and nobody has a clue how probable, that the global warming event now in train will prove, in the very, very long run, from the point of view of the universe, a positively good thing. The fact is, if there is a fact here at all, we simply do not know, from a utilitarian perspective, whether global warming is an urgent and serious problem we should be concerned about.

But we *do* know that global warming is an immensely serious and urgent problem we should be concerned about. This utilitarian *ponens* must be any decent person's *tollens*. If utilitarianism is true, we do not know that global warming is a big deal. We do know global warming is a big deal. So utilitarianism is false. QED.

We are presently living through desperately serious emergencies of our own making: anthropogenic mass extinction and anthropogenic climate change. Utilitarianism, with its imperial ambitions and epistemic hubris is, as we saw in Chapter 4, singularly poor at making sense of the former. We have now seen in the present chapter how it is likewise baffled by the latter. This is not a good philosophy to guide us through our present problems towards our future.

Notes

1 See Knoll 2003.
2 Part X.
3 Lewis 1973.
4 As I once heard John Divers describe it. The turn of phrase comes from Jerry Fodor talking in his 1989 about "those cures philosophers from time to time devise for which there is no adequate disease" (73).
5 Stalnaker 1987.
6 Lewis 1973, 1.
7 Cf. the discussion in Hare 2011.
8 1981, p. vii.

9 E.g. Sagoff 1988, Anderson 1993, chapter 9, Gutmann and Thompson 1996, chapter 5, Hansson 2007.
10 IPCC 2022.
11 Bostrom 2009.
12 MacAskill 2022, 11.

Chapter 8

Beyond Utilitarianism

8.1 Paralysis?

The Cluelessness Considerations are devastating for utilitarianism. Some object that they may be devastating for everyone. After all, doesn't every sensible ethical theory tell us the consequences of what we do matter? Utilitarianism is just the extreme view that consequences matter and *nothing else* does.

Do consequences matter? Well, yes, of course they do. But when I say that, I suspect I don't understand it the way most utilitarians understand it. Consequences matter, but their *being consequences* does not always matter *morally*. The Holocaust, for example, certainly matters, and it certainly matters morally. And the Holocaust is a consequence of Hans and Marthe's lovemaking. But the Holocaust does not feature as an item in Hans and Marthe's moral account book. They are *causally* responsible but in no way *morally* responsible for such remote and unforeseeable consequences of their innocent behaviour. *Moral* responsibility for the Holocaust, *all of it*, belongs to Hitler and his accomplices.

William MacAskill and Andreas Mogensen (2021) argue that the Cluelessness Considerations are a bigger problem for non-consequentialists than they are for consequentialists.

They begin their argument with a thought experiment, the Dice of Fortune, a pair of dice about which you know only that their faces are numbered. You then learn that if you roll them and the value of the sum of the winning numbers is less than a certain value, somewhere an endangered life will be saved. If it is more, then somewhere a stranger will die. (It is all very *Twilight Zone*.)

This, they say (2021, 3), in the light of the Cluelessness Considerations, is "closely analogous to the situation we find ourselves in on a day-to-day basis", in the light of the Cluelessness Considerations, when we roll, as we might say, the dice of history by doing more or less anything at all. But non-consequentialists differentiate between doing and allowing. So non-consequentialists should tell us *not to* roll the Dice of Fortune. By analogy non-consequentialists should also tell us *not to do anything at all*. Stay quite still. Remain motionless in your room. Which does seem an unfortunate result.

It is actually not so clear what the best understanding of the doing-allowing distinction is in this context. The way I motivated it in Chapter 1, you will recall, was in terms of a need for a space of autonomy where we can make our own lives free from the imposing demand to always be doing the thing that will improve the world the most and never anything else. So morality constrains but does not imperiously determine what we should do. There are some things you really must not do, like kill people, or steal from them, or deceive them. And there are things you must do like keeping your promises and caring for your dependent children. But if you stick inside these rules, there is a large space in which you can choose what you do in the light of other non-moral reasons.

Philippa Foot, in a very influential discussion, urges that the doing-allowing distinction is not the same as a simple action-inaction, commission-omission distinction. She gives a nice example.

> An actor who fails to turn up for a performance will generally spoil it rather than allow it to be spoiled.
>
> (2002, 26)

We might compare two actors, Lawrence and Richard. Lawrence is to act a certain part tonight in a certain play. That is his job. But he does not show up. His favourite programme is on the television so he stays at home to watch it.

Richard is not working today. He hears that Lawrence has announced a no-show for tonight's performance and realizes he might save the day. He has no connection with the production but knows the part perfectly from a recent rival production. All he needs to do is call and offer his services, and the audience will not have their night ruined, the company not lose thousands in refunds. But he does not. His favourite programme is on the television so he stays at home to watch it.

The obvious difference between these is that what Lawrence fails to do is one of the things he *must* do: everyone is relying on him to do his job and meet his contract. While what Richard fails to do is a very nice thing he might do, but not one of the things he *must* do.

In the light of that, we can see readily enough why declining to throw the Dice of Fortune, which the Mysterious Stranger puts at my disposal in some pleasingly fantastical narrative, is really not analogous at all to deciding to remain motionless in my room until— I guess until I die or some anxious social worker is called to remove me to some caring institution.

You see, I can refrain from throwing the dice, leave them in their box on the mantelpiece, and get on with my life. But to remain motionless in my room is precisely not to get on with my life and inconsistent with so doing. It is to neglect to feed my children if I have children. It is to neglect my responsibilities to my employer and to those to whom I have professional responsibilities. If no anxious social worker appears, it is to end my own life. If one does appear, it is to make myself burdensome on others in ways that hardly count as an abdication of active influence on the course of the world. Either way, that is an extremely morally grave and active choice, utterly unlike simply refraining from throwing some fanciful dice while things go on as before.

It is a common but serious mistake to see plausible, non-consequentialist ethics as involving an injunction not to *cause harm* or even not to *cause death*. One very familiar reason why this is a mistake is that an injunction not to cause harm is going to entail an injunction not to impose any *risk* of harm.[1] And we risk harm, in small ways, *all the time*, just by imposing the very small risks on others that cannot be avoided in going about the ordinary business of human life. Most of these risks risk harms that will never eventuate. But many such harms do.

Hoping to arrange a lovely evening for us all, I invite my dear friends Albert and Jane to come to my home where I will cook a nice meal. They set out to do so, but on the way to my home, they are involved in a road accident and killed. I did not kill them, but I certainly caused their deaths.

Andy and Fay take their child on a holiday to a lovely resort in some sunny land where some tragic misadventure ends their child's life. These are causings of deaths, but they are morally innocent such causings.

If I am, as people sometimes are in such circumstances, consumed with remorse at being causally upstream of such a tragedy, or if Andy and May are, our friends will rally around and reassure us that, terrible as the tragedy is, it should not be thought to feature as an item in our moral account book.

A less familiar but very important reason why it is a mistake to see plausible non-consequentialist ethics as involving an injunction not to cause harm, or even not to cause death, is that all of us, in the course of our lives, will *certainly* cause *many* deaths. This is just because, as the Cluelessness Considerations make stark, we will all of us cause an awful lot of stuff, way, way more stuff than we can readily foresee.

A consequence of the Cluelessness Considerations is that it is quite futile to have a general injunction against causing harm or death. We can be very sure we all cause a vast amount of harm and a great many deaths. The foreseen consequences of what we do are a tiny drop in the ocean of the total consequences, and the latter, we can be utterly certain, will involve an awful lot of bad stuff, including death, as well as an awful lot of good stuff. We cause a death, after all, whenever we have a child, any child—namely, the death of that child, as well as the deaths of all its lineage, should it have one, in perpetuity. But almost nobody would think this a reason not to have children.

I do not have a worked-out rival ethical theory to offer you as an alternative to utilitarianism, but I have some rough thoughts. The business of ethics, or at least a crucial, central part of it, whether or not we are to think of it as *theory*, is the business of trying to arrive at an understanding of what I may reasonably expect and demand of you by way of taking proper account of me and what you in turn may reasonably expect and demand of me, where a core part of what may be understood by 'reasonably' is that there be a measure of symmetry, of reciprocity, between what I may demand of others and others of me. Ethics is, crucially and centrally, if not exclusively, the business of us trying to arrive together at a shared understanding of what we owe to each other that we can all, if we are reasonable, accept.[2] Our trying to do this has involved, as I noted in Chapter 5, a conversation that has already been going on for a very long time, leaving us with a shared space of normative understanding that shapes our moral relations with each other and in the light of which we stand to be held responsible for our conduct by our fellows.

So what moral demands may we reasonably make on each other? That is a question of what we want our moral relations to be like. I use the word 'want' but urge a certain circumspection. The desires we bring to the table of moral codeliberation are always already moralized ideals, not simply appetites, though intelligent ideals will always give appetite its due. Well, I guess we should treat each other with kindness and respect, with recognition that each of us is a factor in the moral equation. I cannot pursue my aims as if you did not exist. Finding you in my way, I should walk around and not through you. Sometimes I should just stop.

We may demand kindness and respect. But there are things it seems to me we cannot reasonably demand of each other. Here are three.

1. We cannot demand that we do not impose small risks on one another. Such a demand would be paralyzing and would prohibit us from engaging in all the myriad activities that constitute a worthwhile human life.
2. We cannot demand of others a concern for our welfare that demands not just that they give great weight to directing no harm at us, but that they give no less weight to averting harms that threaten us by not allowing them to happen. Again, that would involve an unacceptable level of normative imposition that would unduly confine the sphere of our autonomy to live as we wish. (Which, of course, is not to deny the frequent urgency of taking positive actions, as individuals and as communities, to address the intolerable levels of avoidable suffering and death that burden many of our fellow human beings, or to endorse complacency on that score.)
3. We cannot reasonably be expected not to throw the dice of history by impacting the future in the way we all will where that is ordinarily, beyond a certain not very distant point, utterly inscrutable except for the actuarial certainty that it will be momentous.

We can find many things to reproach our forebears with. Perhaps they have perpetrated great injustices which still cast difficult shadows over our moral relations with each other today. Perhaps they have failed in their stewardship of the natural environment and left us with a poisoned atmosphere and an impoverished biosphere. But the fact that by coupling with their spouses, by moving house, by holding parties, by tentatively opening a conversation with their attractive classmates, they are causally connected in ways they could never have foreseen to every kind of horror, war, murder, and genocide, as well as to countless much nicer things, is not an item on their moral account book. It is simply part of the human condition and not one that we can remotely hope to eliminate that our causal relations to future history are devious, deep, and wholly inscrutable in the ways that they are. And just for that reason, our descendants cannot reasonably demand of us that we should try to do so.

To urge that we should would be, in effect, to embrace a form of species level anti-natalism: to urge that we make ourselves extinct because the harm we cause by perpetuating ourselves into the future is just too much. That may appeal to some people: there is so much suffering; let's just all call it a day. But let us for now not detain ourselves by considering that council of despair and pursue a sensible non-consequentialist approach to ethics that does not embrace it.

A sensible non-consequentialist approach will certainly forbid our *directing* significant harm at other people. I have argued a sensible non-consequentialism will enjoin us to act towards others in ways that are consistent, at least *ex ante*, with the aim of protecting them from harm.[3] But a blanket prohibition on *causing* harm is clearly not an eligible principle. When I exercise my agency in quite ordinary ways, I start countess causal chains that will eventuate somewhere down the line in many people dying.

When we think of a moral landscape where we do not respect or care for each other, where we view each other as simply things to plunder and prey upon, our imagination recoils in horror. We don't, any of us, care to live in such a world. And when we think of a moral community where we live together peacefully and cooperatively in civic friendship, our imagination warms to that possibility, and we think it a desirable thing to which we might sensibly aspire. These aspirations are widely shared and endorsed and prove highly stable under reflective scrutiny.

But when we think of a world where we set out to live our lives, and not just give them up, in such a way that we never stir the pot of history and set in train all manner of remote consequences generations, maybe aeons, hence, we quickly understand that that is an idle fantasy, like a world where we are made of glass or where we are each the size of a large planet, and we simply don't worry ourselves ethically on that score.

8.2 Strong Longtermism and Existential Risk

Consequentialists are left, at best, with the thought that whatever else we do or do not know about the long-term effects of our actions, extinction is forever. So human extinction, at least, we know would be awful because it would, as we already saw, gravely threaten the possibility that we, or something, have a glorious future where we, or something, will colonize space and enable lots of utility to happen for ages and ages. And this is the important thing. Overwhelmingly *the* most important thing. And because extinction is forever, a concern to avert existential risk is distinctively invulnerable to the Cluelessness Considerations. So we should maybe adopt an ethics that gives overwhelming priority to addressing existential risks.[4] Consequentialism can at least make good sense of why *that* is important.

Other animals, as we noted, will survive. But that will be no comfort for those people discussed in Chapter 4 who believe the lives of other animals have no value and the universe would be better off without them. And although other animals might someday evolve that are as smart and important as we like to think we are, perhaps even endowed with the smarts needed to colonize space, we might think the risk too high that that will not happen in time, or perhaps that the cognitively sophisticated descendants of monkeys or whales just aren't interested in doing any of that stuff. (Why ever would they be?)

I do not myself think even a concern to avoid existential risk is distinctively invulnerable to the Cluelessness Considerations. The breezy way in which defenders of strong longtermism spin wildly speculative science fiction stories about the fantastically remote distant future to which they suppose they can assign meaningful values and probabilities is, I think, bewildering in its epistemic complacency. But we can put that thought to one side. For even if we were to grant that in cases where existential risk is saliently at issue, cluelessness can be tamed, the problem remains that it remains untamed *everywhere else*.

So were we to grant (which I think we should not) what was just suggested, we are left with a consequentialism that can make good sense of why it would make poor ethical sense to construct a doomsday machine and detonate it or to develop a supertransmissible killer virus and release it in the population. Which is always nice to know.

But what this consequentialism cannot make sense of is why it is a good idea to make sure your children have enough to eat, or why it is a bad idea to kill your granny and feed her to some nearby pigs, or why you really shouldn't set out to burn down your local primary school or to exterminate the Jewish population of Europe. In contemplating such things, existential threats to humanity are nowhere in sight, just a vast future of endlessly ramifying consequences which we remain utterly clueless how to compute, estimate, and compare. Consequentialism, whatever it says about existential risk, certainly says nothing at all about such things as these. Success that is limited is not success at all.

8.3 Concluding Remarks

The Aristotelian idea that virtue lies in a mean between extremes works better in some contexts than in others. I rather think something like it may apply here. There are two opposing mistakes to be made. On the one hand, you might be so impressed by the thoughts I air here about the feasibility and, indeed, intelligibility of the project of making the world, the whole world, better that you give way to a kind of despairing moral nihilism. Which you should not. On the other hand, you might think there is some number, knowable at least in principle, to God, which is a quantification on some meaningful metric of the amount of value realized in the world from its beginning to its end and that your moral job in your life is to make that number higher than it would otherwise have been, and there is a way of living that will help you make that likelier than otherwise. There is really a kind of deep failure of humility here. Of course, you don't sensibly expect to make a difference at that vast global level. Our lives can be good in a much more local way, and that is far from nothing. It is a splendid thing to make your house, or your city, beautiful whether or not you believe you thereby make a positive addition to the overall beauty of the whole world.

The sphere of your moral responsibility cannot extend beyond the sphere of your control. If you aspire to extend the former to encompass the whole world, you will need to effect an equivalent enlargement to the latter. And that is a dangerous aspiration, the spur to conquer and improve. The world, all of it, is not ours to improve. To suppose otherwise is a hubristic mistake, as I suggested before, a kind of moral imperialism.

If your children are ailing and in need of your attention, you should attend to them. If your city is in danger and needs your service, you should offer it. Of course, there are other children and other cities, remote from you in space and time whom you cannot readily help in these ways, however great are their needs. But mostly, they will have carers and citizens of their own, and it is their job and not yours to step up. You can't do it all and would be foolish to spread yourself too thin. At some point, we rely on the moral division of labour and stick to our own patch. You can't make the world, the *whole* world, a better place.[5] But you can keep your bedroom tidy, your garden beautiful, and you can make life happier for those you love.

You cannot light up the whole world, but you can shine a light in your small corner. Who knows? For some people, it may shine a long way, perhaps a surprisingly long way, but the darkness will, of course, engulf it at last. That is simply one of the limits within which, wise people accept, we all must live.

Which is not to deny that the moral world is bigger than it was. Parfit famously wrote,

> Until this century, most of mankind lived in small communities. What each did could affect only a few others. But conditions have now changed. Each of us can now, in countless ways, affect countless other people.[6]

This is undeniably true, and it is undeniably a game changer. For most people for most of history, and for many people even now, the moral world that made the sphere of their responsibility did not extend much beyond their village and its nearest neighbours. If you were a medieval European villager, if there was an earthquake in China or a famine in the Horn of Africa, you would never have known about it, far less been in a position to help. By looking after your property well, you could make some difference to the likely felicity of your children, your grandchildren, perhaps, your great-grandchildren. By good citizenship and wise counsel, you could help your village thrive and prosper. But much beyond that horizon, your causal capacity to affect in any predictable ways people far away in space or time was effectively zero. It's not that your actions would not ramify down the millennia. They would, but in ways that were quite inscrutable to you and way beyond your control.

We are connected to people very distant from us in space and time in ways that we were not at earlier times in our history, and those connections properly expand the horizons of our moral concern and responsibility in dramatic ways. We have the capacity to mess up the environment in which our children and grandchildren, and their children and grandchildren, will live in new ways and are exercising that capacity in alarming ways that we urgently need to be very attentive to. We are in danger of bequeathing to our descendants a world that has been poisoned and whose finite natural riches have been squandered. We should look after the terrestrial estate we pass on, and that is a far more consequential and far-reaching responsibility than anything in the moral experience of even the most powerful people who lived a few centuries ago. But our reach is still limited. What the world will be like in, say, the 9th, never mind the 90th, millennium of the Common Era is out of our control in a very thoroughgoing way. However much our concerns are expanded from what they were in the past, they fall far, far short of filling the world. Because the world—so much moral philosophy just quietly ignores this fact—is *enormous*.

The sphere of our responsibility is a far bigger village than it once was. But it is still a village. Even our responsibility not to massively boost the carbon dioxide in the atmosphere to the great detriment of future generations is, as noted earlier, a highly local one. Whether that would be a bad thing in the *very* long term is a question we cannot, as we have seen, begin to hope to answer.

We must cultivate our garden. Part of what it is to have the virtue of generosity is to conceive that garden in generous and inclusive ways that reach beyond me, my family, and my ethnic, national, or religious tribe, and we live perhaps in times when the virtue of generosity has never been more important, and our capacity to aid or to endanger distant others has never been greater. If we poison the ocean, life will be unpleasant for our great-great-grandchildren and their contemporaries, so we should not poison it, but that is because we properly concern ourselves with our great-great-grandchildren and their contemporaries, not because we concern ourselves, *sub specie aeternitatis*, with *the world*.[7] If we poison the ocean, something, lots of things, will almost certainly adapt and survive and set life on Earth on a new course that 10, 20 million years from now will people Earth with strange and wonderful things we cannot now imagine. If that should happen, I wish those creatures well, and if I somehow find myself in a position to direct harm their way, I should not do so, but they are not and really cannot be the focus of my active benevolence. They are much too far away, and we will have to trust them to look after themselves. All we can ever do is cultivate our gardens. They, in turn, will perhaps cultivate theirs.

Notes

1 See Kagan 1997, chapter 3 especially 82–4.
2 These remarks, it will be obvious to many readers, draw inspiration from the ideas of the great Harvard contractualist philosophers, John Rawls (1971) and Thomas Scanlon (1998).
3 Lenman 2008.
4 See MacAskill and Mogensen, 2021, 14–15.
5 This might seem dispiriting to many ordinary good people outside the strange world of academic philosophy given to talk of *making the world a better place* by way of expressing a common and admirable moral aspiration. But I do doubt if most folk who say this are really thinking in terms of something so vast as the whole world. Unless perhaps it is being supposed that by doing good deeds, we make the whole world a *very* little bit better as the local times and place of the deeds in question are improved while the rest of the system is left unperturbed. So it is a bit like placing a grain of sand on the top of a huge mountain, thereby making it, ever so very slightly, but certainly, higher. But the point of the Cluelessness Argument is that things are not at all like that.
6 86.
7 See glossary. Here I am remembering Williams: "Philosophers, not only utilitarian ones, repeatedly urge one to view the world *sub specie aeternitatis*, but for most human purposes that is not a good species to view it under" Williams 1973, 118.

II For Utilitarianism

Ben Bramble

Acknowledgements

When I was approached to contribute to this Routledge series, I thought, "Whom would I most like to debate on a given topic?" The answer immediately sprang to mind: James Lenman on utilitarianism! For years, I had read Jimmy's papers and marvelled at them. I love his philosophical style: on the one hand, conversational, colourful, and wry, and on the other, succinct, rigorous, and original. I would have been content only to read his latest thoughts on utilitarianism. The opportunity to engage with them in a format like this was a dream. So, thanks, Jimmy, for agreeing to do this book. It has been every bit as enriching as I'd hoped.

Thanks also to Tyron Goldschmidt and Dustin Crummett, editors of this series, as well as Marc Stratton and Andrew Beck from Routledge.

Thanks also to Roger Crisp and Meredith Rossner.

Chapter 9

Introduction

In this book, I want to introduce you to a new version of utilitarianism, one that seems to me to best capture or express utilitarianism's basic and enduring appeal. This version also gives us new resources to respond to the many serious and influential objections utilitarianism faces.

Utilitarianism makes two key claims:

1. You should always do what will maximise the overall good (that is, perform whatever action will have the best consequences, all things considered[1]).
2. The ultimate good is just **welfare**, well-being, or utility (that is, lives going well *for* their subjects).

Together, these claims give us the following widely used definition of utilitarianism:

> You should always do what will maximise overall welfare.

While simple and accurate enough, this definition is highly ambiguous. There are two main ambiguities.

1.1 The First Ambiguity

The first ambiguity concerns (2), the claim that welfare is the only ultimate good. On one interpretation of this claim, what ultimately matters or has value is just the *amount* of welfare that exists in the universe. Utilitarianism, on this interpretation of (2), says,

> You should always act so as to bring about *as much* welfare in the future as possible.

DOI: 10.4324/9781003300045-11

Following others, let's call this *total utilitarianism*.

Total utilitarian thinking has led many contemporary philosophers to embrace a view called *longtermism*, on which society's current priority should be making it more likely that humanity will survive into the very distant future in conditions conducive to flourishing.[2] If humanity survives for this long and spreads throughout the universe (or into virtual worlds), just think how much future welfare there could be!

But there is a different—and, to my mind, much better—way of thinking of the idea that welfare is the only ultimate good. This is that things go better just when and because they go better *for* some sentient being or beings—i.e., when the lives of some individuals are *improved*. On this interpretation, utilitarianism says,

> You should always act so as to *help* beings as much as possible.

Let's call this *person-affecting utilitarianism*.

1.2 The Second Ambiguity

The second ambiguity concerns the meaning of 'should'. Most philosophers think of utilitarianism as issuing a moral *requirement* or *demand*—i.e., as making a claim about what you morally *must* do, on pain of acting morally *wrongly* (where morally wrong action opens you up to possible charges of being morally *blameworthy* for the action). Call this sort of utilitarianism *requirement utilitarianism*.

But, again, there is a much better way of understanding 'should' in the above definition. Instead of thinking of utilitarianism as the claim that we are morally required to do what will maximise overall welfare, we should think of it as saying merely that we have *most reason* to perform this action or that this is what there is *most point* to doing. Call this *reasons utilitarianism*.

1.3 The Right Version

When people today think of utilitarianism, they often have in mind something like *total, requirement utilitarianism*, on which

> you are morally required to do what would maximise the amount of future welfare.

This is true even of utilitarians themselves, most of whom today are explicitly total, requirement utilitarians.³

But there is, I am going to argue in this book, a better version of utilitarianism available. This is *person-affecting, reasons utilitarianism*, on which

> you have most reason to do what will help beings the most.

In the following pages, I will motivate this view and appeal to it to give new responses to five important objections to utilitarianism. These objections are as follows:

1. *The 'Philosophy of Swine' Objection.* Utilitarianism commends to us a world where we all live long lives consisting purely of intense bodily pleasures.
2. *The 'Cluelessness' Objection.* The consequences of our possible actions stretch so far into the future, it is impossible to form reasonable beliefs about what actions would be overall better than others.
3. *The 'Demandingness' Objection.* Utilitarianism implies that you should devote the rest of your life to earning money to give away to charities that will spend it on distant others.
4. *The 'Alienation' Objection.* Accepting utilitarianism is incompatible with having friendships, interests, or projects of your own.
5. *The 'Harming to Help' Objection.* Utilitarianism implies that, in some cases, you should harm some people to help others when (in such cases) you should not do so.

To be clear, my main goal in this piece is not to provide a decisive or definitive argument for utilitarianism. It is to introduce you to a new version of utilitarianism, one I believe is its best expression. That said, I hope you will come away thinking that *if* utilitarianism is true, it will probably be the sort of utilitarianism outlined here.

1.4 The Plan

Here is the plan for my part of this book. I will start, in Chapter 10, by explaining why person-affecting utilitarianism is preferable to total utilitarianism.

In Chapter 11, I will respond to the 'Philosophy of Swine' Objection.
In Chapter 12, I will respond to the 'Cluelessness' Objection.
In Chapter 13, I will explain why reasons utilitarianism is preferable to requirement utilitarianism.
In Chapter 14, I will respond to the 'Demandingness' Objection.
In Chapter 15, I will respond to the 'Alienation' Objection.
In Chapter 16, I will respond to the 'Harming to Help' Objection.
Finally, in Chapter 17, I will sum up my argument.

Notes

1 'Consequences', here, includes any intrinsic value in the action itself.
2 For work on longtermism, see William MacAskill, *What We Owe the Future* (Basic Books, 2022) and Toby Ord, *The Precipice* (Bloomsbury, 2020).
3 Peter Singer is a prominent example.

Chapter 10

Total or Person-Affecting Utilitarianism?

According to total utilitarianism, all that ultimately matters is the *amount* of welfare that exists in the universe. We should do whatever will bring about *as much* welfare in the future as possible.

The Problem With Total Utilitarianism

The problem with total utilitarianism is that it *instrumentalises* people in an objectionable way. It regards people as valuable only because they make possible the existence of welfare. On total utilitarianism, if you could somehow have welfare *without* people—and more cheaply, let's say—then it could be best to dispense with people altogether. They'd be a waste of space. This is highly counterintuitive.

Total utilitarians reply that, of course, there *cannot* be welfare without people—welfare is necessarily the welfare *of* somebody, some subject. But total utilitarians must still regard this—i.e., the impossibility of welfare without people—as a *shame*. "It is regrettable", they must think, "that we cannot have welfare without people. If only it *were* possible!" This seems clearly the wrong way to think about things.

There is another way to frame this worry: for total utilitarians, the point of *helping* people is just to add more welfare to the world. This seems wrong. The point of helping people, of making their lives go better for them, seems rather to be the *helping* itself. The fact that helping people adds more welfare to the world seems incidental or beside the point, not part of why we should be doing it.

Moreover, since for total utilitarianism, the fundamental point is to add more welfare to the world, not to help people, if you were in a

DOI: 10.4324/9781003300045-12

situation where you could add more welfare to the world by creating a bunch of new happy people than by helping existing people, then you should add the happy people. This is immensely implausible.

It is even more implausible when you consider that there are cases where the happy people in question would have to be only *slightly* happy—i.e., have lives that are only slightly positive in overall lifetime welfare—say, short-lived animals with mostly bland experiences. If you could make *zillions* of them, then it could be the case, on total utilitarianism, that you should do that instead of greatly helping millions of existing people who are badly in need of help. This is an absurd (or, as some have put it, repugnant) result.[1]

Person-Affecting Utilitarianism to the Rescue

Fortunately, total utilitarianism is not the only form of utilitarianism. There is another: person-affecting utilitarianism. On person-affecting utilitarianism, the right way to interpret the claim that welfare is the only ultimate good is that things go better just when and because they go better *for* some sentient being or when somebody's life is *improved*. We should be acting not to maximise the amount of welfare in the future but to help beings or improve lives as much as possible.

Person-affecting utilitarianism does not instrumentalise people in the way mentioned earlier. It does not regard them as valuable merely as conditions of the existence of welfare—the people themselves are *absolutely* necessary. The point of helping people, according to person-affecting utilitarianism, is not to add more welfare but the help itself. And person-affecting utilitarianism does not say that there can be cases where you should add more happy people rather than help existing people. You should always help the existing people.

I agree with Tatjana Višak when she writes,

> Can utilitarianism consistently be person-affecting? I think it can be, and indeed should be, person-affecting. A widely accepted basis for utilitarianism is that *it extends the principle of prudence for one individual to society as a whole*. It is considered prudent for me to benefit myself and, by extension, those I care about. The moral point of view, according to utilitarians, requires extending this concern to society as a whole.[2]

Why is utilitarianism attractive in the first place? We start with a clear intuition that there is some reason to benefit ourselves and our loved ones, some point in doing so. We then realise that we ourselves are not intrinsically special—there is no relevant difference between us and others that makes it intrinsically more important that we are benefited than that they are. From here, it is natural to think that perhaps what there is *most* reason or point to doing is benefiting beings *generally*, and as much as possible. This conclusion is nothing other than person-affecting utilitarianism. The most natural route to utilitarianism is an argument for person-affecting, not total, utilitarianism.

For many total utilitarians, the case for utilitarianism begins with the idea that we should act so as to maximise the amount of good stuff in the world, *whatever it might be*. The good stuff happens to be welfare, they think, so we should maximise that. Had the good been something else, we should be acting so as to bring about as much of that other stuff as possible.

By contrast, while I do find it plausible that we should be acting so as to make things go as well as possible, this seems to me to be the case only *because* I am thinking of the good as welfare. My thinking of welfare as good or worth promoting *comes first*, and it is only because of this thought that I come to think that we should act so as to maximise overall welfare.

Which version of utilitarianism did classical utilitarians like John Stuart Mill and Jeremy Bentham accept? Unfortunately, their writings do not clearly distinguish between these two different versions. But they seem to have been driven by a powerful desire to help beings as much as possible. It is hard to believe they might have thought we should be helping people only as a means of maximising the total amount of welfare in the universe.

Human Extinction

If total utilitarianism is so implausible, why do so many current utilitarians subscribe to it?[3] One reason, I suspect, is that many utilitarians—especially younger ones who have grown up in the heyday of total utilitarianism—do not even realise that person-affecting utilitarianism is an option.

Many total utilitarians, of course, do realise that person-affecting utilitarianism is an option but prefer total utilitarianism. Why? It is because they think there are a number of things that person-affecting utilitarianism cannot explain. The main thing here is *the badness of human extinction*. On person-affecting utilitarianism, if humanity went extinct tomorrow, this would be a bad thing only because of the harms caused to current people. But this, according to total utilitarians, is deeply implausible. Intuitively, they say, the badness of extinction would go well beyond this.

Total utilitarians appeal here to two famous thought experiments. The first is Derek Parfit's ***Two Wars***.[4] Parfit asks us to consider the following three scenarios: (1) peace, (2) a war that kills 99% of the world population, and (3) a war that kills 100% (resulting in human extinction). According to Parfit, while (2) is obviously much worse than (1), the difference in badness between (2) and (3) is far greater still. To fully account for the badness of (3), it is not enough to appeal to the additional harms caused to the final 1% of humanity. Intuitively, says Parfit, its badness has to do also with the *loss of all the happy people who would have come to exist had humanity kept going*. Parfit and others conclude that there must be tremendous positive value in the creation of all these happy lives and so some positive value in the addition of each new happy life. What ultimately matters, then, is not improving lives but maximising the amount of welfare that exists in the universe.

The second case is Larry Temkin's ***Extinction Pill***:

> If we developed a pill enabling each of us to live wonderful lives for 120 years, it would be terrible for us to take the pill if the cost of doing so were the extinction of humanity. Moreover, this is so even if taking the pill were better for each individual who took it, and hence, collectively, for everyone who was alive then or later lived. We think the outcome where people lived wonderful lives for 120 years would be much worse than the outcome where people lived lives of 80 years, but human life continued on for countless centuries.[5]

Jonathan Glover, whose original case inspired Temkin's, says our deciding to take such a pill would be "about the worst thing it would be possible to do".[6] Total utilitarians complain that person-affecting utilitarianism cannot explain why this is so since taking the pill would be best for all affected parties. Why would it be so terrible if we all took such a pill, according to total utilitarians? Intuitively, they say, it is because it would prevent zillions of new happy lives.

Here are some things total utilitarians and their sympathisers say. Nick Beckstead, Peter Singer, and Matt Wage write,

> [If we go extinct] we will have blown the opportunity to create something truly wonderful: an astronomically large number of generations of human beings living rich and fulfilling lives.[7]

Jeff McMahan writes,

> To most of us, it is appalling to think that instead of this incalculable number of people enjoying these incalculable benefits, there might instead be only the emptiness of a world devoid of consciousness.[8]

Will MacAskill writes, in a section of his book entitled "Bigger Is Better",

> We should...hope that future civilisation will be *big*. If future people will be sufficiently well-off, then a civilisation that is twice as long or twice as large is twice as good. ... The future of civilisation could be literally astronomical in scale, and if we will achieve a thriving, flourishing society, then it would be of enormous importance to make it so.[9]

And Toby Ord asks us to imagine, if we went extinct, all

> the children and grandchildren we would never have: millions of generations of humanity, each comprised of billions of people, with lives of a quality far surpassing our own. *Gone*. A catastrophe would not *kill* these people, but it would foreclose their very existence. It would not *erase* them, but ensure they were never even written.[10]

This, Ord thinks, would be an immense loss.

I think, however, that extinction would not be bad by preventing the existence of all these happy beings. We can see this by considering the following case:

> **Utopian Extinction.** Many millennia into the future, after years of slow but steady progress, humanity finally achieves a utopia on Earth, where everyone lives long lives as good as it is possible for anyone to live. At this point, there is nothing

more for humanity to discover in the arts, sciences, philosophy, or physically elsewhere in the universe (beyond our solar system). These humans really have done it all and *have* it all. As such, they become, not bored exactly, but satiated, thoroughly content. They decide they do not want to have children or raise a further generation. They would prefer to wrap up the human experiment, go out on a high. One sunny day, they do so, and humanity ends.

Utopian Extinction does not seem regrettable at all. It might be regrettable that 'this is all there is' (cosmically speaking)—that there is no bigger purpose, plan, or meaning for humanity, no afterlife that might somehow make sense of our lives or bring us even closer to each other. But *given* (as we are assuming) that there isn't anything bigger in this sense, I see nothing to regret in these utopians wrapping things up. And yet—here's the crucial point—this extinction *also* (let's assume) prevents the existence of trillions of new happy beings. So, it cannot be the case that the loss of trillions of new happy beings *itself* makes an extinction bad, including the extinctions in the Parfit/Temkin cases.

So, what *is* going on in the Parfit/Temkin cases? After all, these extinctions do seem extraordinarily *sad*, much sadder than Utopian Extinction, and sad in a way that cannot be fully accounted for in terms of harms to the final people.

Here is my suggestion: the Parfit/Temkin extinctions *are* extraordinarily sad and sad in a way that goes beyond these harms, but they are not *bad* in a way that goes beyond these harms. Total utilitarians, I suspect, are picking up on the sad or (in a certain respect) tragic nature of these extinctions—they are *feeling* the immense sadness of these extinctions—and then being led by their emotion here to mistakenly conclude that these extinctions are *bad* or *regrettable* over and above these harms.

How can something be sad without being bad? There are many examples. Here's one: suppose an old person who has no living friends or relatives passes away, and her things are simply tossed in the trash. Their being thrown out like this is clearly not a bad thing. It does not make things worse in any way. There is no reason not to do it—no reason to, say, preserve them instead. Yet it is *deeply* sad.

To say that things are sad, I believe, is simply to say that sad emotions are fitting or appropriate in response to them. This can be true even when the things in question are not bad.

Why exactly are the Parfit/Temkin extinctions so sad? What is it about them that makes appropriate sad feelings or emotions? I think it has to do with the fact that in these cases—unlike in Utopian Extinction—*humanity's story has been cut short*. There is still a great deal more for humanity to achieve, so much progress—social, political, scientific, cultural, artistic, and so on—yet to make. Utopian Extinction, by contrast, is not sad or tragic for the simple reason that, here, humans have achieved it all already.

Jonathan Bennett takes a similar view. He says that while there is no value in humanity carrying on independently of the effects of this on people's welfare, he very much *likes* the idea of our carrying on since he wants humanity's *story* to keep on going or progress further. He writes,

> I am passionately in favour of mankind's having a long future. ... This is a practical attitude of mine for which I have no basis in general principles. ... I just think it would be a great shame...if this great biological and spiritual adventure didn't continue: it has a marvellous past, and I hate the thought of its not having an exciting future. ... This attitude of mine is rather like my attitude to pure mathematics and music and philosophy: even if they didn't have their great utility, I would want them to continue just because they are great long adventures which it would be a shame to have broken off short. ... My attitude to mankind's future is conditioned by my attitude to its past: my sense that it would be a shame if the story stopped soon is nourished by my sense that it has been an exciting story that involves some long-term endeavours that aren't yet complete. I would probably care less about the 21st century if I didn't love the 17th so much.[11]

Jan Narveson takes a similar view about a different but related subject matter. He notes that some philosophers (including total utilitarians) believe that it would have been a bad thing had humans never evolved in the first place. Narveson rejects this idea, writing,

> We might *prefer*...a universe containing people to one that does not contain them...but...this [is not] a moral preference... and...the effort to make it one is a mistake.[12]

It is worth emphasising an important difference between myself, on the one hand, and Bennett and Narveson, on the other. Bennett and Narveson regard their sentiments or feelings here as *merely personal*—idiosyncratic or rationally contingent. Narveson, for example, uses the phrase "a matter of taste" to describe them. And Bennett says that if somebody happened not to share his feelings on this, they wouldn't be mistaken in any way or missing something. He writes,

> When I imagine myself having a different attitude to mankind's future. ... I don't see myself as *spoiled* but just as *changed*.[13]

By contrast, I believe there is an important sense in which sentiments like Bennett's and my own concerning humanity's future are right or appropriate. It is this that explains why the Parfit/Temkin extinctions are truly sad.

Once we realise that we can say that these extinctions are sad—deeply sad or even (in a sense) tragic—without having to say that they are bad (over and above the harms they involve), this, it seems to me, greatly reduces our tendency to feel that they are bad.

In sum, we should prefer person-affecting utilitarianism to total utilitarianism. Total utilitarianism faces devastating objections, while the main worry total utilitarians have about person-affecting utilitarianism is not a good one. Moreover, it is person-affecting utilitarianism, rather than total utilitarianism, that fits better with the proper reason to be a utilitarian in the first place.

Notes

1 For the classic discussion of the 'repugnant conclusion', see Derek Parfit, *Reasons and Persons* (Oxford, 1984).
2 Tatjana Višak, "Do Utilitarians Need to Accept the Replaceability Argument?" in Tatjana Višak, and Robert Garner (eds), *The Ethics of Killing Animals* (New York, 2015; online edn, Oxford Academic, 22 October 2015). For another person-affecting utilitarian, see Narveson, Jan, (1973). "Moral problems of population". *The Monist* 57 (1):62–86.
3 I have in mind especially the many utilitarians in the **effective altruist** (EA) fold.
4 Parfit (1984), 452.
5 Larry Temkin, *Rethinking the Good* (Oxford, 2012), 414.
6 Jonathan Glover, *Causing Death and Saving Lives* (Penguin, 1977).

7 Nick Beckstead, Peter Singer, and Matt Wage, "Preventing Human Extinction", *Effective Altruism Forum* (2013), accessible here: https://forum.effectivealtruism.org/posts/tXoE6wrEQv7GoDivb/preventing-human-extinction.
8 Jeff McMahan, "Causing People to Exist and Saving People's Lives", *Journal of Ethics* (2013), 26.
9 MacAskill (2022), 201.
10 Ord, (2020), 143.
11 Jonathan Bennett, "On Maximizing Happiness", in R. I. Sikora and B. Barry (eds) *Obligations to Future Generations* (Philadelphia: Temple University Press, 1978), 66.
12 Narveson, Jan 1967. "Utilitarianism and New Generations". *Mind* 76:301, 72.
13 Bennett (1978).

Chapter 11

Philosophy of Swine

One of the most famous objections to utilitarianism is that it is a 'philosophy of swine'. The best-known statement of the objection is John Stuart Mill's:

> [Utilitarianism] excites in many minds, and among them in some of the most estimable in feeling and purpose, inveterate dislike. To suppose that life has (as they express it) no higher end than pleasure—no better and nobler object of desire and pursuit—they designate as utterly mean and grovelling; as a doctrine worthy only of swine, to whom the followers of Epicurus were, at a very early period, contemptuously likened.[1]

We can frame this objection more precisely as follows:

1. Utilitarianism commends to us a future where we all live long lives consisting purely of intense bodily pleasures, like those of sex, drugs, and so on.
  However,
2. Such a future does not seem good at all. Actually, it would be lousy. It would lack many things of great value, like love and deep relationships, science and understanding, achievement and striving for worthwhile goals, great works of art and their appreciation, virtue and its exercise, and so on.
  Therefore,
3. Utilitarianism is false.

The Right Theory of Welfare

How should a utilitarian respond? Total utilitarians often *accept* that utilitarianism commends to us such a future. Such a future *would* be an extremely good one, they say. If it doesn't seem good to us, this is only because we are unduly 'into' things like love, friendship, art, virtue, and so on, and our attachments here are clouding our judgement.

But this seems pretty clearly the wrong response. Instead, a utilitarian should deny that a future where we all live like pigs would be good, *no matter how much pleasure it involves.*

How can they consistently deny this? It is because your welfare is not a matter of experiencing *as much* pleasure as possible—it is not about the *quantity* of pleasure you experience during your lifetime. To have a life high in welfare, you must have or encounter *many of the sorts of things the critic mentioned earlier as so valuable or important*, things like love, friendship, science, great art and natural beauty, achievement, virtue, and so on. These things are indeed vital, but they are vital precisely for *welfare*.

How exactly are these things vital for welfare? Here is one answer a utilitarian *cannot* give. A utilitarian cannot say that striving for worthwhile goals or achieving things is good for you because these goals or achievements are *themselves* ultimately or intrinsically good. That would be to posit ultimate goods other than welfare (which a utilitarian cannot do). Similarly, a utilitarian cannot say that encountering great works of art is good for you because these works are *themselves* ultimately good or valuable. That, again, would be to posit other ultimate goods. Utilitarians, in other words, cannot endorse the now popular view of Susan Wolf and others that

> the world [is] full of things of immeasurable [intrinsic] value, including objects and environments of the natural world, works of supreme human accomplishment, not to mention people themselves, and *it is a kind of good fortune to be able to interact with these, in a way that involves going some way toward understanding and appreciating their value.*[2]

I will come back to this view shortly (in order to try to explain what is wrong with it). But first, I want to further flesh out the sort of positive account of welfare I believe utilitarians should hold.

Why are things like love, science, art, etc., so vital for welfare? A utilitarian should say that it has to do just with the *pleasures* associated with these things. This was, of course, Mill's own favoured reply to the swine objection. According to Mill, you need some "pleasures of the intellect; of the feelings and imagination, and of the moral sentiments"[3]—**higher pleasures**, as he called them—to have a life high in welfare.

What explains why these particular pleasures contribute so much to a person's welfare? For Mill, it had to do with the preferences of what he called "competent judges". He says,

> Of two pleasures, if there be one to which all or almost all who have experience of both give a decided preference, irrespective of any feeling of moral obligation to prefer it, that is the more desirable pleasure. ... Now it is an unquestionable fact that those who are equally acquainted with, and equally capable of appreciating and enjoying, both, do give a most marked preference to the manner of existence which employs their higher faculties. ... What is there to decide whether a particular pleasure is worth purchasing at the cost of a particular pain, except the feelings and judgment of the experienced?[4]

But this explanation has been rightly pilloried over the years—for reasons I won't go into here. If 'competent judges' agree in their preferences between pleasures, it is because they *recognise* which ones are more valuable.

Instead of appealing to people's preferences, a utilitarian should simply appeal to the *qualitative character* or *feel* of the pleasures in question. This feeling alone is what makes these pleasures so wonderful or valuable for us.

The Wonderful Pleasures

Let me say some more about the sort of pleasures I have in mind, the ones with the special sort of qualitative character or feel I am talking about. Start with the pleasures of love and friendship. These are pleasures associated with really getting to know other people well or deeply and appreciating what is so good or wonderful about them in their particularity as individuals. In the case of friendship, these pleasures also involve having some kind of relationship with the other person—ideally, one where *they* also know *you* well, appreciate you, and express it.

Next are pleasures of understanding—understanding abstract ideas like those of science and philosophy but also more concrete things like properties of different kinds of birds, plants, histories and achievements of various cultures, and so on. Perhaps the most valuable pleasures of all here are the pleasures of understanding humanity itself. Human nature is immensely complex, of course. But in my view, we are, at heart, *good* in the following sense: most of us are not purely self-concerned or self-interested. We genuinely care about (at least some) others *for their own sakes*, including beings who might be quite distant or different from ourselves in various respects—say, spatially, temporally, socially, culturally, economically, or even biologically. A central theme of a huge amount of great literature is the disinterested love or concern some of us have for others who are different from us in certain ways. It is sublimely wonderful that we have this ability to so care, and, accordingly, wonderful to recognise this fact. To understand this about others, and about ourselves, is a source of some of the most wonderful pleasures possible.

Next, there are pleasures of making the world a better place, of waking up in the morning and believing you can make a positive difference to the lives of others.

Last, but not least, there are the pleasures of appreciating great works of art, music, literature, and so on. To understand these works and appreciate them can clearly be deeply enriching.

Earlier, I said that these pleasures are so good for us just because of their qualitative character or feel. What is it *specifically* about their feel that makes them so beneficial? Part of it, I think, is that these pleasures—or some of them, at least—are *very* pleasurable. It is common to assume that the most pleasurable pleasures are intense bodily pleasures. But this is a mistake. Bodily pleasures can be very *gripping* or *attention-grabbing*. They can shout at you. You often can't miss them. But it doesn't follow—and I suspect it is not the case—that they are really all that pleasurable (at least when compared with what I'm calling the wonderful pleasures).

The wonderful pleasures, mostly, do not grip or shout at you in the same sort of way. Most of the time, they are quite difficult to attend to or focus on. For many of them (in contrast to most bodily pleasures), you can be having them *only if you are focused on or attending to something else*—namely, the *object* of the pleasure (say, a piece of music, a bird, a puzzle, etc.). As such, it is possible, indeed likely, that there is a lot more to them—in terms of pleasurableness itself—than meets the (introspective) eye. Their pleasurableness goes deep. The part of them you can easily introspect is the tip of the phenomenological iceberg, so to speak.[5]

The other part of the feel of the wonderful pleasures that makes them so valuable for us is, I believe, that many of them are qualitatively *unique* among pleasures. That is, they feel *unlike any other pleasures you can experience*. As such, they add to the overall *richness* or *diversity* of the set of pleasures you will end up having felt during your lifetime. This, it seems to me, makes them more valuable for you than 'lower' pleasures, which are mostly just 'more of the same'.[6]

To see what I mean, consider the pleasures of great works of art. The pleasures of lesser works—say, airport novels, B-grade movies, muzak or elevator music—are all qualitatively very similar to each other. Their characters, plots, themes, and so on are none too original—they are, in their essential features, just the same as or very similar to what one finds in many other works, with only relatively minor superficial differences. These works are just different vehicles for what are qualitatively roughly the same sorts of pleasures. 'Same product, different packaging', you might say.

By contrast, great works are all original in various ways. This is one of their defining features. If they are especially immersive, they take you to places no other work does. If their characters are highly realistic, they will be like real people, individual or unique. If they are highly thought-provoking, they are offering us thoughts or a perspective on the world that no other works impart. These differences all have direct implications for the qualitative character or feel of the pleasures that are associated with these works. Most importantly of all, great works help you to get inside the skin of others—often people in very different times or places—and vicariously experience the unique sorts of pleasures that are possible for them in their way of life.

Turn, next, to the pleasures of friendship. These involve, as I mentioned earlier, understanding and appreciating other people in their particularity or as individuals. Accordingly, the pleasures associated with them are qualitatively unique or original. The pleasures of knowing one good friend and spending time with them are fundamentally different in kind or character from those of knowing and spending time with a different person or friend. And friendships, as they evolve and deepen over time, offer further new sorts of pleasures. By contrast, mere acquaintances are far more generic, and for this reason, their pleasures are of less value for you.

Consider, finally, the pleasures of understanding. There are many different kinds of pleasures that are possible from understanding the ideas of science and philosophy, the intricacies of the natural world, and the social and cultural histories of humanity. The possibilities here are almost endless.

These wonderful pleasures can be contrasted with bodily pleasures, which quickly become 'just more of the same'. There just isn't that much qualitative diversity possible in bodily pleasures. Don't get me wrong—bodily pleasures have real value. Having *some* such pleasures in your life adds *something* to the richness or diversity of the pleasures you will experience. A life without any pleasures of, say, food, sex, or alcohol is missing something of value. But the main value of bodily pleasures, it seems to me, is *instrumental*. They are valuable by helping you to get through each day, and so on to the next day, when you might be able to experience some qualitatively new pleasures (or, alternatively, help some other people to experience some).

My answer, if true, would explain a lot. But there are some serious objections to it. I will now consider and respond to two important objections that have been made to my general idea—i.e., to the idea that the value of love, knowledge, art, nature, science, and so on, can be fully explained or accounted for in terms of their associated pleasures.

The Order of Explanation Worry

As we have seen, for Susan Wolf and others, encounters with nature, art, science and philosophy, other people, etc., are so very good for us just *because* these things are valuable *in themselves*. If they were not ultimately valuable, they would not benefit us so greatly. Wolf's remarks here are highly evocative and worth quoting at length. Concerning great works of art, she writes,

> At least some of the time, our early acquaintance with a poem or a novel or a painting—like our early acquaintance with a person—has the character of a discovery of something valuable in itself. Learning about an art form, one can feel a whole realm of value opening up before one. For many of this essay's readers, I suspect, the introduction to philosophy felt the same way: Here were questions and problems, or ways of looking at the world which you (and I) found challenging and worth exploring

further. We were drawn to them; they called out to us—not as forms of entertainment we found ourselves to enjoy, but as problems and ideas that were worthy of study and contemplation. ... *These objects do not strike us as good because they please or interest us, much less because they yield more separable instrumental benefits; rather, it seems that they please or interest us because we perceive them to be good in some other way.*[7]

Concerning nature, Wolf writes,

> We are moved by the beauty and desolation of a desert landscape, awed by the power and majesty of a towering mountain, charmed by the delicacy and variety in a meadow filled with wildflowers, much as we are moved, awed, charmed by works of art. Other experiences of the wonders of nature, however, are not aesthetic in this narrow and familiar sense. Birders and botanists, so far as I can tell, find interest and value in every sort of bird or plant, and do not discriminate very much on the basis of straightforwardly aesthetic distinctions. Any of these experiences may have the character of bringing us into contact with objects that merit our interest and concern. When we marvel at a species of plant or stand in awe overlooking a mountain range, we seem to recognize a value in these phenomena that is independent of our welfare, a value that is not grounded in our happening to find them interesting or beautiful. Rather, in finding them interesting or beautiful, it seems to us that their value is revealed.[8]

Wolf, I think, is undoubtedly right that when we are having such experiences—i.e., experiences of being "moved, awed, or charmed" by the objects in question—we are not thinking of their value *for* anyone. Instead, we are focused on their intrinsic properties—what they look or sound like, the ideas they involve, express, or explore, and so on. But it does not follow—and it does not seem plausible to me—that in these moments, we are aware of or responding to the independent *value* of these objects. What we are aware of or responding to here, I believe, is simply their *beauty* or *interest*. That they are beautiful or interesting does not entail that they are ultimately valuable.

There are certainly times when we *are* struck by their value and even well up with emotion at how wonderful it is that the things in question exist. But now these *are* times, it seems to me, when we have suddenly caught sight of how these objects are making us feel and the great value of such feelings for us (and, by extension, how many others might benefit from encounters with the things in question). We are not necessarily having such thoughts *consciously*—in fact, usually we are not. But the thoughts are nonetheless there.

Suppose I am listening to The Beatles' song "Michelle" and greatly enjoying it or even feeling deeply moved by it. Here, I might be responding simply to the song's intrinsic properties and great beauty without any thought of its tendency to benefit anyone. Suddenly, though, I might find myself welling up with emotion at how wonderful it is that this song was written or exists. When this happens, it seems to me I have temporarily noticed how this song is making me feel, and with this, the immense value for me (and, by extension, for many others) of the feelings in question.

Wolf might object that my account still does not capture the way we seem to care about these objects *for their own sakes*—i.e., over and above their ability or tendency to benefit anyone—and our loyalty, commitment, or devotion to them. As Thomas Hill Jr. notes, many of us are deeply uncomfortable about the destruction of natural environments *even when no harms will result*. We are even willing to make substantial sacrifices in our own interests to protect and preserve such environments. Hill writes,

> Uprooting the natural environment robs both present and future generations of much potential use and enjoyment. Animals too depend on the environment; and even if one does not value animals for their own sakes, their potential utility for us is incalculable. Plants are needed, of course, to replenish the atmosphere quite aside from their aesthetic value. These reasons for hesitating to destroy forests and gardens are not only the most obvious ones, but also the most persuasive for practical purposes. But, one wonders, is there nothing more behind our discomfort [at uprooting natural environments]? Are we concerned solely about the potential use and enjoyment of the forests, etc., for ourselves, later generations, and perhaps animals? Is there not something else which disturbs us when we witness the destruction or even listen to those who would defend it in terms of cost/benefit analysis?[9]

For Wolf, this 'something else' is their intrinsic value. But, as Hill points out, there is no need to attribute intrinsic value to nature in order to explain our feelings and concerns here. According to Hill, these feelings or concerns are a natural result or upshot of traits like "humility, self-acceptance, [and] gratitude [for what enriches our lives]".[10] Those who have such traits will naturally love nature and care about it even when it is clear that a given part of nature *won't* benefit anyone and *doesn't* have any intrinsic value itself.

It is easy to be led by our deep feelings about things to think that there must be intrinsic value in their object. But this is a mistake. It is a little like how religious people are often led by their feelings of awe whilst in church to believe that God exists. They shouldn't be led in this way. Better explanations of such feelings exist. We, similarly, should not be led by our feelings about humanity's survival or the existence of great works and natural environments to conclude that there is intrinsic value in these things.

The Experience Machine

According to Robert Nozick, it is important not only that we have *experiences* of love, friendship, knowledge, art, nature, achievement, and so on but that these experiences are *real* in some sense. In particular, Nozick says, it is important that we "*do* certain things, and not just have the experience of doing them".[11] He goes on to say,

> There is more to life than feeling happy. We care about what is actually the case. We want certain situations we value, prize, and think important to actually hold and be so. We want our beliefs, or certain of them, to be true and accurate; we want our emotions, or certain important ones, to be based upon facts that hold and to be fitting. We want to be importantly connected to reality, not to live in a delusion.[12]

Nozick argues by appeal to the idea of an "experience machine", which you can plug into for the rest of your life. This machine is designed by brilliant scientists to produce the most pleasurable future course of experiences possible for you. Whilst in the machine, you won't know you're in the machine. You will think it's all really happening. Would it be good if we all plugged into such machines? Not at all, says Nozick. It would be a lousy future. It would be lousy because we wouldn't really be doing anything, our beliefs would all be false, and our emotions would not be fitting or based on the facts. Moreover, he says, it is vital that we each

> *be* a certain way,...be a certain sort of person. Someone [who is plugged into an experience machine and] floating in a tank is an indeterminate blob. There is no answer to the question of what a person is like who has been long in the tank. Is he courageous, kind, intelligent, witty, loving? It's not merely that it's difficult to tell; there's no way he is. Plugging into the machine is a kind of suicide.[13]

How should we respond to Nozick's worry? The first thing to say is that for the machine to truly give us the set of future pleasures that will be most valuable for us, it would have to give us the 'higher' or 'wonderful' pleasures mentioned above. But to give us these, it will not be enough that it merely gives us the *impression* of understanding science, philosophy, humanity, or great works. For the machine to truly succeed in giving us the pleasures in question, it will have to ensure that we truly *understand* the things in question. Someone who merely *thinks* they are understanding a Shakespearean play but is mistaken is not gaining the deep pleasures this play can confer. Someone who merely *thinks* they understand the intricacies of a particular species of bird and doesn't really is not able to have the relevant pleasures. For this reason, we must imagine the machine as *greatly boosting our understanding of the world*—including science, philosophy, and other people, as well as great works of art, literature, and so on.

How could the machine do this? Well, the idea is that if you plug into the machine, you will gradually (so you don't suspect you are in a machine) become smarter and find yourself becoming more interested in science, philosophy, and the world at large. The machine won't *force* you to be more interested in these things. The idea is rather that by helping you to better understand the things in question, it will nudge you in the direction of such interests. As a result, you will very likely choose to read more about these things and come to an even deeper understanding of them, gaining a new-found appreciation of the beauties and complexities of nature and ideas of major thinkers. In order to improve your understanding of humanity—its richness or complexity, as well as our capacity for genuine concern for each other—the machine will give you representations of others that are incredibly nuanced and authentic, including wholly true or faithful representations of many existing people in your real life.

The machine will also make it possible for you to 'visit' parts of the world you would never visit in reality. You might have experiences, say, of climbing Everest, diving in the Great Barrier Reef, or visiting cultures you had no knowledge of or access to in the real world. These experiences will be fully informed by the nature of these real places, and so be indistinguishable from experiences of them that someone might have if they were to visit them in real life.[14]

What am I getting at? While there is a way in which the machine will take you out of reality, *there is also a way in which it will bring you closer to reality by giving you a deeper understanding of the real world, as well as access to deeply true or faithful representations of it*. It will *have* to do so if it is to have any hope of giving you all the wonderful pleasures. Understanding all this, I believe, makes it seem far more plausible that a future in which we are all plugged into individual experience machines could be a good one.

Still, some people will not like the idea of us all plugging in. "How terrible", they will think, "to leave your friends and loved ones behind forever, to never see, touch, or talk to any of them ever again, and to hang out with mere simulacra".

I agree this is a troubling thought—and, in a way, deeply sad. But we must also remember that the machine is so sophisticated that it knows *your friends and your loved ones* much better than you yourself know them—better, indeed, than anyone knows them, including these people themselves. As such, the machine will be able to create representations of these special people in your life that will do an even *better* job of communicating their essence to you than these people could do themselves in reality.

The real world, you see, is set up in such a way that it is easy to slip into friendships with people who aren't truly well suited to being your friends at all. The machine will phase many of these people out of our lives. The real world can also conspire to put distance—physical and emotional distance—between you and people who *are* well suited to being your friends or lovers. This is a major theme of many tragic plays and real-life tragedies. The experience machine can ensure that the situations in which you encounter your friends and loved ones (or rather, representations of them) are ones in which their true nature can shine through. For this reason, the machine might bring us *closer*—at least, in a certain respect—to the people who are truly important in our lives. Consider, also, that your loved ones will be in machines of their own, machines that are giving *them* wholly true or faithful representations of *you* that will help them to better understand who you are than encounters with the actual, real-life 'you' could possibly do. In this way, these machines, taken collectively, might succeed in bringing us all much closer to each other *by* separating us from each other or by taking us out of the real world. An odd but plausible thought.

Of course, not everything will be rosy inside the machine. The machine will have to put you in some situations where there are strains or difficulties of various kinds, for its overriding priority will be to give you a rich, accurate, and as complete as possible understanding of humanity in order to help you experience the pleasures of truly understanding what is so good and interesting about us all.

So, yes, we'll never actually see our loved ones again, but in a way, we'll see them even more clearly, closely, and deeply than before. And we'll even (in a way) do things *with* them that would not be possible in the real world. It will all take place with doppelgangers. But in a way, it will still be with each other (especially if they themselves, in their machines, are doing the same sorts of things with doppelgangers of *us*).[15]

My point, to emphasise, is that reality, given the limitations it puts on us—intellectual and emotional limitations, limitations in where we can go in the world, and, more generally, the distance it puts between us and others as a result of poverty, stress, and the difficulty of finding people who are well suited to be our friends—is not all it's cracked up to be. Reality is actually not all that good at helping us connect *with reality (or, at least, with the really important parts of it)*. The machine can do better. And it will have to if it is to succeed in giving us all the wonderful pleasures.

What about Nozick's worry that we wouldn't be *doing* anything in the machine and, in fact, wouldn't even *be* anyone? This is a mistake. The machine should not work by giving us the mere *impression* that we are making choices. Instead, it should give us real choices between simulated possibilities. Since we are making real choices, there is a real and important sense in which we are doing things and being someone. We can read books and listen to music. We can 'visit' different parts of the world and learn more about them. We can develop and pursue our individual tastes and proclivities. We can hone skills or develop new interests, talents, and so on. We can even strive for things, as well as achieve certain things, such as moral growth, a better understanding of the world, or even the creation of artistic works of our own.

Actually, since the machine will (as I have argued) have to boost your knowledge of the world, you are likely to make *better* decisions than you would in reality. You are *more* likely to grow as a person, develop new skills or interests, create new artistic works of your own, etc. It is true that you cannot help anyone else. But you can certainly *do* things and *be* someone. Indeed, there is a sense in which you can be your *best* self. The machine will not make any of this *easy* for you. It will merely remove certain obstacles that reality puts in our way, obstacles that can make living one's best self too hard or even impossible.

You might object: but *why* must the machine give us real choices rather than just the impression of choosing? The answer is that if the machine merely gave you the impression of choosing, then you would indeed be nobody at all. And in that case, the machine could not give *you* the most pleasurable possible future. You must *survive* in order to be benefited by the machine.[16]

To conclude, I do agree that there is something incredibly sad about the thought of everyone being plugged into individual experience machines and never seeing each other again. But as I have been at pains to point out in this book, *sad* does not entail *bad*. It is, I am more than willing to concede, fitting and right to have mixed feelings about the thought of plugging in. Just as somebody who knows and loves the environment will be sentimental about it, and somebody who knows and loves humanity will be sentimental about it, so someone who knows and loves other people will be sentimental about *them* and the thought of leaving them.

But once you keep in mind all the things I've said in this chapter—in particular, the fact that the machine will help you know your friends and loved ones even better than you could know them in reality, and help you to have (in a sense) wonderful experiences with them that you could not have in reality—it seems much more plausible that everyone being plugged into the machine (without their knowledge) might well be the best outcome for humanity. The technology would need to be incredibly sophisticated, not to mention absolutely failproof. But if it was, this outcome might be best.

Notes

1 J. S. Mill, *Utilitarianism*. (Oxford University Press UK, 1861). Edited by Roger Crisp.
2 Susan Wolf (2010). "Good-for-nothings". *Proceedings and Addresses of the American Philosophical Association* 85 (2):47–64. See also Thomas Scanlon (*What We Owe to Each Other* (Cambridge: Harvard, 1998), p. 143): "If I devote my life, or a part of it, to research in pure mathematics or to mastering the rudiments of theoretical physics, these activities contribute to making my life better. But what makes these pursuits worthwhile is not *that contribution* (or the possible contribution that their applications might make to the well-being of others) but rather the fact that they constitute serious attempts to understand deep and important questions". Scanlon says that such pursuits make a person's life go better for them *because* they are "successful [pursuits] of worthwhile goals". If these goals weren't worthwhile in this sort of way, being successful at them *wouldn't* be the sort of thing that so greatly benefits us.
3 Mill (1861).
4 Mill (1861).
5 Ben Bramble, (2013). "The Distinctive Feeling Theory of Pleasure". *Philosophical Studies* 162 (2):201–17.
6 Ben Bramble (2016). "A New Defense of Hedonism about Well-Being". *Ergo: An Open Access Journal of Philosophy* 3.
7 Wolf (2010).
8 Wolf (2010).
9 Thomas E. Hill Jr., (1983). "Ideals of Human Excellence and Preserving Natural Environments", *Environmental Ethics*, 3.
10 Hill (1983), 213.
11 Nozick, Robert, *Anarchy, State, and Utopia* (New York: Basic Books, 1974).
12 Nozick, Robert, *Examined Life: Philosophical Meditations*. (Simon & Schuster, 1990).
13 Nozick, Robert, *Anarchy, State, and Utopia* (New York: Basic Books, 1974).
14 The machine might also invent new wonderful places for you to visit (a very nice friend's farm or island or library), places that do not exist in the 'real' world. As David Chalmers argues, these would then be real in a significant sense (David John Chalmers, *Reality+: Virtual Worlds and the Problems of Philosophy* (New York: W. W. Norton, 2022). In this case, you'd have access to real places that nobody else would and that would be impossible for you to visit if you stayed in reality. By doing so, the machine would be *expanding* reality.
15 Nozick might complain, "But no one will really love you in the machine. Isn't *that* a terrible thing?" Well, your friends and loved ones

in *their* machines will still love you (and, having come to know you better, perhaps love you *more deeply or more truly*).

16 Also, it seems possible that there is necessarily a felt or phenomenological difference between genuinely deciding or trying to do something, on the one hand, and merely having a false impression that you are trying or deciding to do something, on the other. It is not clear that you can fully or adequately simulate for somebody the phenomenology associated with their truly trying or deciding. In this case, the machine, in order to give you the most pleasurable future course of experiences possible, would clearly have to allow you to make real choices in the machine. Otherwise, there would be a whole host of important pleasures you'd miss out on.

Chapter 12

Cluelessness

When deciding what to do, we can usually make decent guesses about *some* consequences of our possible actions. Right now, for example, I could either keep working or take a break (say, go for a walk). If I keep working, I will probably make some progress, but my headache will get worse, I might start to feel restless from working too long, and so on. By contrast, if I go for a walk, I will probably enjoy some fresh air or views along the way; I might bump into some friends, make some new ones, etc.

A Drop in the Ocean

However, as James Lenman points out, 'the foreseeable consequences of an action are so often *a drop in the ocean* of its actual consequences'.[1] This is because the consequences of your actions go on for a *very* long time. And these longer-term consequences, which constitute by far the majority of their overall consequences, are *utterly unpredictable*—we have no hope of making decent guesses about them.

Why are they so unpredictable? A big part of it, as Lenman explains, has to do with the fact that so many of our actions (perhaps all of them) are *identity-affecting*—that is, they will change the identities of certain people who will exist later on. Changing identities radically alters the distant future since different people will live very different lives (including making choices that will themselves change further people's identities).

Why are our actions identity-affecting? Some actions affect which people meet others and have children together. Other actions affect merely the *timing* of when couples conceive their children, but by doing so, they alter the sperm-egg combinations that give rise to future people. Our actions affect these things due, in part, to the complex (and in certain cases chaotic) nature of causal systems. Small changes in your behaviour can cause large fluctuations in other events, which can in turn amplify exponentially. As Tyler Cowen notes, even the simple act of stopping at a traffic light rather than going through it on one occasion will "affect the length of other commutes and thus change the timing of millions of future conceptions".[2] Cowen adds,

> Our traffic behavior need only lead other male drivers to jostle enough to redistribute their sperm. ... Given that a male body holds millions of sperm, it is unlikely that various jostlings will have no affect on the genetic identities of future children. Again, only the smallest of changes are needed to have long-term repercussions.[3]

In virtue of these sort of facts, Lenman says, the foreseeable consequences of our actions are, in the context of trying to work out the overall consequences of our actions,

> [clues] of bewildering insignificance bordering on uselessness—like a detective's discovery of a fragment of evidence pointing inconclusively to the murderer's having been under seven feet tall.[4]

For this reason, according to Lenman and others, we cannot hope to form even reasonable guesses about what actions available to us will have overall better consequences than others.

According to these philosophers, this poses big problems for utilitarianism. For one, Lenman says, it means that a view like utilitarianism cannot vindicate basic moral judgements like that Hitler should not have acted as he did. Lenman writes,

> [T]he full consequences of each death [due to Hitler] are...vast and impenetrable. ... How many [even worse dictators] might have been among the descendants of [Hitler's] victims? Not that it would help us to know this. For the causal ramifications of [*these* dictators' actions] are so astronomically great that [their] moral value is—by consequentialist standards—utterly inscrutable.[5]

A second reason is that it means that utilitarianism is, as Shelly Kagan puts it, "unusable as a moral guide to action".[6] If utilitarianism were true, the worry goes, then any attempts to get closer in action to what you should do are futile.

I will now respond to these worries in turn.

Person-Affecting Utilitarianism to the Rescue

We must surely accept that because the consequences of our actions go on for so long and will change identities in the ways described earlier, the foreseeable consequences of our actions are a mere drop in the ocean of their overall consequences. However, it might still be possible, I believe—*if person-affecting utilitarianism is true*—to live in such a way that we can be reasonably confident of doing more good than bad.

Recall that on person-affecting utilitarianism, your actions make things better in some respect just in case they *help* or *benefit* somebody or *improve* their life in some way. Now, take a case where your action alters a future person's identity—say, makes it the case that a certain couple's child will be John rather than Sally. Here, your action benefits and harms this *couple* in various ways (by altering their child's identity, and so all their future interactions with their child), as well as anyone who encounters John (and anyone who would have encountered Sally). But your action does not benefit or harm *John*. This is because had you not performed this action, John would never have existed.[7]

This point generalises. As the consequences of your actions ripple out, changing future people's identities, they thereby *stop* benefiting and harming future individuals. The identity changes act as a sort of buffer, preventing your actions from benefiting and harming still further people. As they do so—if person-affecting utilitarianism is true—their *good* and *bad* consequences run out. If person-affecting utilitarianism is true, while the *consequences* of your actions might go on forever, their *good and bad consequences* run out on the first generation of people they affect (since, by affecting them, they change the identities of their children). At some point in the future, as a result of *whatever* action you perform, there will be not a single person alive who would otherwise have existed. At this point, the good and bad consequences of your action will have entirely ended.

With this in mind, let's return to Lenman's example of Hitler. If person-affecting utilitarianism is true, Hitler certainly did *not* act as he should have since the effects of his actions on the *first generation* of people they affected were, on balance, *hugely* bad. Their further effects are indeed massive and unknowable. But these further effects are normatively irrelevant because the relevant future people would not have existed at all had Hitler acted otherwise (other people would have existed instead). Hitler's actions do not make these future people any better or worse off than they would otherwise have been.

'Kindness Is Catching'

A critic might respond: "OK, *Hitler's* actions were clearly overwhelmingly bad, on balance, for the first generation of people they affected. But what about the sort of actions most of us have to choose from in our everyday lives? *Their* consequences for the first generation of people they will affect are far less clear. As such, if person-affecting utilitarianism is true, we still have virtually nothing to go on when choosing between our various possible options".

I agree that most of the *details* of the consequences of our actions for the first generation of people they will affect are utterly unguessable. But I believe it might still be possible to live in such a way that we can be confident *enough* that our actions will help people more than they will harm them.

Consider that 'kindness is catching'. Jonathan Haidt and his collaborators describe how witnessing prosocial or helping behaviour can lead a person to experience a particular kind of positive emotion—'elevation'—which can in turn lead this person to perform prosocial actions towards others.[8] Haidt writes of the subjects in one of his studies:

> Elevated participants were more likely to report physical feelings in their chests, especially warm, pleasant, or tingling feelings, and they were more likely to report wanting to help others, to become better people themselves, and to affiliate with others.[9]

Many further studies have since borne this out. Research conducted by James Fowler and Nicholas Christakis suggests that

> cooperative or uncooperative behavior...can create cascades of similar cooperative or uncooperative behavior in others, spreading from person to person to person, even when reputations are unknown and reciprocity is not possible.[10]

And the extensive study of Joseph Chancellor et al. suggests that

> although everyday prosocial acts may be small, they are not insignificant. The benefits of prosociality do multiply, favoring not only those who give but also those who receive and observe.[11]

It is not altogether clear how this works. One possibility is that witnessing prosocial behaviour can inspire in you (unconsciously) *a greater optimism about humanity* and with this a greater confidence that your efforts to build a better world are not in vain. Many of us have a disinterested concern for others and want to build a better world, but when others seem mean or narrowly self-interested, this can make us feel that the project of building a better world is unfeasible or not worth it. So, we tend to keep resources for ourselves. By contrast, when others act kindly or generously (towards us *or* others), this boosts our confidence that the goal of building a better world might indeed be feasible. This can lead to a greater willingness to make personal sacrifices to this end.[12]

The idea that 'kindness is catching' is a key theme of many classic films and works of literature. In these works, acts of kindness inspire positive change in beneficiaries or observers, who in turn act kindly towards others or even do something momentous. In *Les Miserables*, for example, an ex-convict, Jean Valjean, steals the silverware of a priest (Bishop Myriel) who had welcomed him into his home. The police apprehend Valjean, and report him to Myriel. Myriel lies to the police that the silverware was a gift to Valjean. Valjean is freed, and Myriel tells him to keep the silver and use it "to become an honest man". Valjean responds by transforming himself, going on to help many other people throughout his life, many of whom are in turn inspired by Valjean's actions (including, notably, inspector Javert).

Another well-known illustration of the idea that kindness is catching is George Bailey in the film *It's A Wonderful Life*. Bailey is about to commit suicide when his guardian angel, Clarence, suddenly appears and shows George what his town of Bedford Falls would have been like had he (George) never existed. It is worse in many ways. George's friends and family are all much worse off. They lead dark, despondent lives. The town, more generally, has become a bleak place, rife with gambling, alcoholism, and poverty. Part of George's positive effect on the town had to do with his Building and Loan, which allowed the citizens of the town to live independently of capitalist Mr Potter. But it goes much further than this. There are many everyday acts of kindness George performs throughout his life—risking his own life to save his brother's, preventing his boss Mr Gower from accidentally poisoning someone, etc.—that have huge beneficial flow-on effects. But perhaps most significantly of all, we are led to believe that it is simply George's everyday positivity and bigheartedness, his devotion to his community and willingness to always lend a hand, that has made such a difference to his town. George, in his daily encounters with his fellow townsfolk, radiated a kindness, concern, and goodwill that spread to many others, changing their lives, touching the lives of many others in turn, and eventually transforming the town as a whole.

As Skott Brill brilliantly puts it,

> This film shows the great extent to which an ordinary, decent person can have a positive effect on part of the world, in this case his family, workplace, home town, and even beyond. Most remarkable about the film is its illustration of the snowball effect, both the positive snowball effect virtuous acts can have on parts of the world and the negative snowball effect the removal of virtuous acts can have. The film shows that while the immediate effects of good acts done are impressive enough, the ensuing chain reaction can multiply the significance of good acts exponentially. The film also nicely illustrates how easily an ordinary person's positive impact on the world can be overlooked, even by that person.[13]

Of course, George Bailey is an exceptional person. He is both exceptionally kind and involved in his community, and the difference he makes is, accordingly, much greater than many of us are capable of making. But there is nonetheless reason to think that we, lesser folks, are able, by acting kindly or generously in our everyday lives, to have a positive impact on the world that will inspire many other such acts in others, and in this way, benefit many people in the short to medium term.

If this is right, *and* person-affecting utilitarianism is true, then we might be able to live in such a way that we can be reasonably confident that our actions will help people more than they will harm them. If you live in a kind or bighearted way, immersed in your local community, your kindness will snowball, influencing others to have such traits and exercise kindness in turn, and further spread such traits. You can make a very great positive difference over time, via this snowballing effect, by being a decent person living a normal life and having the good effects of this flow onto others. Such a life, over the long run, is likely to cause more benefits than harms to the first generation of people your actions will affect.

Of course, we cannot be *certain* that living in such a way will help people more than it will harm them. There are possible worlds where even Bailey's total life ends up doing more harm than good (say, by causing some freak harms in neighbouring towns). But certainty isn't required. It is enough that we can be reasonably confident. We are, then, not entirely clueless. We have more than a mere clue.

To emphasise, my conclusion here is not that we can be confident *on any given occasion* that acting kindly on this occasion will be best or help people more than it will harm them. It is rather that we can be confident that living a life like Bailey's will, over time, help people more than it will harm them. It's like playing poker. A good player will lose some hands, even many of them, but if they play this way for long enough, they are very likely to win the long game.

Notes

1 James Lenman, (2000). "Consequentialism and Cluelessness". *Philosophy and Public Affairs* 29 (4):342–70.
2 Tyler Cowen, (2006). "The Epistemic Problem Does Not Refute Consequentialism". *Utilitas*, 18 (04):383–99.
3 Cowen (2006).
4 Lenman (2000).
5 Lenman (2000).
6 S. Kagan, *Normative Ethics* (Westview Press, 1998).
7 The fact that John exists (rather than Sally) will change a whole host of other people's identities, too, which will again benefit and harm some people, but not the people whose identities will be changed.
8 Jonathan Haidt, "The Moral Emotions", in R. J. Davidson, K. R. Scherer, & H. H. Goldsmith (eds) *Handbook of Affective Sciences* (Oxford), 852–70; Dacher Keltner & Jonathan Haidt, (2003). "Approaching Awe: A

Moral, Spiritual, and Aesthetic Emotion", *Cognition & Emotion*, 17:297–314; Sara Algoe and Jonathan Haidt, (2003). "Witnessing Excellence in Action: The 'Other-Praising' Emotions of Elevation, Gratitude, and Admiration", *Journal of Positive Psychology*, (4): 105–27.

9 Jonathan Haidt, "Elevation and the Positive Psychology of Morality", in C.L.M. Keyes & J. Haidt (eds), *Flourishing: Positive Psychology and the Life Well-Lived* (Washington, DC: American Psychological Association, 2003).

10 James Fowler & Nicholas Christakis, (2010). "Cooperative Behavior Cascades in Human Social Networks", *Proceedings of the National Academy of Sciences of the United States of America*, 107(12):5334–8.

11 Joseph Chancellor, Seth Margolis, Katherine Jacobs Bao, and Sonja Lyubomirsky, (2018). "Everyday Prosociality in the Workplace: The Reinforcing Benefits of Giving, Getting, and Glimpsing", *Emotion* 18(4):507–17. See also Simone Schnall, Jean Roper, and Daniel M.T. Fessler, (2010). "Elevation Leads to Altruistic Behavior", *Psychological Science* 21(3):315–20; Sigal G. Barsade, (2002). "The Ripple Effect: Emotional Contagion and Its Influence on Group Behavior", *Administrative Science Quarterly*: 644–75.

12 Nothing hangs on this particular explanation being correct. The point is that the sort of reproduction in question seems plausible and is borne out by a large and growing body of scientific work.

13 Skott Brill, (2007). "Does It Matter That Nothing We Do Will Matter in a Million Years?' *Dialogue*, 46:19.

Chapter 13

Reasons or Requirements?

I have just been arguing that if person-affecting utilitarianism is true, then it might be possible to live in such a way that you can be confident enough that, over time, your actions will help people more than they will harm. But I also admitted we cannot hope for certainty here.

There is something else to admit: it is entirely futile to try to work out what action available to you on any given occasion would be overall *best*. Given the complex and chaotic nature of causal systems, the very *best* action available to you at any given time is likely always to be something very odd, like jumping five times on the spot, yelling at a stranger, or phoning a particular overseas phone number, etc.

This, I think, provides decisive evidence against *requirement utilitarianism*, the view that we are morally *required* to do what would be best. Why? If requirement utilitarianism were true, then virtually *all* the actions we in fact perform are morally wrong, something which is intuitively unacceptable. Return to George Bailey. It is hard to take seriously a view on which all *his* actions are morally wrong, especially if we are thinking that a person is morally to *blame* for acting morally wrongly (at least, without a good excuse).

Requirement utilitarians might respond, "All of our actions *are* morally wrong, but this is intuitively acceptable since we always *have* a good excuse—nothing other than our cluelessness itself".

But, here, I struggle to understand what is being claimed by the requirement utilitarian when they say that such actions are morally wrong, as opposed to these actions merely falling short of what the agent has *most reason* to do. Why not simply say that we are always failing to do what we have most reason to do and leave it at that?

What does it add to say these actions are morally wrong? The idea that every time we act, we are doing something other than what we have *most reason* to do is intuitively acceptable—indeed, it is intuitively plausible, given the chaotic nature of causal systems. Reasons utilitarianism is not embarrassed at all by the idea that it is futile to try to work out what action available to us would be *best*.

There is a further problem with the requirement utilitarian's response here. It is obvious that we *are* sometimes blameworthy for our actions *even though we have no hope of performing the best action*. Hitler, certainly, was to blame for his actions, notwithstanding his inability to know what actions available to him were the very *best*.

For these reasons, I think, the Cluelessness Objection refutes requirement utilitarianism while leaving reasons utilitarianism intact.

It might be said, "But surely we need a theory of moral requirements and wrongness?" Some reasons utilitarians (notably, Alastair Norcross) deny this. But I do agree that we need such a theory. It's just that I do not think utilitarianism is best understood as a theory of such things. The key insight of utilitarianism is just about what we have reason (and most reason) to do. *This* is the sense of "we should maximise overall welfare" that has both plausibility and significance.

Duty and Wrong Action

So, what is the right theory of moral requirements and wrongness? What *are* we doing at times when we wonder whether a given action is morally required or, by contrast, morally wrong? I will not here offer a complete theory of this, but I want to offer some thoughts.

Suppose you told a friend last week that you would meet them for lunch today, but now you feel more like watching a live sports match than going to see them. Or suppose you have spent an hour trying on different pairs of shoes at a locally owned and run shoe store and are about to buy a pair when your friend tells you that you could buy the very same pair for much cheaper from an online bargain warehouse. Or suppose you would like to recycle a bottle you've been drinking from, but the only recycle bin is all the way over on the other side of the building. Or suppose you are trying to work out whether to become a vegetarian.

When deliberating in such cases, what are you deliberating about? Yes, you are trying to work out what to *do*. But more fundamentally, I think, you are trying to work out what sort of a person to *be*. In particular, you are trying to work out how a good or virtuous person—someone like, say, George Bailey—would *feel* about performing the actions in question. Would it 'sit well' with them? Or would they rather feel uncomfortable about it or even be unable to bear it? Would a Bailey-type figure be able to *enjoy* watching the sports game knowing they are doing so at the cost of disappointing their friend? Would a Bailey-type figure feel just too awful at the thought of buying the shoes online rather than at the local store? Would a Bailey-type figure who knows all about the lives of animals and the suffering they experience in factory farms feel comfortable eating meat? And so on.

Normally, when acting, our level of comfort with performing given actions is relatively settled. But sometimes we encounter situations where we're not sure how to feel. We might feel conflicted. Or we might not have been in such a situation before and have no precedent to draw on. *These* are times when we are deliberating about whether certain actions are morally wrong or, by contrast, required. The question of whether they are wrong *is* the question of how to feel in such cases.

Morally wrong actions, then, are ones that our George Bailey–type figure who understands the relevant facts would feel a certain kind of discomfort performing. Morally required acts are ones a George Bailey–type figure who understands the relevant facts would feel uncomfortable *not* performing.

In such moments of deliberation, I think, we are trying to come to better approximate a George Bailey–type figure in our *feelings* or *sentiments* about things so as to become better at living our everyday lives in such a way that we positively influence others (in the sort of ways identified as important in the previous chapter). Most of the time, we do not stop to consciously deliberate about what to do—we are running on autopilot in a certain sense. When we do stop to deliberate (in such cases as these), we are trying to become better autopilots.

Chapter 14

Demandingness

Many philosophers have objected to utilitarianism on the grounds that it is too demanding—i.e., that it requires too much of us. In particular, many complain that utilitarianism implies that as someone living in a wealthy country today, you should devote the rest of your life to 'earning to give'—i.e., taking the highest paying job you can and giving almost all your income away via 'effective charities' to poorer people in distant parts of the world. By doing so, you can help people far more than you can by living a normal life with personal relationships, interests, and projects of your own. But this implication, they say, is wildly counterintuitive. You are required to do no such thing. You do not act morally wrongly by not devoting your life to earning to give. You are allowed to have a life of your own. It may be awfully nice of you to give up so much, but you are not required to do so.

However, as we saw in the previous chapter, utilitarianism should not be understood as a theory of moral requirements but rather one strictly of *reasons for action*. We should be *reasons utilitarians*, not *requirement utilitarians*. So, utilitarianism, properly understood, does *not* imply that you are morally required to devote yourself to earning to give. It does not imply anything about your moral duties at all.

Still, it might be said, reasons utilitarianism is vulnerable to a similar worry. It is counterintuitive even that you have most *reason* to devote your life to earning to give.[1]

But as I pointed out in the previous section, the series of actions available to you that would be *best*—i.e., that would help people the most—is likely to be a series of very odd and unpredictable actions, like jumping five times on the spot, yelling at a stranger,

DOI: 10.4324/9781003300045-16

then phoning a particular overseas phone number, etc. It is almost certainly *not* earning to give. So, reasons utilitarianism does not imply that you have most reason to devote your life to earning to give.

Even so, you might say, the worry can be framed (or reframed) in a way that does make genuine trouble for reasons utilitarianism. Surely, your best *bet* for maximally helping others—the *subjectively* rational thing to do, on utilitarianism—is to devote your life to earning to give. This is what you should *choose* to do *if you accept utilitarianism and live consistently with its principles*. However, so the objection goes, this is clearly *not* what it is subjectively rational for a person to do. It can be entirely reasonable to choose to live something like a normal life with friends, interests, and projects of your own. Indeed, the critic might continue, there seems something odd or even *irrational* about somebody who gives up all of this in order to devote themselves to earning to give. As Susan Wolf puts it, a life of earning to give is not one that is "reasonable or healthy or desirable for human beings" to aspire to, strive toward, or lead. Such a life is not good as a "personal ideal". It is not "a model… which it would be particularly rational or good or desirable for a human being to strive".[2]

For Wolf, the reason it is subjectively rational to live your own life rather than devote it to earning to give is that there are special reasons of self-interest, as well as ultimate reasons to interact with, sustain, and appreciate intrinsic goods other than welfare—goods such as art, beauty, and knowledge. Wolf writes,

> [N]onmoral values, such as beauty, knowledge, love, as well as self-interest, [give] us goals and reasons for action that [are] independent of morality, and I [know] of no argument…that [establishes] that reasons grounded in moral values should always take precedence. … Nonmoral values compete directly with moral ones and…no sound arguments give us reason to assume that moral values should take absolute precedence over others.[3]

As a utilitarian, I disagree with Wolf that there are these other sources of reasons. All reasons, I believe, are provided just by your ability to help beings (yourself or others), and there are no special reasons of self-interest.

But I do agree that it can be subjectively rational to live something like a normal life. In what follows, I will explain how this can be true—on my sort of utilitarianism.

Person-Affecting Utilitarianism to the Rescue

My explanation of this is nothing other than a more developed version of the answer I gave earlier to the Cluelessness Objection. There, I suggested that despite our utter ignorance of the very distant consequences of our actions, it might be possible to live in such a way that it is reasonable to think that you are helping people more than you are harming them. This is by living a life, roughly, like George Bailey's—a kind and generous life immersed in your community. This is because kindness is catching. It snowballs.

How exactly does this account justify spending time on your own relationships, interests, projects, etc.? Wouldn't it instead recommend spending all your time walking around town performing kind acts like opening doors for people, helping elderly people with their groceries, and so on?

Well, small acts of kindness like these certainly do spread goodwill. But their effects are small. The sorts of actions I have in mind are instead more sustained interactions, especially multiple interactions with the same people over time, where the others in question come to better understand you as a person—especially your concern for, and commitment to, beings other than yourself—and also come to find you and your approach to life attractive and worth emulating.

This can happen in friendships but also with colleagues, peers in an educational system, and even in certain kinds of interactions with acquaintances. To see the difference between what I'm talking about, on the one hand, and a life of walking around opening doors for people, on the other, consider again George Bailey. Bailey did not spend his time walking around opening doors for people or performing 'good deeds' like that. Instead, he lived more or less an ordinary life, yet one where he was a good friend and fellow citizen to many others in his town. Over time, as people got to know him, his bigheartedness and concern for others rubbed off on them. What I'm talking about is being a good ambassador, in a regular sort of life, for a socially engaged life of kindness and concern for others.

Such a person, note, will not be indifferent to the welfare of distant others. On the contrary, they will be concerned indeed about them. It's just that their concern for them will not lead them to devote their lives to earning to give but rather to advocating, in some of their daily interactions (when contextually appropriate), for greater government assistance to such people or even a restructuring of the whole system to improve their welfare.

How exactly does my account justify spending time on your own relationships, interests, projects, etc.? There are several ways. First, unless you have some interests, passions, and projects of your own, as well as deep personal relationships, you're unlikely to *learn* enough about the world to understand others and care about them in the ways I'm talking about. You're not, that is, going to *be* a kind, wise, or bighearted person in the first place. You won't have depth. Having some relationships and activities of your own deepens your understanding of the world—indeed, they are necessary for such depth. You must engage in some experiments in living of your own and learn about the world and others through trial and error. You can learn this only through involvement in such things. Otherwise, you won't be the sort of person we should *want* people to emulate.

Second, unless you have some interests, passions, or projects of your own, as well as deep personal relationships—not to mention qualities like a sense of humour!—you're not going to be *attractive* to others as somebody to spend time with or emulate. If you're not likeable or relatable, you might even alienate others from your good approach to the world.

Third, spending time with others in regular sorts of situations is precisely *how* your values get spread. This is the primary setting in which others come to understand you better and like you enough to want to emulate you.

Fourth, it is important to have some relationships and interests or activities of your own in order to stay cheerful enough to keep learning about the world and be likeable enough that others will want to emulate you. If you're not somebody who takes pleasure in various aspects of life, you'll get stuck in a rut and then be no good to anyone. Friendships and activities, in other words, can be needed to rejuvenate you or keep you interested and immersed in life.

Fifth, spending quite a bit of time with your friends or near and dear, as well as a greater proportion of your resources on them, is important in helping *them* to realise *their* potential to be good ambassadors for a socially engaged life of kindness and concern for others. Your friends and near and dear are, for the most part, not merely people you have chosen at random to spend time with. They are, in most cases, people whom you like and respect—this is *why* you are (or stay) friends or close with them. They are people who— if *you* have wisdom or depth—are the sort of people who are themselves spreading kindness in society. It is only when such people are themselves deep, happy, secure, and doing well that they can engage with others in a positive way. You can contribute to this by spending time with them. It is extremely valuable to nourish these special people.

Ask yourself, how do you feel when you think about one of your best friends deciding to give up their existing relationships and interests to devote their lives to earning to give? If you are like me, you will not like the idea of it at all. Intuitively, this is not only from a concern for *them* or *yourself*. It is also because you immediately recognise the loss to *society* of having such a special person leave their existing communities and cease contributing in the ways they are. Right now, this person is making important contributions in their everyday lives, simply by being themselves. Their contributions are making an enormous difference over time, as their flow-on effects spread positivity and kindness to others. We need such people *in* society. Without them, other people with worse values will fill the gap.

Not Just Any Kind of Life

To emphasise, I am not saying that it is subjectively rational to live *any* sort of life of your own, but only one where you are striving to understand things better, are kind, generous, and immersed in your community. A life of, say, sitting at home playing video games all day is not such a life. A life of watching Fox News and spreading untruths at Little League games is also not such a life.

Wolf and some other critics of utilitarianism think that interests or activities like fine dining and high fashion can be legitimate. I disagree. The enrichment such activities provide does not justify their cost, given that you can gain similar enrichment from much cheaper dining and fashion options.

A George Bailey–type figure, I believe, would not be able to *enjoy* fine dining or high fashion, given their awareness of the suffering of others in the world and the fact that much cheaper forms of dining and fashion are comparably enriching for you as fine dining or high fashion.

More generally, while a Bailey-type figure might feel comfortable spending *some* time and money on improving their house, car, or garden, etc., they might not feel comfortable driving a flashy BMW, living in an opulent mansion, or having extensive landscaped private gardens at great cost, when so many others have so little. Instead, if they have surplus money, they would spend it on other, more socially useful things—say, investing it in socially worthwhile projects or businesses.

What About Earning to Give?

Our critic might complain, "While I accept that you can do a lot of good by living a kind life immersed in your community, surely you can do even more good by earning to give?"

I doubt this for a few reasons. First, when you give money away like this, you cannot effectively convey kindness or goodwill. The beneficiaries will—almost inevitably, and quite reasonably from their perspective—take a cynical view of why you are helping. So, while *they* will benefit from the money, and there will be *some* good flow-on effects of this, your contribution is unlikely to have anything like the sort of ripple effects described earlier.

Second, even if some of the people your money will benefit are inspired or enabled by your action to perform acts that will pass on certain kinds of values through their own societies, you can have no idea what these values will be. Your money might be helping religious zealots or others who are taking their communities in the *wrong* direction. By contrast, in spending your time and resources on your friends or near and dear, you can be far more confident that you are nourishing or strengthening people whose contribution to society through their everyday actions is a net good one.

Third, societies in poorer countries are far less influential in world affairs and for this reason less influential in determining the future course of the planet than wealthier societies. Making a small contribution to a positive cultural shift in the US or UK is likely to be far more consequential than contributing to one in a poorer country.

The Right-Wing Family Member Objection

You might object: But what about friends or relatives who *aren't* kind or bighearted, or worse still, who have only bad or toxic values? How can utilitarianism justify your spending time and resources on *them*?

The short answer is that it can't. If you can't influence them to hold better views or become a better person, then you shouldn't be wasting your scarce time or resources on them. This might be sad, but it's what you should do.

The Bed-Ridden Mother Objection

What about a loved one who is kind and good but who, due to some kind of illness or impairment, can no longer contribute much to the world? Consider, for example, a parent who is old and needs looking after. Surely, it can still be subjectively rational to spend time and resources on looking after them. But utilitarianism, you might say, cannot say this. It implies you should abandon such a person.

But a George Bailey–type figure surely could not *bear* abandoning someone they love who is in such a position. They would recognise that were they to do so, they themselves would be so broken or traumatised by doing so that they would no longer be of much use to anyone.

Why would they be so broken or traumatised? Simply as an offshoot or by-product of their love for this person. As I've mentioned many times in this book, those who richly understand things (for example, the nature and value of humanity and individual human lives, the nature and value of natural environments, the nature and value of great works of art, and so on) are necessarily *sentimental*. They feel and want things out of proportion to the value these things have.

The George Bailey Objection

Next, you might object that the character of George Bailey does not actually help to make my point, for Bailey himself explicitly *gives up* his own personal hopes and dreams (to travel the world and become an engineer) in order to stay home and help others. Bailey, then, is more like an ***effective altruist*** or someone who chooses to earn to give. If we hold him up as a model, we should hold up the effective altruists of today who devote themselves to earning to give.

But while it is true that Bailey made certain kinds of sacrifices, he still led a very full life in Bedford Falls, with a loving partner and family, many friends, friendships, and enjoyable activities. Had Bailey been an 'effective altruist', he would instead have taken up Mr Potter's offer of working for him at a high salary and then spent all his time working for Mr Potter and sending his money abroad. *That* choice, it seems to me, would have been subjectively irrational, given the huge amount of good he could do through a normal life with the right kind of involvement in his local community.

Still Demanding in a Way

I want to finish this chapter by pointing out that while utilitarianism does not recommend a life of earning to give and makes no moral demands on you at all, it nonetheless does call you to a life that can be *hard* in various ways.

In my version of utilitarianism, you might need to work hard on educating yourself on better informing yourself about the world and other people in order to ensure that you are the sort of person who is spreading good values in your everyday life. Such an education will be harder for some than for others and might involve, for example, reading a lot about the world, travelling to foreign places, meeting and chatting with people who hold different points of view, being a good listener, having an open mind, etc. But hopefully, even if it is hard, it will be fulfilling.

Similarly, on my version of utilitarianism, you should go to the trouble of being sociable or involved in your local community in various ways. For many people, it is easier to stay home all day and watch TV. This is a mistake.

Living as you should can involve considerable sacrifices, not only of interests you might have in, say, expensive cars, fine dining, or high fashion but of time and resources that might be needed to better inform yourself about the world and spend more time with other people.

Notes

1 For interesting discussion, see Brian McElwee (2010). "The Rights and Wrongs of Consequentialism", *Philosophical Studies: An International Journal for Philosophy in the Analytic Tradition*, 151(3):393–412.
2 Susan Wolf, (1982). "Moral Saints", *The Journal of Philosophy*, 79(8):419–39.
3 Susan Wolf, *The Variety of Values: Essays on Morality, Meaning, and Love* (Oxford Academic, 2015).

Chapter 15

The Alienation Objection

Perhaps you were reading the previous chapter and thinking to yourself: "What a horrid idea that we should have friends, interests, and projects of our own *in order to become better ambassadors for the good*. George Bailey was not motivated by any such goals! He was simply *immersed* in his friendships and projects, and *passionate* about them. He had a wife and family out of *love*, and friendships out of *affection*, not out of a conviction that such relationships would help to make him a deeper or more relatable person and so improve his ability to promote the good or help people as much as possible. If Bailey *had* been motivated by such goals or convictions, he wouldn't have truly loved these people at all. And if we were *all* like this, the world would be a lousy place indeed".

Michael Stocker famously expresses this sort of worry about utilitarianism in the following passage:

> Suppose...you embody [utilitarianism] as your motive in your actions and thoughts toward someone. Whatever your relation to that person, it is necessarily not love (nor is it friendship, affection, fellow feeling, or community). The person you supposedly love engages your thought and action not for him/herself, but rather as a source of pleasure.[1]

Likewise, Bernard Williams asks us to imagine a case where we face a choice between saving our spouse or a stranger. A utilitarian, Williams admits, might be able to consistently hold that "in situations of this kind it is at least all right (morally permissible) to save one's wife". However, he goes on, this construction *provides the agent with one thought too many*: it might have been hoped by some (for instance, by his wife) that his motivating thought, fully spelled out, would be the thought that it was his wife, not that it was his wife, and that in situations of this kind it is permissible to save one's wife.[2]

Response

I am not suggesting, however, that we should be getting into friendships and relationships, or sustaining them, from any sort of *conscious* calculation that this will be for the best. If, on seeing your wife drowning, you pause for a moment to consider whether you should save her or a stranger instead, then something has gone seriously wrong indeed.

But what has gone wrong, I believe, is that if you are like this, then you are clearly not the sort of person who is flourishing in your daily life or bringing much joy to others. *Of course*, George Bailey did not hang out with his friends and family as a result of conscious calculation that this would be an effective way of doing good. It was from love and affection. This is *why* he was doing so much good.

Utilitarianism, in other words, does not entail that you should *think* like a utilitarian. Actually, it entails that you should *not* think like a utilitarian when thinking like a utilitarian would interfere with your ability to do good.

This idea was famously expressed by Henry Sidgwick as follows:

> If experience shows that the general happiness will be more satisfactorily attained if men frequently act from other motives than pure universal philanthropy, it is obvious that these other motives are reasonably to be preferred on Utilitarian principles.[3]

More recently, this idea has been developed in sophisticated ways by Peter Railton and Philip Pettit. Railton writes,

> [T]he best outcome [sometimes] requires action so swift as to preclude consequentialist deliberation. Thus a sophisticated consequentialist has reason to inculcate in himself certain dispositions to act rapidly...The disposition is not a mere reflex, but a developed pattern of action deliberately acquired.[4]

Pettit argues for *Standby Consequentialism*, on which there are many contexts in which, to do good, I should

> let natural affection carry the day [or] pilot my behavior [,]... offload control to the movements of my sensibility [, or involve myself] in the spontaneous swirl of everyday choice.[5]

This might involve, Pettit says, "responding without a second thought to the request of friends, and to the other demands of friendship". It might involve privileging "a motive or trait like generosity or courage, giving more or less free rein to its promptings". During such times, I "[deny] myself the opportunity to reflect, case by case, on whether doing so is for the best overall". However, at certain times, "the red lights go on" or "[signal] the alarm". Here, we snap back again into thinking like a consequentialist. For example, Pettit says,

> The red lights do not go on when you ask me to move apartment but they would go on if you asked me, in the old joke, not to move apartment, but to move a body.[6]

Pettit cites John Austin, who says,

> Though [the utilitarian] approves of love because it accords with his principle, he is far from maintaining that the general good ought to be the motive of the lover. *It was never contended or conceived by a sound, orthodox utilitarian, that the lover should kiss his mistress with an eye to the common weal.*[7]

Stocker Again

While I agree with this general approach, there is something I find unsettling about the ways in which Railton and Pettit flesh out the idea. What's unsettling is talk of 'inculcating' dispositions in ourselves, 'allowing' our natural affection to pilot our behaviour, 'privileging' certain motives, and 'denying' ourselves opportunities to reflect. Just as there is something objectionable about the idea of getting into friendships as a result of conscious calculation, there is something unappealing about the idea of allowing ourselves to feel affection or inculcating, say, spontaneity. You shouldn't have to allow, inculcate, or privilege any such things. You should get into, and be into, friendships, loves, and so on more *organically* somehow than this. Bailey himself did not allow or inculcate any such things. What we seek is a justification for being a regular person like Bailey *with the same sorts of mental states he himself possessed*.

Stocker seems to be on a similar wavelength when he writes,

> Once we begin to believe that there is something beyond such activities as love which is necessary to justify them, it is only by something akin to self-deception that we are able to continue them.[8]

And,

> [i]t is bad enough to have a private personality, which you must hide from others; but imagine having a personality that you must hide from (the other parts of) yourself.[9]

The correct moral theory, intuitively, should be one that a George Bailey–type figure can accept and then *go back to being the sort of way they were before*. It should justify precisely the same sort of immersed life they already had. "Carry on, as you were", the right theory should say to Bailey. And if he came to accept the theory, he could, following its advice, go back to being this way.

But if Railton and Pettit were right, then even if Bailey, on accepting their theories, was able to return to an immersed life of love and affection, he would return to them a changed man, somebody who thought of things—including his friends and loved ones—fundamentally differently than before. His acceptance of the theory would have implanted something in the back of his mind, something, intuitively, that acceptance of the right moral theory should *not* put in one's mind: a kind of permission or allowing. He would be, in a way, ruined.

We can put the point this way: the right moral theory, intuitively, should not only justify a life that is *outwardly* like Bailey's but one that is entirely *inwardly* like it as well. Moreover, it should be such that accepting this theory would not lead a Bailey-type figure to be inwardly different.

Love

There is, I think, a solution to this problem. To explain it, I want to start by considering the nature of love. What is it to love someone? Many philosophers believe that love is a purely *conative* state—i.e., that it is fundamentally about, or constitutively involves, *dispositions to feel and do certain things*, like, say, take pleasure in another person's happiness and try to secure it.[10]

However, it seems to me that the heart of love is quite different. It is something *cognitive*. When you love someone, I want to suggest, you are aware of and rejoicing at this person's having a certain kind of *value*.

I am not the first person to suggest such a theory of love. David Velleman famously argues that love is "an arresting awareness of [value inhering in its object]".[11] He writes,

> This description of love seems right, to begin with, as a piece of phenomenology, just as the conative analysis of love seems implausible, to begin with, on phenomenological grounds. Love does not feel (to me, at least) like an urge or impulse or inclination toward anything; it feels rather like *a state of attentive suspension, similar to wonder or amazement or awe.* ... According to this hypothesis, the various motives that are often identified with love are in fact independent responses that love merely unleashes. ... The responses unleashed by love for a person tend to be favorable because they have been unleashed by an awareness of value in him, an awareness that is also conducive to a favorable response.[12]

I agree entirely. But what *sort* of value are we aware of when we love somebody? According to Velleman, it is

> the value that he possesses solely by virtue of his being a person—by virtue, in fact, of what Kant calls his rational nature.[13]

Velleman goes on:

> Before balking at this statement, recall the following tenets of Kantian theory: that the rational nature whose value commands respect is *the capacity to be actuated by reasons* [that is, *the capacity for appreciating the value of ends, including*

self-existent ends such as persons]; that the capacity to be actuated by reasons is also *the capacity to have a good will*; and that the capacity for a rational and consequently good will is that better side of a person which constitutes his true self. I find it intuitively plausible that we love people for their true and better selves.[14]

He sums up his theory as follows:

I find it plausible to say that what we respond to, in loving people, is *their capacity to love*: it's just another way of saying that what our hearts respond to is another heart.[15]

I do not share Velleman's Kantianism, but I find very attractive his claim that in loving someone, we are responding to their capacity to love. On my view, to love somebody is to think—and rejoice in the fact that—*here is somebody who cares not only about themselves, but disinterestedly about others as well*. We rejoice in this thought because somebody's being like this, we recognise, *is a condition of their truly flourishing, as well as a condition of the possibility of there being a good society at all*. We care so much about the possibility of others flourishing and the possibility of a good world. So, when we encounter somebody who clearly has the capacity to care disinterestedly about others, this leads us to a joy like no other. "People really *can* live lives high in welfare", we think. "There really is some hope we can cooperate with each other and build a better world". It is this recognition and our rejoicing in it that explains not only our feelings here but why we want to *express* these feelings to the person in question, care for them, nurture them, nourish them, or interact with them.

The Solution

Suppose this theory of love is right. It makes possible a solution to the Alienation Objection. If I'm right, then while we do not *consciously* or *explicitly* get into our friendships and relationships with a view to helping us promote the good—rather, we are (often) led directly by affection—*such affection itself is animated by an (unconscious) awareness of, and concern for, value that we see here*. When we are drawn to others in the first place, or come to develop affection for them, we are thinking (unconsciously), "Here is someone truly wonderful, someone who can really flourish and is the sort of person who can help to make this world a better place". If we want them as our friend, what we want here is, in effect, to join forces with them in trying to nudge the world in a better direction.

What about our other interests, passions, or projects? As I argued earlier, I do not think that we are interested in or "moved, charmed, or awed" by the natural world, physics, or great works of art because we see or think there is value in these things. We find these things interesting and beautiful just because of their intrinsic properties—simply because they *are* interesting or beautiful. But I do think that when we *pursue* these things—e.g., decide to learn more about them, develop skills in them, incorporate them as parts of our lives—we are doing so because we have become aware of the ways in which they can enrich people's lives and so of their value. We sense that there are things or activities here which can help us to lead a more productive life or that fit well with our unconscious background project of trying to nudge the world in a positive direction.

Bailey, then, upon coming to accept my form of utilitarianism, can return to *exactly* the sort of life he led beforehand, not only outwardly but inwardly as well. This is because his life beforehand was already one in which he was drawn to other people and certain activities from an unconscious sense that there was great value here. He was not *consciously* calculating. But these thoughts were nonetheless present in an unconscious form under the surface.

Now we can better see my differences from Pettit. According to Pettit, when your friend asks you to move a body, this sets off 'the red lights' because it sets up a *conflict* between your friendship or affection for your friend, on the one hand, and your ultimate underlying concern for the good, on the other. But on my view, when your friend asks this of you, it *destroys* your affection for your friend by making you question whether they really are (as you had previously thought) a force for good in the world. Your affection for them crucially involved such an approval.

What of Austin's claim that no utilitarian will say that we kiss our lover with an eye to the commonweal? Certainly, a lot of kissing involves no such thoughts. But when kissing involves real love, I actually do think that there is a way in which we are thinking of the common good. We are aware of this person's ability to flourish, how wonderful it is that such people exist, and how this person is making things better. In such a kiss, we rejoice at their existence—and this *because* of their capacity to flourish and their kindness. There is passion, but evaluative thoughts are animating the passion.

In loving someone, we are thinking not only of them but of their relation to value and to society as a whole. For this reason, I think that loving somebody—in the relevant sense—may be possible *only* for those who do care about the world *at large* or the direction of society.

If my account is right, the "spontaneous swirl of everyday choice" *is* a swirl of value thoughts. There is no need for a utilitarian to put their concern for the good into 'standby mode'. Such a concern is already present, doing essential work, in everyday immersions.

In sum, someone who accepts utilitarianism does not have to be self-deceived, inauthentic, or divided against themselves at all. On the contrary, if they stopped having value thoughts, this would destroy or interfere with their love and immersion in everyday life.

Demandingness Again

In the previous chapter, I discussed the **Demandingness Objection**, which says that utilitarianism asks too much of us. Intuitively, we are not required—and do not even have most reason—to give up our loves, interests, projects, etc., in order to devote ourselves to helping others.

A famous expression of this objection (which I did not mention at the time) is Bernard Williams's:

> [An agent] is *identified* with his actions as flowing from projects or attitudes which…he takes seriously at the deepest level, as what his life is about. … *It is absurd to demand of such a man, when the sums come in from the utility network which the projects of others have in part determined, that he should just step aside from his own project and decision and acknowledge the decision which utilitarian calculation requires.* … It is to make him into a channel between the input of everyone's projects, including his own, and an output of optimific decision; but this is to neglect the extent to which *his* projects and *his* decisions have to be seen as the actions and decisions which flow from the projects and attitudes with which he is most closely identified. It is thus, in the most literal sense, an attack on his integrity.[16]

I agree with Williams that there is something absurd about asking somebody to step aside from their existing loves and projects in order to devote themselves to helping others—that to do so does constitute a kind of attack on their integrity. In light of my response to the Alienation Objection, we can now see how utilitarianism—far from being in conflict with this idea—actually helps to explain its truth.

The reason it is absurd to ask somebody to step aside from their loves and projects in order to do the best they can is that their loves and projects *are* their way of trying to do the best they can. We are already, in these things, trying to do the best we can. So, naturally, it sounds absurd for someone to come along and say, "You need to give up all these things in order to do the best you can". What's absurd is not the suggestion that they should be doing the best they can, but the idea that they could be expected to think that earning to give would be best. It would be absurd to give up the whole life project we are invested in, in order to do good, given that we are invested in this project *because* we think it good.

Notes

1 Michael Stocker, (1976). "The Schizophrenia of Modern Ethical Theories", *The Journal of Philosophy*, 73(14):453–66.
2 Bernard Williams, "Persons, Character, and Morality", in James Rachels (ed) *Moral Luck: Philosophical Papers 1973–1980* (Cambridge University Press, 1976).
3 H. Sidgwick, *The Methods of Ethics* (7th ed.). (Hackett Publishing, 1981).
4 Peter Railton, (1984). "Alienation, Consequentialism, and the Demands of Morality", *Philosophy & Public Affairs*, 13(2):134–71.
5 Philip Pettit, "The Inescapability of Consequentialism", in Ulrike Heuer & Gerald R. Lang (eds) *Luck, Value, and Commitment: Themes from the Ethics of Bernard Williams* (Oxford University Press USA, 2012).
6 Philip Pettit, "The Inescapability of Consequentialism", in Ulrike Heuer & Gerald R. Lang (eds) *Luck, Value, and Commitment: Themes from the Ethics of Bernard Williams* (Oxford University Press USA, 2012).
7 Austin, John, *The Province of Jurisprudence Determined and the Uses of the Study of Jurisprudence.* (London: Weidenfeld & Nicolson, 1954). Edited by John Austin.
8 Michael Stocker, (1976). "The Schizophrenia of Modern Ethical Theories", *The Journal of Philosophy*, 73(14).
9 Michael Stocker, (1976). "The Schizophrenia of Modern Ethical Theories", *The Journal of Philosophy*, 73(14).

10 For discussion, see H. Frankfurt, "Autonomy, Necessity, and Love", in *Necessity, Volition, and Love* (Cambridge: Cambridge University Press, 1999), 129–41.
11 J. D. Velleman, (1999), "Love as a Moral Emotion", *Ethics*, 109:338–74.
12 J. D. Velleman, (1999), "Love as a Moral Emotion", *Ethics*, 109:338–74.
13 J. D. Velleman, (1999), "Love as a Moral Emotion", *Ethics*, 109:338–74.
14 J. D. Velleman, (1999), "Love as a Moral Emotion", *Ethics*, 109:338–74.
15 J. D. Velleman, (1999), "Love as a Moral Emotion", *Ethics*, 109:338–74.
16 Williams Bernard. "A Critique of Utilitarianism", in J.J.C. Smart and Williams Bernard (eds) *Utilitarianism for and Against* (Cambridge: Cambridge University Press, 1973), pp. 77–150.

Chapter 16

The 'Harming to Help' Objection

Many of us accept that there can be cases where you should harm someone in order to prevent certain kinds of harms to others. So, for example, if the only way to prevent a nuclear blast from destroying a city is for you to slap a stranger in the face, you should do so.

However, critics of utilitarianism complain utilitarianism entails that you should harm people *whenever* this will help others more, which is not so. Consider the famous *Transplant* case, described well here by Peter Singer:

> Imagine that you are a surgeon. ... One day you walk into the hospital and find that you have a patient who will die shortly because she needs a heart transplant and there are no hearts available. In the next ward is another patient who has an equally pressing need for a liver transplant, but, again, you cannot do the operation because there is no prospect of finding a suitable liver donor in time. In a third ward is a patient on which you are about to operate to remove a brain tumour. You have done many of these operations, and have no doubt that you can perform the operation successfully on this patient, but you also know that you could contrive a little slip, for which no one could really blame you, that would result in the death of your patient's brain. Then the patient would become a suitable donor of both heart and liver. Thus you would take one life, but save two. All three lives in question could be expected to be of similar quality and length, and all three have much the same kind of family connections.[1]

Utilitarianism, critics say, implies that you should contrive the slip. But intuitively, you should not do so.

Or consider another famous such case, a *Trolley* case: there is an out-of-control trolley car headed for five people who are stuck on the tracks through no fault of their own. The only way they can be saved is if you push a stranger off a footbridge onto the tracks in front of the trolley. This would stop the trolley but kill this person. The stranger is already leaning over the edge, and there is no one else around. You could easily push them, and the police would assume they had slipped. Utilitarianism, critics say, implies that you should push the person off the footbridge, but you should not.

1 Cluelessness to the Rescue

Here's what I think a utilitarian should say about these two cases: while it is certainly worse that one person dies than that several do, other things equal, *these are not cases where other things are equal.* The action you perform here will have *all sorts of other far-reaching consequences—both good and bad ones—consequences you are in no position to anticipate.* As Lenman might put it, the deaths of the people in these cases are mere drops in the ocean of the overall consequences of these actions. When it comes to what action would help people the most, even these deaths are clues so small as to be worthless. While preventing a city from being destroyed is clearly what helps people the most (in the example with which I started this chapter), things are very different in Transplant and Trolley. It is entirely unclear what action in these cases would help people the most in the long run.

There is something important to add. As I've been arguing throughout this book, your best bet for maximally helping people is to live a life of your own, one of kindness and generosity, immersed in your local community. However confident you might be that you could perform the actions in Transplant and Trolley without being found out, there will always be at least a slim chance you will be found out, and if you are, then this would destroy any chance you have of influencing society for the better by living a kind and generous life immersed in your community. Your personal brand will be forever tarnished. Nobody will listen to you again.

Also, performing actions such as these can affect *you* in very bad ways, ways that might greatly damage your ability to live in a helpful way during the rest of your life. It could, for example, be traumatising for years to come, which could prevent you from being the sort of cheerful, good-natured person who can succeed at spreading values like kindness throughout your community. Or it could desensitise you to inflicting suffering or embolden you to perform similar actions in situations where you don't possess such certainty.

Kant was concerned about humans harming non-human animals because he thought this could damage the humanity in us in a way that might lead to our mistreating humans. Well, my suggestion here is similar: we should not perform actions like those in Transplant and Footbridge because doing so could damage the humanity in us in a way that might compromise our ability to live in the sort of way that is most helpful to humans (and other beings) later on in our lives.

There is still more to say. The sort of person who is living a kind life immersed in their local community—someone like George Bailey—would not even have the thought of performing such actions *occur* to them, or if these thoughts did occur to them, they would not seriously *entertain* them, or if they did entertain them, they would realise that they would not be able to *bear* performing such actions. Someone like Bailey might slap, or even shoot, a stranger to prevent a nuclear bomb from destroying a city, but I cannot imagine such a person pushing a stranger off a footbridge to save five strangers. They would be too *soft*—in a good way.

So, if you are having such thoughts and seriously entertaining them, your priority should be *to urgently change yourself and your approach to the world*. If you find yourself having such thoughts, you must stop everything and take actions that will make it more likely that you will become the sort of person who would not have such thoughts in the first place, or if you do, to banish them immediately. You should fight even the thought of doing such things; try to ensure that the idea of it is abhorrent or repugnant to you. If you are having such thoughts, *run and revise*.

Note

1 Peter Singer, *Ethics* (Oxford University Press, 1994), 11.

Chapter 17

Conclusion

In this book, I have outlined what I believe to be the most plausible version of utilitarianism: *person-affecting, reasons utilitarianism.* Utilitarianism should be understood as saying that we have most reason to do what will maximally help beings.

Some of utilitarianism's most eloquent critics have argued against utilitarianism by pointing to the fact that our actions are identity-affecting, and we are clueless about the overall consequences of our actions. I have argued that, on the contrary, these facts are central to the case *for* utilitarianism.

On the view I have defended, you shouldn't obsess on each occasion of acting about choosing the action that will be best or help people the most. You've no hope of working that out or even making a decent guess about it. Instead, you should strive to live a life like George Bailey, a life of kindness immersed in your local community, where you are influencing others to be empathetic and loving in *their* everyday lives. To achieve this, you will need to work hard at educating yourself—reading, thinking, travelling, talking with others, having an open mind, and so on. When you encounter cases where you are unsure what, *morally* speaking, you should do, you should think about what someone like Bailey would *feel* in such situations—would they feel uncomfortable doing the action? Could they bear it? Or might they feel uncomfortable *not* doing it? Deciding correctly here can help you to become a better autopilot—i.e., increase the chance that, in the long run, your life will be helping people more than you will be harming them.

III Reply to Bramble

III Reply to Bramble

1 Utilitarianism: The Bramble Variation

My co-author and disputant, Ben Bramble, has written a rich, original, and extremely interesting essay defending a distinctive and original form of utilitarianism. It is a rather nonstandard form of utilitarianism, nonstandard in ways that make it less vulnerable than more standard versions to the objections I have raised to utilitarianism above. But it is certainly eminently worth discussing in its own right.

Indeed, Bramble's utilitarianism is, to my mind, in many ways, significantly more credible and attractive than more standard variations. In some ways, Bramble comes across less like a good Bethamite than a good Confucian. He thinks we are morally required not to maximize utility but to conduct ourselves virtuously where that is unpacked by reference to morally exemplary persons such as—his endearing central example—George Bailey in Frank Capra's popular and delightful classic film *It's a Wonderful Life*.[1] And he emphasizes the power and importance of moral contagion, the potential for morally exemplary people such as Bailey to transform those around them, an idea the ancient Chinese texts express in the core notion of 德 dé, which we might translate 'moral power'.[2] And he is perhaps somewhat Confucian in a further way, which we'll come to.

My own main objections to standard forms of utilitarianism are mostly about the issue of cluelessness, appreciating the depth and seriousness of the epistemic difficulty of engaging with the consequences of our acts in their totality. Bramble puts up no resistance to this argument but rather simply accepts it and endeavours to construct a version of utilitarianism that is relatively invulnerable to it. To begin to see how this works, we can recall a famous philosophical puzzle, the so-called non-identity problem.

2 The Non-identity Problem and Person-Affecting Utilitarianism

Here is a familiar, fanciful example.[3] Mary and Kevin want to have a baby together. Let us stipulate that by a 'winter baby' we mean a baby conceived in the months between the clocks in the UK going back in October and their going forward in March. And let us call a baby conceived at any other time a 'summer baby'. And let us suppose that, never mind why, it happens to be the case that if Mary and Kevin have a summer baby, its prospects of happiness will be significantly greater than if they have a winter baby. And let us suppose, never mind how, that Mary and Kevin know this.

Now it is natural to think it would be wrong of Mary and Kevin, knowing this, to have a winter baby. Or at least that they have a strong reason to have a summer baby. They should then use contraception during the winter months and have a summer baby instead. Because the summer baby would be happier. But there is a problem: the non-identity problem. The problem is that the person the summer baby would be *happier than*, the winter baby Mary and Kevin might have instead, is *not the same person* as the summer baby. Indeed, if they do not have a winter baby, the winter baby they do not have is not a particular person at all. All there is here is just a generic description of a person.[4] So there is no person who is better off for being born in the summer. And if Mary and Kevin have a winter baby, there is no person that baby is worse off than.

And here is an example that is not fanciful at all but only too real. Suppose we are living in ways that are damaging and degrading the terrestrial environment which our descendants will inherit from us. Because of this, we feel we have an obligation to take significant steps to change our behaviour so as to stop damaging and degrading it. The changes we need to make will be pretty large and extensive. Straight away, these changes can be relied upon to start having swiftly amplifying direct and indirect effects on exactly when exactly which of exactly whose sperm is fertilizing exactly which of exactly whose eggs. So we can be pretty confident the decision we make will affect not only the conditions in which, say, being conservative, our great-great-grandchildren live, but also who our great-great-grandchildren are. So failing to do the right thing will not actually make anyone in that generation worse off than they would otherwise be. The better-off people who would otherwise have lived happier lives are just absent from that world, so nobody is worse off there than they would otherwise have been.

Bramble distinguishes what he calls total and person-affecting utilitarianism. Total utilitarians think that if Mary and Kevin decide to have a child they should have a summer baby, not a winter baby. They also take the view that so long as the result is a positive addition to the totality of happiness, Mary and Kevin *should* decide to have a child. The person-affecting utilitarianism isn't bothered whether Mary and Kevin have a child or not. They are also not that bothered, if Mary and Kevin do decide to have a child, whether the child is a summer or a winter child. Because the choice to have a winter child *harms* nobody. Bramble prefers the person-affecting version as a way of avoiding what he takes to be the absurdities of total utilitarianism.

It is worth noting that within utilitarianism, there are alternatives here. There is space for a view that says, with Bramble, that it is just fine if Mary and Kevin decide to remain childless. They have no obligation, as it were, to the universe to fill it up with potential containers of utility. But *if* they are to have a child, they should prefer to have a summer child as it is better if their child is happier than their child would otherwise have been, even though the identity of that child is not invariant across the possibilities being compared. Not being a utilitarian, I have no dog in this fight, but I suspect many utilitarians would think this third view deserving of more consideration and would perhaps be unconvinced that the classical utilitarian injunction that everyone should be as happy as possible does not enjoin that we seek a world where the actual people, whoever they may be, are as happy as we can make them, even if, like myself, they lose no sleep over the welfare of merely possible people.

A strict person-affecting understanding of ethics, utilitarian or otherwise, certainly looks counterintuitive. It is natural to suppose we have at least very strong moral reason not to damage and degrade the environment in which our great-great-grandchildren will live. I myself am quite happy with the idea that we can have obligations to people identified generically. The sign in the public lavatory asks us to leave it in good condition for the next user, and so we should, whoever that might be. And I am happy with a young person making life choices with a view to the health and happiness of their future children, or with my generation of humans rightly feeling an obligation to our great-great-grandchildren to bequeath a planetary environment to them that has not been unduly polluted, climactically disrupted, or ecologically impoverished, even where the identities of these people will not be fixed independently of the decisions in question.[5]

But it may be that the implausibility of person-affecting views can be tamed, at least to a degree. With Mary and Kevin, we might think if the winter child will certainly be not just less happy but positively wretched, they should avoid having a child, as having a child with an expectation of a wretched life is perhaps a bad idea without needing to be compared to anything. And it is significant too here that the example is fanciful. We almost never in reality have such certain information about the felicific prospects of our future children.

The case of responsible environmental policy is less fanciful. A lot less. Maybe something on the scale of doing the right thing for the future of the environment will be so impactful on the identities of future people that it will affect the identities of all our great-great-grandchildren, so the person-affecting view says we have no obligations here based on consideration for *them*. But we do surely have an obligation to our grandchildren to bequeath them a planet in decent nick. It is hard to imagine identity-affecting ramifications kicking in on that scale that fast—when there will be many people reading this whose grandchildren exist *already*. And plausibly, our grandchildren will in turn have an obligation to *their* grandchildren (*our* great-great-grandchildren) to *leave* them a planet in decent nick. In which case, maybe we have an *obligation* also to *our* grandchildren to make sure, if we can, that their obligations to *their* grandchildren are not intolerably burdensome. So we don't do too much violence to moderate longtermist moral common sense.

Bramble seeks then to tame cluelessness:

> If person-affecting utilitarianism is true, while the *consequences* of your actions might go on forever, their *good and bad consequences* run out on the first generation of people they affect (since, by affecting them, they change the identities of their children). At some point in the future, as a result of *whatever* action you perform, there will be not a single person alive who would otherwise have existed. At this point, the good and bad consequences of your action will have entirely ended.

This is a very interesting point. One thing that starts to matter here might be timing. Armchair common sense reasoning will indeed tell us it is true enough that "at some point in the future, as a result of *whatever* action you perform, there will be not a single person alive who would otherwise have existed." What it tells less clearly is how *quickly* we can ordinarily expect to reach that point. We know human affairs are complex and chaotic, but are they complex and chaotic for this to happen, even for quite minor actions, quite fast, or might it take rather a long time? That is a tough question, the answer to which is likely to make a difference here.

Enough cluelessness remains, on Bramble's account, to tame other worries—notably, the worries thrown up by cases like Bridge, Transplant, and Sheriff. Cluelessness is reined in by going person-affecting, but even while the time horizon on which we need to consider consequences is thus limited, it is still long enough to warrant a good measure of epistemic humility, certainly enough to make us wise up to the folly of sandboxing these examples to give them a simplicity no real cases could ever have. So in the spirit of Mackie-style moderate utilitarianism, we can avoid making ourselves unpalatably ready to, as Bramble has it, harm to help. We should not push people off bridges, kill them to harvest their organs, or judicially murder them to appease a mob. George Bailey would never do these things, and we should be like him.

3 Reasons and Requirements

This person-affecting turn is not, Bramble thinks, itself enough to tame the cluelessness concern. Two other things come into play here. The first is the phenomenon, already noted, of moral contagion. The light good people like Bailey shine often, Bramble suggests, shines a long way because the good people in our midst can inspire us all to raise our moral game. That happy, optimistic thought I have no plans to contest.

But this is not yet enough to tame cluelessness. A second modification to utilitarian orthodoxy is needed. Even when we go person-affecting, Bramble writes,

> it is entirely futile to try to work out what action available to you on any given occasion would be overall *best*. Given the complex and chaotic nature of causal systems, the very *best* action

available to you at any given time is likely always to be something very odd, like jumping five times on the spot, yelling at a stranger, or phoning a particular overseas phone number, etc.

This is right, of course. The objective act utilitarian idea that we are *required* to do whatever is best is for the birds. The last example is telling. Forget the long term. Even if we only concern ourselves with quite short-term benefits, it is plausibly rather likely that an awful lot of the time, the most useful thing you could possibly be doing is ringing the number of some imperilled person or persons somewhere in the world to say, "*There is about to be an earthquake, get outside! There is a bomb; evacuate the theatre! You haven't put that cigarette out properly, fix it or there will be a terrible fire!*" Or some such thing. But none of us has the superpower we would need to know what numbers those are so we cannot do these things. We cannot even try to do them. For this form of strict requirement utilitarianism, cluelessness *can* kick in pretty fast.

There is a problem here for objective utilitarianism that we might seek to tame by going subjective. Instead, Bramble opts for a shift in focal point to give what he calls *reasons utilitarianism*. The central claim here, I think, is,

> [a]ll reasons, I believe, are provided just by your ability to help beings (yourself or others).

Now the thought is that, while we cannot be remotely sure, even on a person-affecting understanding, that doing the things Bailey does will maximally promote the good, we can be pretty confident that they will help people more than they will harm them. If what we want to do is help people as much as we can and harm them as little as we can, then trying to live like a morally exemplary person like Bailey is the best way to go about it.

Bramble does not have a utilitarian theory of moral requirements, only of moral reasons. But he still needs *some* account of moral requirement. Moral requirement is still a thing. And Bramble does have an account of this. It is a nonutilitarian, virtue-theoretic account:

> Morally wrong actions, then, are ones that our George Bailey–type figure who understands the relevant facts would feel a certain kind of discomfort performing. Morally required acts are

ones a George Bailey–type figure who understands the relevant facts would feel uncomfortable *not* performing.

Now we are in danger of a little trouble here: "a certain kind of discomfort" is a bit vague. *What kind?* Suppose George, like his brother in the film, goes off to fight in a war. Suppose he thinks, and suppose we agree, that it is a just war and that the means by which he is being ordered to conduct it by his commanding officers are legitimate, just means. But still, he has to kill enemy combatants. He thinks about those young men. Many of them are, he supposes, decent young men like himself, with friends and family and local ties who have simply been born in a different country where they have found themselves conscripted into an awful conflict no more of their making than of his. Because George is a decent man, the thought of killing these people makes him uncomfortable. *Very* uncomfortable. But he still thinks it is, on balance, the right thing to do. Or perhaps he is a doctor who needs to perform some very unpleasant but vitally urgent medical procedure on a child who does not understand why this is being done to them and finds it intensely distressing. Again, *very* uncomfortable. But he doesn't think these things are morally wrong. So we need to specify the state of mind more precisely. But of course, we might not want to specify it as the state of mind of thinking the thing is *morally wrong* if that presupposes George has some sound but independent handle on what that means.

4 Love

Let us put that worry to one side. I think there are perhaps deeper problems. One thing about Bramble's ideal of a virtuous person, a person like Bailey, is that he or she is not a utilitarian agent. Bailey is immersed in his family and his community. He isn't focused on making the world a better place so much as making his little town Bedford Falls a better place. And so he does.

Bramble's utilitarian theory thinks the only thing with genuine intrinsic value is welfare—and in particular what he calls the wonderful kind—and the only genuine reasons are reasons to help people have more wonderful welfare. And he thinks virtuous people will be motivated by rather larger landscapes of value and reason than the starkly monistic one he affirms as real. Here are a couple of key passages:

I do agree that there is something incredibly sad about the thought of everyone being plugged into individual experience machines and never seeing each other again. But, as I have been at pains to point out in this book, *sad* does not entail *bad*. It is, I am more than willing to concede, fitting and right to have mixed feelings about the thought of plugging in. Just as somebody who knows and loves the environment will be sentimental about it, and somebody who knows and loves humanity will be sentimental about it, so someone who knows and loves other people will be sentimental about *them* and the thought of leaving them.

* * *

What about a loved one who is kind and good but who, due to some kind of illness or impairment, can no longer contribute much to the world? Consider, for example, a parent who is old and needs looking after. Surely, it can still be subjectively rational to spend time and resources on looking after them. But utilitarianism, you might say, cannot say this. It implies you should abandon such a person.

But a George Bailey–type figure surely could not *bear* abandoning someone they love who is in such a position. They would recognise that were they to do so, they themselves would be so broken or traumatised by doing so that they would no longer be of much use to anyone.

Why would they be so broken or traumatised? Simply as an offshoot or by-product of their love for this person. As I've mentioned many times in this book, those who richly understand things (for example, the nature and value of humanity and individual human lives, the nature and value of natural environments, the nature and value of great works of art, and so on) are necessarily *sentimental*. They feel and want things out of proportion to the value these things have.

In my own contribution, I proposed to understand value as what a good or virtuous person would, stably under reflective scrutiny, welcome. Bramble has a different story. He thinks there are things a virtuous person, a person plugged into human moral community, would value and considerations such a person would recognize as reasons. But many of these things are not really valuable or reasonable.

There are the values recognized by utilitarianism which are exclusively welfarist and reasons recognized by utilitarianism which are exclusively concerned with advancing people's welfare in impartial ways. Call these the U-values and the U-reasons.

And there are the values and reasons that engage someone like Bailey. Someone like Bailey is not a utilitarian agent. They care about and cherish the natural world. They would not be willing permanently to retreat from real human relationships into a fake but agreeable virtual reality. And they care in very partial and particular ways about the people they love. Call these the B-values and the B-reasons.

Bramble thinks these B-values and B-reasons are not real values and reasons. But he also seems to think these nongenuine values and reasons work to determine the sphere of the morally obligatory, the *genuinely* morally obligatory, because he wants to characterize the genuinely morally obligatory in terms of what would occasion certain emotional responses in a virtuous person, a person like Bailey.

I find this all a bit of a rum do. Let's just think about the second of the passages I quoted. There are two ways we can think about the very same circumstance.

> Perspective 1. MOTHER. Here is my mother. She is a person connected to me by the most profound intimacy. I grew in her womb, and she fed me at her breast. She made it a core project of her adult life over many decades to nurture me and do all she could to promote and enhance my well-being and happiness, often at very great cost to herself, a cost she bore willingly and uncomplainingly (OK, maybe sometimes she complained *a bit*) because she loves me and has loved me, intensely and unconditionally, through all my childhood tantrums and insufferable adolescence. Even after I grew to adulthood, when there was a problem, I could call her and there she was. And now here she is nearing the end of her life and needs help and support, and I should give it to her. *Of course*, I should give it to her. I owe her a debt of love and gratitude I can never adequately repay. I can at least do this, and so I should.

> Perspective 2. SOME OLD LADY (SOL). Here is some old lady who would like me to help her. Of course, I could help her. But

there are also many other things I might do with the resources I will use to help her. And many of those things will be much more effective uses of those resources than helping this old lady who is not much use to anyone anymore and who will be dead soon. Helping her would be a bit like giving money to the guide dog charity or to helping women in Ethiopia with obstetric fistulas,[6] an inexcusably inefficient way of converting resources into utility. I should abandon her and go do some other, more effective thing.

MOTHER, obviously, is how good, morally decent human beings with good, kind mothers think about their good, kind mothers. Again, it is tempting to recall Confucianism: MOTHER is the proper perspective of *xiào* 孝, filial respect, that core virtue that constitutes the root of our humanity.[7] SOL is, I hope no less obviously, deranged, callous, inhuman, and morally shallow. And I really don't feel remotely inclined to say that, while MOTHER is an expression of what a virtuous person, understanding the nature and value of humanity, will think about the case, there is still something *correct* about SOL: that SOL is what we get when we strip everything merely sentimental away and see the intrinsic value and genuine reasons that are really there. Rather, I think what the virtuous person sees here, namely MOTHER, is the only moral reality there can intelligibly be. If a moral theory says something that is deranged, callous, inhuman, and morally shallow, then it's false.

5   Two Kinds of Values. Two Kinds of Reasons

Bramble writes,

> Utilitarianism, in other words, does not entail that you should *think* like a utilitarian. Actually, it entails that you should *not* think like a utilitarian when thinking like a utilitarian would interfere with your ability to do good.

MOTHER, not SOL, is how the virtuous person should think. We should not think like utilitarians. We should not think in this way even, as the *standby consequentialist* might have it, on special occasions. We should not cultivate a kind of split personality where the utilitarian part of me gives the nonutilitarian, (it is to be hoped) virtuous part of me permission to carry on as normal most of the time. Where does that leave us?

Some theories in ethics and other fields are said to be self-refuting. They themselves tell us they are false. For example, the theory that it is objectively true that nothing is objectively true is a view that seems to shoot itself in the head pretty swiftly and straightforwardly.[8] Some ethical theories in particular are self-defeating. They tell us, perhaps along with certain empirical facts about the world, not to be guided by them because being guided by them is not likely to be the best way to do as they tell us we should. A case in point is ethical egoism, which tells each of us to pursue our own happiness to the exclusion of everything else. This gets us into trouble because it is very plausible that someone who pursues their own happiness to the exclusion of everything else is unlikely to be very happy.

Some philosophers think that a theory can be self-defeating in this way but not quite self-refuting. The fact that accepting and seeking to live by a theory is not the best way to do as it tells us we should does not necessarily mean the theory is false. Perhaps it is merely self-effacing: that is, true, but by its own lights, not a good thing to go believing.[9] Others[10] maintain that in the case of ethical theories at least, seeking to live by it being a very good idea is just what truth is, and there is no space for self-defeat to be anything but self-refutation.

In any case, even self-effacement looks quite embarrassing. Ever since Henry Sidgwick explored the possibility in his *Methods of Ethics*, there has been much discussion of the possibility that utilitarianism is like this, that being a utilitarian is perhaps not at all a good way to realise utilitarian ends. This leads to what we might call Bernard Williams, Dilemma: as that philosopher put it half a century ago:

> So, if utilitarianism is true, and some fairly plausible empirical propositions are also true, then it is better that people should not believe in utilitarianism. If, on the other hand, it is false, then it is certainly better that people should not believe in it. So, either way, it is better that people should not believe in it.[11]

6 More Love

Bramble does not quite think utilitarianism is self-effacing, though he seems to come very close to thinking this. He thinks we should live in a way that is not only outwardly like Bailey but inwardly as well. But Bailey is still psychologically in affinity with utilitarian values as are we as we seek to emulate him. Why? Because utilitarian values are what lie at the root of our motivation. He writes,

> If I'm right, then while we do not *consciously* or *explicitly* get into our friendships and relationships with a view to helping us promote the good—rather, we are (often) led directly by affection—such affection itself is *animated by an (unconscious) awareness of, and concern for, value that we see here*. When we are drawn to others in the first place, or come to develop affection for them, we are thinking (unconsciously), "Here is someone truly wonderful, someone who can really flourish and is the sort of person who can help to make this world a better place".

Can this really be right? Claims about unconscious motives, notoriously, are very easy to make and very difficult to test. But certainly when we are drawn to others to seek their friendship, it is not always the case that we are drawn to their goodness. That seems way too rose-tinted a picture. We can certainly be attracted to form relationships with people who are manifestly not very good. When the young David Copperfield is drawn into friendship with his callous and egotistical classmate James Steerforth, he is attracted less by Steerforth's virtue than by what we might call his *lustre*: his charm and popularity and power and the fact that the teachers at their school are afraid of him. Recalling a moment when Steerforth successfully humiliated one of their teachers over the latter's family's financial circumstances, David, as fictional narrator, writes,

> I could not help thinking even in that interval, I remember, what a noble fellow he was in appearance, and how homely and plain Mr. Mell looked opposed to him.[12]

This rosy view of friendship extends even to the case of erotic love. Here it might seem an especially big stretch. Bramble likes old movies so he must remember the love between Walter and Phyllis in *Double Indemnity* or Anna's love for Harry Lyme in *The Third Man*. Very bad people can often be sexy as hell, as every lover of Gothic fiction or film noir knows all too well.

> What of Austin's claim that no utilitarian will say that we kiss our lover with an eye to the common weal? Certainly, a lot of kissing involves no such thoughts. But when kissing involves

real love, I actually do think that there is a way in which we are thinking of the common good. We are aware of this person's ability to flourish, how wonderful it is that such people exist, and how this person is making things better. In such a kiss, we rejoice at their existence—and this *because* of their capacity to flourish and their kindness. There is passion, but evaluative thoughts are animating the passion.

Importantly, the claims here are qualified. "Certainly, a lot of kissing involves no such thoughts. But when kissing involves real love, I actually do think..." So we are not talking about *every* kind of passionate erotic attachment, but only about what Bramble calls *real* love. He goes on:

> In loving someone, we are thinking not only of them, but of their relation to value and to society as a whole. For this reason, I think that loving somebody—in the relevant sense—may be possible *only* for those who do care about the world *at large*, or the direction of society.

We are, it seems, not talking about love but only love 'in the relevant sense', *real* love, and this is something only good people can do. Here again, I am reminded of Confucius who, it is reported at Analects 4.3, said, "It is only the good person who can love other people. Or hate them" (唯仁者能好人, 能惡人). It is an intriguing passage. Confucius, we can be very confident, was an extremely clever and judicious man. And yet, what he is saying here is surely obviously false. Commentators seek to minimize the implausibility by reading Confucius as saying that only good people are able to love the right people in the right way. As Amy Olberding reads the passage, "[I]t takes a truly virtuous person to distinguish good people from bad".[13] While Edward Slingerland quotes from Jiao Xun (1763–1820) elaborating on the commentary of Kong Anguo (156–74 BCE): "The good person loves what is really worthy of admiration in others and despises that which is genuinely despicable in them. That is why such a person is said to be 'able to love others and despise others'".[14]

We can perhaps go some way to defend something like the face-value reading of *Analects* 4.3. A police officer dealing with an erotically obsessed young man who has made someone's life a misery by stalking her asks him, "What do you think you are doing, acting this way?" and gets the reply, "Don't you see, I love her!" And the officer will think, as we think, do we not, "No, he doesn't. Love doesn't behave like that. Not *real* love". Or a controlling, abusive husband, seeing his wife at last deciding enough is enough, packing her bags and heading for the front door, perhaps begs her to stay: "Don't leave! Can't you see? I love you". And she might very intelligibly reply, "Do you? *Really*? Can you really call what you have directed my way over these years *love*?"

But such thoughts get us, it seems to me, only so far, and it remains right to be resistant to an overly moralistic understanding of these matters. Perfectly real love and affection can be found in many places. Nomy Arpaly addresses these matters with characteristic good sense.

> One does not need to be a radical skeptic on the subject of character in order to admit that it is possible for a person with a decisively mediocre record in matters of honesty and altruism to make exceptions for specific individuals and groups. It might be strange, in the same way that it is strange that a person who eats beef and pork can be selflessly devoted to her dog or cat (even dog and cat welfare generally), and yet the latter sort of strangeness is such a part of normal life that until recently very few people have noticed it at all. Even downright dubious individuals (who are not actual psychopaths) often have one or two people in their lives for whom they will act unselfishly and to whom they are loyal and substantially honest. This is both obvious to anyone who knows such people personally and is obvious through oblique measures, such as the fact that it is possible to blackmail and coerce such individuals by threatening these special relationships. [15]

We could perhaps persevere in the insistence that these things cannot be real love, but now we are dangerously close to **No True Scotsman** territory where troubling counter-examples are in danger of being too conveniently stipulated out of existence.

7 Alienation

It is certainly true that virtuous people are liable, if anyone is, to be motivated by virtuous considerations. Considerations like these (this is the splendid list provided by Rosalind Hursthouse[16]):

"I could probably save him if I climbed up there", "Someone had to volunteer", "One can't give in to tyrants", "It's worth the risk", "It would be cowardly not to" (courage), "This is an adequate sufficiency", "I'm driving", "I'd like you to have some", "You need it more than I do", "She said 'No'", "That would be greedy" (moderation), "He needed help", "He asked me for it", "It was his twenty-first birthday", "She'll be so pleased", "That would be mean" (generosity), "He's my friend", "He's expecting me to", "I can't let him down" (friendship), "It was the truth", "He asked me", "It's best to get such things out into the open straight away", "This is the honest thing to do" (honesty), "It's his", "I owe it to her", "She has the right to decide", "I promised" (justice), "It would be a bit low not to", "This is what any decent person would do".

These are plausibly the kind of thoughts a good person is typically motivated by. And the picture they paint is one of the world of B-reasons. They certainly make reference to helping and pleasing particular people, but they do so as part of a much richer normative landscape. But then why does Bramble insist the unconscious motivation is all about not B-reasons but U-reasons? It seems rather odd and ad hoc.

Bramble writes,

> What about our other interests, passions, or projects? As I argued earlier, I do not think that we are interested in, or "moved, charmed, or awed" by, the natural world, physics, or great works of art because we see or think there is value in these things. We find these things interesting and beautiful just because of their intrinsic properties—simply because they *are* interesting or beautiful. But I do think that when we *pursue* these things— e.g., decide to learn more about them, develop skills in them, incorporate them as parts of our lives—we are doing so because we have become aware of the ways in which they can enrich people's lives and so of their value. We sense that there are things or activities here which can help us to lead a more productive life or that fit well with our unconscious background project of trying to nudge the world in a positive direction.

So we don't—even unconsciously—think the natural world, for example, has value. We just care about it because it has properties that make us love it, properties that will inspire love in any good human being seeking to understand and appreciate it. But recognizing this is not recognizing value. That we do only when we think about welfare. When considerations of welfare motivate us, that is an unconscious recognition of real value. So unconsciously, all people are utilitarians. Or rather, all good people are. But that is just to describe the claim we are being presented with. I'm not clear what reason there might be for anyone to believe it.

Bramble continues:

> Bailey, then, upon coming to accept my form of utilitarianism, can return to exactly the sort of life he led beforehand, not only outwardly but inwardly as well. This is because his life beforehand was already one in which he was drawn to other people and certain activities out of an unconscious sense that there was great value here. He was not *consciously* calculating. But these thoughts were nonetheless present in an unconscious form under the surface.

I find this quite puzzling. We are asked to imagine a Bailey who has come to accept utilitarianism. *Consciously* come to do so, I take it. But he is happy to carry on just as before, living the B-values and the B-reasons? But now he appreciates that living by the B-values and B-reasons is the best way to live the U-values and U-reasons, so his, now utilitarianism accepting, outlook is one where he can happily, we might say, *allow himself* to live by the B-values and B-reasons. But this now looks vanishingly close to the 'schizophrenic' picture Bramble has already, in his discussion of Railton and Pettit, agreed with Stocker in rejecting. So I am struggling to understand how Bramble's solution to the alienation problem, even if we believe the extremely questionable empirical claims involved, is a solution at all.

8 Conclusion

I continue then to prefer the simpler and more natural story I already defended. The values and reasons we need to affirm, honour, live by, and recognize if we are to be good people are not the U-values and reasons but the B-values and reasons. If we are to be good moral philosophers, we should surely do the same, and that is to leave utilitarianism behind with no ifs and no buts.

Notes

1. On exemplarist virtue theory, see Zagzebski 2017. On the significance of moral exemplars for Confucianism, see Olberding 2012.
2. Analects 2.1: Our teacher said: Someone who governs by their moral power (德) is like the Pole Star that keeps its place while a multitude of stars revolve around it. 12.18: Ji Kang Zi was worried about people stealing and asked our teacher Kong about it. Our teacher Kong said: If you yourself were only free of desire. Then people would not steal even if you offered to reward them for it. 12.19: Our teacher Kong said: In the conduct of government, why be killing anybody? If you fix your desire on goodness, the people will be good. The moral power (德) of the person of noble character is the wind. The moral power (德)of the person of mean character is the grass. When the wind is over the grass, the grass must bend. See further Olberding 2019, 83–90.
3. My examples are variants on those in Parfit 1984, chapter 16.
4. If I had never existed, it could not have been said, of me, that I did not exist. There would have been no referring to me at all. It would have been possible to say that Andrew and Frances Lenman did not have a son, even that they did not have a very tall son called 'James' who grew up to be a philosopher who liked sticky toffee pudding and walking in the countryside and disliked bananas and air travel, but these would not have been thoughts *about me* or about any particular person.
5. Cf. Kumar 2003.
6. MacAskill 2015, chapter 2 offers these things as examples of what he considers reprehensibly ineffective altruism.
7. Analects 1.2.
8. Plato: *Theaetetus*,151d–187a.
9. Parfit 1984, part 1 is a classic discussion of these matters.
10. Michael Stocker, "How Emotions Reveal Value and Help Cure the Schizophrenia of Modern Ethical Theories", in Roger Crisp (ed) *How Should One Live?* (Oxford: Clarendon Press, 1996), 173–90.
11. Williams 1973, 98.
12. Dickens 1850, chapter 7.
13. 2019, 74.
14. 2003, 30.
15. Arpaly 2018, 154.
16. 1999, 128.

IV Response to Lenman

IV Response to Lenman

1 Lenman's View

Jimmy Lenman has written an extremely clear, powerful, and original critique of utilitarianism. It synthesises earlier work of his on this topic while further developing some of its key themes. Lenman and I agree on a surprising amount. In some ways, I am closer to him than I am to most contemporary utilitarians. We agree, for example, that current people should be focused on the state of the world today and in coming centuries and millennia rather than (as utilitarians in the longtermist tradition maintain) on the world eons from now. Neither Lenman nor I see any point in creating trillions of new beings in the very distant future, let alone robotic ones like Lenman's 'Digital Dickie', designed to sit around feeling as much pleasure as possible.

We agree also that for most individuals today, the right thing to do is (in some sense) 'tend your own garden' rather than sacrifice a life of your own in order to devote yourself to trying to solve the world's biggest problems. 'Tending your own garden', note, is not to focus exclusively on yourself or your loved ones. It involves (as Lenman puts it) some "reach beyond myself, my family, and my ethnic, national or religious tribe"-for example, living as a kind, generous, and involved member of your local community.

The big difference between Lenman and myself concerns the *justification*s we give of these basic prescriptions. On my view, there is an objective normative truth in some sense woven into the fabric of the universe: you should do what helps sentient beings the most. This fact has existed for all time (including before any humans came to exist), and it applies to all possible beings who are capable of having reasons to act. Why, in light of this principle, should we tend our own gardens? It is because doing so is—given our own individual epistemic limitations—your best shot at helping beings the most (for reasons I go into in my main contribution to this book). Why should we focus on the present and near-term rather than on creating trillions of future happy beings? It is because creating new beings—even very happy ones—does not *help* these beings one jot.

For Lenman, by contrast, there are no normative truths woven into the fabric of the universe in this sense. The universe has no 'point of view' or morality of its own. There are only the individual viewpoints of particular beings (albeit beings who will, ideally, agree on quite a lot). How does Lenman seek to justify his aforementioned prescriptions? According to him, what justifies them is the fact that we would end up endorsing such prescriptions after a process of reflective equilibrium—a process where we take our existing desires and intuitions and "regiment [them] into something systematically coherent and attractive". That we would end up in this place has, according to Lenman, to do crucially with our existing or starting desires and intuitions. And what are these starting desires and intuitions? Lenman says they "express what we are, biologically and culturally and as such are shaped by all the forces that have shaped us". Some species have made it through evolution up until today by being, say, especially tall, strong, or fast, or (in the case of R-selected animals) by having as many babies as possible (most of whom die in infancy). Humans, by contrast, have survived by having a small number of offspring whom we are close to over many years and, more generally, by being social animals who like to live together cooperatively in smallish-sized communities (while at the same time having interests and projects of our own). Our concerns, while more diachronic than most animals' (many of whom live entirely in the moment), are still basically for the here and now (understood broadly). Otherwise, we would not have survived to this point. Starting with these desires and intuitions, Lenman thinks reflective equilibrium will take us to a place where we like the idea of an arrangement where we can live our own lives (within certain limits), and we are not making sacrifices for the distant future.

Lenman says his main objection to utilitarianism is his well-known *Cluelessness* Objection—the worry that the consequences of our actions go on for so long that we cannot form reasonable beliefs about what actions will be overall better than others.[1] But it seems to me that he has an even deeper worry. He seems to think that *even if* (somehow) you or I attained a god's eye perspective and were able to see all the consequences of our possible actions throughout the ages, still—given the sorts of creatures we have evolved to be—we wouldn't *care* very much about their very distant consequences. Our concerns would remain local. His cluelessness worry seems an additional worry to this.

Lenman, it is also worth noting, is highly skeptical of the scientific credibility of the idea that there are moral truths woven into the fabric of the universe, in the sense utilitarians like myself accept. He writes,

> [Our] intuitions are not credibly seen on the model of a kind of perception where by means of a faculty we understand nothing about how we somehow detect some independent body of moral truths out there in the world. There is no credible picture of how this supposed faculty came into being and how it might be supposed to work that allows the moral truth to shape and explain our moral beliefs.

And further:

> Goodness, so understood, is a very elusive property. Scientists have not devised an instrument for measuring it, and it does not seem to be something we observe by sensory means.

In my following response to Lenman, I will address the most important of his concerns and explain why I am not ultimately dissuaded from utilitarianism.

2 Is Utilitarianism Scientifically Credible?

Lenman says there is 'no credible picture' of how we could perceive normative truths that are woven into the fabric of the universe. But I think there is a very credible picture of this, one mentioned by Lenman himself: that of Peter Singer and Katarzyna de Lazari-Radek. The idea here is that we can detect independent normative truths because we have evolved *intelligence*—for *its* tremendous utility—and it is our intelligence that allows us to detect these truths. Just as our intelligence allows us to understand complex mathematical truths in a way that goes beyond the understanding of mathematics that is fitness-enhancing for beings like us, so it allows us to understand normative truths as well.

Not only is this picture available, it also has much to recommend it. It would explain, for example, why many of us have at least some concern for beings who are very distant or different from ourselves—not only other human beings elsewhere in the world (geographically, ethnically, or socioeconomically different from ourselves) but also different kinds of animals. Many of us care deeply about other species of animals. Lenman himself expresses great concern for animals as diverse as

> [the] Spix's macaw, the northern white rhino, the Pyrenean ibex, the Chinese river dolphin, the Bramble Cay melomys, the splendid poison frog, the ivy-billed woodpecker, the South Island kōkako, the Hawaiian crow, the slender-billed curlew, the robust burrowing mayfly, the Santa Cruz pupfish, the Lake Lanao freshwater fish, the smooth handfish, etc., etc.

He says that preventing the extinction of animals like these "seems to me and to many to be one of the grimmest and more urgent problems facing human beings". Singer and Lazari-Radek's picture can explain why so many of us (including Lenman himself) care so deeply about these animals. We care because we see that they have lives that can go well or badly for them, and we implicitly understand that their welfare matters.

By contrast, it is unclear what explanation Lenman can offer of our concern for such distant and different sorts of creatures, and our willingness to make sacrifices to protect them. There seems little or no fitness advantage in caring about creatures so remote from us.

Finally, Lenman is perfectly right that we cannot (at this stage) detect or measure goodness in any kind of scientifically rigorous or satisfactory way. The way in which these truths are woven into the fabric of the universe, and our ability to pick up on them, remain a mystery. But there is *a lot* that is mysterious that science has yet to understand and explain. What is the nature of consciousness? Why is there something rather than nothing? Why is there precisely *this* rather than something else? And so on. Perhaps, in time, science will improve enough to allow us to detect or measure goodness in a better way.

3 Accordance with Common Sense

Lenman says that a big strike against utilitarianism is that it has implications that are deeply counterintuitive and take us very far from commonsense. If you start with the claims that "the good of any one individual is of no more importance...than the good of any other...[and that] as a rational being I am bound to aim at good generally...not merely at a particular part of it", and build on these, your theory will "[keep] coming into conflict with basic features of moral common sense, widely shared intuitions about, e.g., autonomy, justice and the wrongness of pushing people off bridges". We should not, according to Lenman, when faced with these results, say, "*So much the worse for moral common sense. It is doubtful and insecure. Our axioms cannot be wrong*". Instead, we should reject the starting point, utilitarianism.

I agree it is a major problem for a moral theory if its implications diverge too greatly from common sense or what is intuitive. It is *highly* intuitive, for example, that it can be reasonable to have interests, projects, loves, and relationships of your own. It is also highly intuitive that it would be great folly for current generations to make enormous sacrifices to create trillions of new happy beings eons from now. It is not *impossible* that these things could be false, but we would need a very good argument indeed to reject them. But as I have argued in my main contribution to this book, utilitarianism is entirely consistent with these things, and indeed can explain why they are so. Lenman is right that contemporary utilitarians like Singer, Lazari-Radek, and many effective altruists and longtermists accept that utilitarianism has deeply counterintuitive consequences, arguing that intuitions aren't so important. But I have argued for a different sort of utilitarianism—one that starts with the axioms mentioned earlier but interprets them in a different way. In particular, the point is to help people as much as possible, not create as much welfare as possible.

Actually, it seems to me that Lenman's view is the one with counterintuitive consequences. Lenman says we deplore the Holocaust because of "our complex endowment of emotions and concerns" and that these in turn were "a consequence of our evolutionary history". This strikes me as deeply counterintuitive. I think we deplore the Holocaust because we see that it was objectively bad. Our attitudes towards it are a response to our recognition that it is bad independently of our attitudes. If there had never been any humans, it would still have been true that if humans came to exist and carried out actions like that, those actions (and the death and suffering they caused) would have been horrifically bad. It is not merely that we hate what happened in the Holocaust because it was fitness-enhancing in our ancestors to hate that sort of thing. Someone who doesn't think the Holocaust was bad is making a mistake, and not simply because most animals like us would happen to deplore the Holocaust after a process of reflective equilibrium. (Note that Lenman agrees that what *makes* the Holocaust bad is—at least, in part—the suffering it involved, and not facts about our evolutionary history. My worry, to be clear, is that on Lenman's account, what ultimately *explains our attitudes* towards, say, the Holocaust is our species' utterly contingent evolutionary history rather than our having come into appreciative contact with truths woven into the fabric of the universe.)

Lenman says that, due to the cluelessness worry, utilitarianism cannot make sense even of

> why it is a good idea to make sure your children have enough to eat, or why it is a bad idea to kill your granny and feed her to some nearby pigs, or why you really shouldn't set out to burn down your local primary school or to exterminate the Jewish population of Europe.

In my main contribution to this book, I have argued that utilitarianism is able to make sense of these things. I now want to add that it seems to me that it is Lenman's account that cannot make sense of them.

If I imagine for a moment that we have the instincts, emotions, and intuitions we do only because of what sort of instincts, emotions, and intuitions happened to be fitness-enhancing for our ancestors—that, as Lenman puts it, 'the shaping of human nature was not a process that tracked any truths'—then I struggle to see why it really matters whether we feed our children or ourselves, kill our grannies, or commit genocide. My sense that there is a reason to treat others well, or even get out of bed in the morning, is premised or dependent on a background belief that these things matter in some deeper or independent way. If I truly came to accept Lenman's picture of the origin of our attitudes, then I think much (or perhaps all) of my motivations to live would be sapped. I think that most people are in the same boat as me. Depression or ennui is often the result of a loss of the ordinary, everyday conviction (mostly taken for granted) that some things matter in the sort of objective or independent way I have been arguing for in this book.

4 Well-Being

Lenman does not regard the notion of well-being as very important. He writes,

> I like Tiberius's view that welfare is living well in accordance with our values. But the more I reflect on it, the more I come to suspect that I like her view not so much because it is necessarily my favourite answer to the question, *What is welfare*, more because I think, *How can we live well in accordance with our values?* is just a more interesting question to put in the centre of ethical inquiry than the question *What is welfare?* Once I have figured out how to live well in accordance with my values, I don't know what residual difficulty there might be for *What is welfare?* to engage with. Of course, some ways of living well in accordance with my values might be a lot easier than others. And of course, there are always more particular questions. *What might be fun to do this weekend?* But such questions, while they can be very important, are going to lack the sweeping generality of a question like *What is welfare?*

By contrast, it seems to me that without the notion of well-being—without already thinking that there are beings (including us) with lives that can go well or badly for them—there just wouldn't be any thoughts about how to live in the first place. I struggle to see the point of anything in a world without beings for whom things can go better or worse. It is the capacity for well-being that is the ultimate foundation of anything that matters.

As for the question, "How can we live well in accordance with our values?", I find it much less interesting. I have little interest in what I in fact value and much more interest in what I *should* value. The fact that I value something is itself of little intrinsic significance to me.

One of Lenman's concerns with the notion of well-being is that there is no good way of comparing welfare across different kinds of creatures. He writes,

We have perhaps an idea of what a good life might be like for a tiger or a panda insofar as we have studied these creatures and formed a sense of what it is for them to flourish. But there is no clear metric for comparing these things to say if my life is better or worse and how much than that of a certain tiger or a certain panda. Never mind the extraterrestrial or the piece of sentient AI that may sit on my shelf one day. And so, of course, no clear metric by which to sum them as we need to if the utilitarian is to do their sums.

Even welfare comparisons between *humans* are tricky, he says. He writes,

> Interpersonal comparisons are notoriously a headache for utilitarians even before we start to concern ourselves with creatures other than human beings. Even when we deal in preference satisfaction as represented by utility functions, while certain formal assumptions…allow us to represent a given person's utility on a scale, that scale is an interval scale, where that is a scale which yields a whole family of functions unique only up to positive linear transformation, i.e., transformations that scale our function up or down and/or change which point in the scale we count as the "zero" point while preserving the order and proportion of utility values.

The problem here seems to me not a problem with utilitarianism but with the assumption of some desire or preference-based theory of welfare. If we instead adopt (as I propose in my main contribution to this book) a sophisticated hedonism about welfare, on which welfare is about experiencing a large array of different kinds of wonderful pleasures, then it becomes very possible to compare welfare across humans and even across different species. Humans have a greater capacity for well-being than most other animals do by virtue of our higher faculties. We can feel pleasures—from love, art, science, striving, and so on—that enrich our lives in ways most other species cannot. Yes, we have pains they cannot feel either. But it is better to have loved and lost than never to have loved at all.

Again, the problem is not with utilitarianism itself but only with utilitarianism understood or built on in implausible ways.

One reason Lenman finds utilitarianism so concerning is that he thinks of utilitarians as eager to let go of our existing human culture and natural environment in order to issue in a world of very different sorts of creatures than us, who are able to feel more pleasure and less pain. He writes (sarcastically),

> Come to think, why not replace *ourselves* with sentient synthetic things that have a more potent capacity for whatever we think welfare is? And now we *really* don't need plants. Synthetic sentience doesn't need oxygen to breathe and doesn't care if climate change has made everything a bit hot. And it doesn't need organic matter to eat and convert into energy. It can run on solar-powered batteries. Yay! Let's do that. Let us make a brave new *postbiological* world where technology liberates us (I use the word 'us' extremely loosely) from nature. Our synthetically sentient successors will go on to colonize space, harvesting the energy of the stars to make a vast utopian utilitarian future, one devoid of organic living things, to be sure. Such organic living things are the product of the blind, purposeless process that is evolution by natural selection. Technology will someday, perhaps someday very soon, get smarter than evolution at making psychological systems and physical systems to realize them. That is what will save us. Or at least save something. Filostrato's dream will come true. I am not making this up. People really do say these things.

I am with Lenman here. I find the apparent eagerness of some utilitarians to issue in such a future concerning. But the problem here is not with utilitarianism. We do not need to junk utilitarianism and decide to embrace our own partialities or (as Lenman puts it) 'prejudices' in order to stick up for existing human culture, values, and the natural environment. Instead, we should recognise that the reason these existing things are so special is that actually, while there is a lot wrong with the world, the way we do things is pretty good in many ways since it is a source of many objectively wonderful pleasures. The world as it is now makes possible welfare that is (in Mill's term) much *higher* than the welfare of a being like Digital Dickie, who sits on the shelf feeling the same kind of pleasure all day long and no pain whatsoever. We shouldn't want a world full of Digital Dickies, but this is not because utilitarianism is false. It is rather because Digital Dickie is not well off at all. His is an extremely narrow life, missing all the wonderful sorts of pleasures that are available to more complex (though fraught) beings like us.

That said, while Digital Dickie is not a model for any of us, I can imagine certain ways technology might be used to enlarge our capacities for welfare. But this would have to be done extremely carefully. There are huge dangers here, dangers for *welfare*.

Incidentally, there is no worry that my version of utilitarianism could imply that current humans should be replaced, even by beings who could experience much more welfare. This, again, is because, on my version of utilitarianism, the point is to *help* beings as much as possible. We do not help current people by replacing them with other beings who can have more welfare.

5 The Natural World

This leads me to my next point. Lenman mentions that some utilitarians and utilitarian sympathisers would like to reengineer the natural world. In particular, they would like to intervene in nature to prevent predation or, more generally, replace animals whose lives are nasty, brutish, and short with animals for whom things are better. (Lenman cites, among others, a paper of mine in this context.) However, he says, to do so would be the height of hubris.

I absolutely agree with Lenman here. We should not go messing around in such big ways with ecosystems. Certainly, we should not do so now, with our relatively poor understanding of the effects such interventions would have on other parts of ecosystems. We could harm beings greatly. But even if we attained mastery over nature, it might still be the case that we should not exercise it. There is something extremely valuable for *us* to have contact with realms we have no control over. Moreover, I suspect that a human being with the highest capacity for welfare—or a George Bailey–type figure—would simply not want to go messing around with nature. They would feel a reverence, awe, or humility before it. We should want to be (since these are the best-off beings) the sort of beings who would, as a byproduct of the ways they are, want not to completely control nature. Finally, again, my form of utilitarianism does not prescribe replacing beings with happier ones. That doesn't *help* anyone.

That said, I do think we should be deeply concerned about the lives of most wild animals and that it should pain us to contemplate what they endure. Many of their lives *are* largely awful. We should be moved by this. Perhaps not to *do* anything. But we should be moved by it all the same.

6 Some More Problems for Lenman

I want to raise two more problems for Lenman's positive account. Suppose he is right that creatures like us would, after a process of reflective equilibrium, converge in our feelings or attitudes. This, I think, would be hard to explain unless we posit a realm of objective values that, during such a process, we would be coming to understand better. While we are all human beings, it is by no means clear that we are so alike that, without such a realm, we would end up in anything like the same place at the end of such a process.

The other problem is that such a process of reflective equilibrium might fundamentally change the sorts of people we are. We might, that is, continue to *evolve* through such a process into very different sorts of beings than we are now, with very different basic intuitions or concerns. Even if Lenman is right about the sorts of beings we are today as a result of evolutionary pressures, what reason is there to think that through a process of reflective equilibrium—involving vastly greater understanding of the physical facts, as well as hashing things out with each other potentially for years—we would not all become beings who are much more impartial or who even have strictly utilitarian instincts?

7 Conclusion

Lenman's worries are deep. In fact, I think that in many ways they succeed against the sort of utilitarianism that is in vogue today. But I continue to think that they do not touch the version of utilitarianism I defend in my main piece, a utilitarianism on which the point is to help beings as much as possible rather than to create as much welfare as possible.

Note

1 As he puts it, "My own core objections to standard forms of utilitarianism are mostly about the issue of cluelessness, appreciating the depth and seriousness of the epistemic difficulty of engaging with the consequences of their acts in their totality".

Glossary

Act consequentialism: *See* consequentialism.
Act utilitarianism: *See* utilitarianism.
Adam and Eve: An objection to average utilitarianism. Adam and Eve know that if they reproduce there will be many resulting future generations of people who are very happy but slightly less happy than Adam and Eve themselves. Average utilitarianism seems to imply, absurdly, that Adam and Eve should not then have children.
Agent-neutral consequentialism: *See* consequentialism.
The Alienation Objection: The objection to utilitarianism that accepting it is incompatible with having friendships, interests, or projects of your own. The Integrity Objection is a version of this.
Anti-natalism: Anti-natalists are people who think it is wrong to bring new life into the world. They think it is wrong to have children and look favourably on the prospect of the extinction of human and other life.
A posteriori: *See* a priori.
A priori: Something can be known—or justifiably believed—a priori if it can be known without the need for any specific empirical evidence or data. Stuff that can only be known—or justifiably believed—with such evidence is known or believed *a posteriori*.
Aretaic: Of or pertaining to virtue (From Greek *aretē*—virtue).
Attributive: An adjective is used *attributively* when it does not, as we say, *detach*. So *Nina is a small whale* cannot be rewritten as *Nina is a whale* and *Nina is small*. *Flambeau is a good burglar* does not mean *Flambeau is a burglar* and *Flambeau is good*. As opposed to a **predicative** use—*Daffodils are yellow*

flowers permits us felicitously to infer that *Daffodils are flowers and they are yellow*.

Average Utilitarianism: *See* utilitarianism.

Axiology: Inquiry about goodness or value. (From Greek *axios*—worth.)

Axiom: A proposition that is taken as fundamental in some field of knowledge, sitting on the ground floor of justification, to be used—usually along with other axioms—as a basis for the derivation of everything else. An axiom is not itself amenable to discursive justification, but it is usually hoped that it is so manifestly and obviously right it makes little sense to doubt it.

Bridge: A famous thought experiment due to Thomson. An out-of-control trolley car is hurtling down the tracks towards where it will hit and certainly kill five people who are trapped on the line ahead. But first, it will pass under a bridge. There is a big person standing by the edge, quite unsuspecting. You could push him in the trolley's path. (Thomson compared cases like this to a case where a runaway trolley hurtling towards five can be deflected onto a side track where it will kill just one. Many people think it is permissible to sacrifice one person in the deflection case but not in the bridge case. The notorious *Trolley Problem* is the problem of finding a principled reason to account for the cases differing in this way. If they do.)

Central Limit Theorem: This is an important theorem in statistics that says (put very informally) that the cumulative result of combining large numbers of independent random variables over many trials will tend to conform to a **normal distribution**.

Chaos: A causal system is said to be chaotic when a small change in initial conditions can make a large difference over time to what happens downstream. The term echoes Lorentz's famous illustration where a butterfly flapping its wings ends up causally responsible, later on and afar away, for a storm.

Cinema: An example used by Kagan to illustrate the Demandingness Objection to utilitarianism. Utilitarianism seems to imply we may never go to the cinema because there is always some more effective use to which we might put the resources of time and money that going to the cinema uses.

The Cluelessness Objection: The objection to utilitarianism—and other kinds of consequentialism—that the consequences of our actions ramify massively into the distant future, making it impossible to form reasonable beliefs about what actions would be overall better than others.

Consequentialism: The view that the fundamental aim of ethics is the maximization of goodness. It is standardly presented as a theory of the rightness of actions.

Agent-neutral consequentialism: Consequentialism that does not think the goodness different agents should be concerned to maximize can be different for different agents. Goodness can be understood in terms of a single ranking of worlds which is the same for everyone.

Act consequentialism: The view that any given action's rightness or moral value is to be understood in terms of the goodness of its consequences. Philosophers sometimes distinguish **objective** forms of act consequentialism, where it is the goodness of consequences an act will in fact have that determine this from **subjective** versions, where it is the expected value of the act's consequences that determines it.

Rule consequentialism: Rule consequentialism claims first that what we should do is *obey the ideal moral code*. And secondly, it says that we should understand the ideal moral code as the code general acceptance of which would generate as much goodness as possible.

Standby consequentialism: A view defended by Pettit on which we should not think like consequentialists most of the time but temporarily snap back into consequentialist thinking in certain conditions.

Cost-benefit analysis: Analysis applied to projects and policies by corporations and governments that seeks to quantify and compare expected costs and benefits. In normal current economic practice, costs and benefits are measured in monetary value as determined either by market prices or by people's willingness to pay.

Counterfactuals or counterfactual conditionals: Conditional sentences about how things might have been, of the general form, *If P had been the case Q would have been the case* where P is something that is not the case. Such as, *If David had stayed at home, Sadie would have married him.*

德 (dé): 'Moral power'. In classical Chinese philosophy, this word, sometimes simply translated as 'virtue', is often used to signify the power of morally exemplary people to transform people around them.

The Demandingness Objection: The objection to utilitarianism that it is way too imposing.

Deontic: Of or pertaining to what is right (or wrong) or what ought (or ought not) be done. (From Greek *deon* neuter participle of *dein*, used to say of a thing that it is needful or fitting or ought to be done.)

Description, under a: When I think about a thing, I think of it in a certain way under a certain aspect. As George Orwell, as Eric Blair, as the author of 1984, as the only son of Richard and Ida Blair, or whatever. So I might think George Orwell is my favourite author but (not knowing Orwell was Blair) not think Eric Blair is my favourite author. Or one might want to get to know the handsome man standing near the piano (as one very naturally might—he is *very* handsome) but not want to get to know the only person in the room with a conviction for murder. Of course, if the convicted murderer is the handsome man, then there is a sense in which one does want to get to know the convicted murderer but not, we say, under that description.

Determinism: A metaphysical hypothesis to the effect, roughly, that the world is governed by very strict laws, such that given that the state of the world at a given time, the state of the world at all later times is fixed.

Doing-allowing distinction: Moral common sense seems to attach importance to the distinction between doing harm—actively inflicting it—and allowing harm—failing by inaction to prevent it.

Dominance Addition: Take a world with some people in it and make all those people better off. Also, add some other people with positive welfare. The result says Dominance Addition is an improvement.

Effective altruism: A movement founded in the early 21st century by a group of philosophers at Oxford University to advance the project of bringing about maximally efficient improvements to the world where improvement is understood in an impartial and welfarist way. Effective altruists like to sharply differentiate themselves from utilitarians, for example, by stressing that it is a project and not a normative claim (*see*, e.g., MacAskill 2019). It's not quite clear what this comes to. The idea may be that I can be committed to a project, like the project of organizing an annual music festival in my local park, without necessarily thinking that the project is of overriding importance, that it trumps all other concerns and interests I might have, with no other considerations, moral and otherwise, properly constraining it. Something like that may make some sense, but it remains pretty clear from their many writings that effective altruism's leading advocates, well, advocate it and embrace it. Their writings are conspicuously awash with normative claims, making it evident that leading effective altruists are none too keen on people doing a given thing when some other thing they might be doing would be "doing good better". While effective altruism may be a 'project', it is a project driven by the relentless application of utilitarian ideas—maximization, impartiality, welfarism—and clearly and unmistakably identified with the utilitarian philosophical tradition, not least through the influence of the utilitarian Peter Singer who may be viewed as its secular godfather and who wrote it an influential manifesto in Singer 2015.

Emotivism: The view that when I call a thing 'good', I simply express my approval for or liking for it and invite you to approve of or like it also.

Ethics: The discipline that studies how we should live.

Eudaimonia (εὐδαιμονία): An Ancient Greek word that plays a central role in Greek thought. It is usually translated as 'happiness' or, perhaps better, 'flourishing'. To be *eudaimon* (the adjective cognate to eudaimonia) is not just to feel good at a given time but to be doing well over time. Aristotle took it to be the ultimate end at which human life is aimed.

Expected utility: The expected utility of a choice is what you get by summing all the numbers obtained when the utility of each possible outcome is multiplied by its probability.

Expected value: The expected value of a choice is what you get by summing all the numbers obtained when the value of each possible outcome is multiplied by its probability.

Experience machine: An imaginary scenario described by Nozick where you are plugged into a machine in which you then live out your days in a kind of virtual reality world, having the most wonderful time while simply lying there, not doing anything at all.

Extinction pill: A thought experiment of Temkin inspired by Glover. We can all take a pill that will cause us to have very long and very happy lives, but the price is that human beings will become extinct when our long and happy lives end. Temkin, like Glover, thinks it would be very wrong to agree to this.

False dichotomy: A fallacious kind of argument where we are presented with two alarming eventualities which purport to be mutually exclusive and exhaustive of the relevant space of possibilities, but on closer examination, it turns out they are not.

Final goodness: Something has final goodness if it is good in and of itself and not just as a means to or way of realizing some other good thing or things.

Foundationalism: A bottom-up understanding of moral justification where our moral beliefs are supposed to draw their ultimate support from fundamental axioms which we take to have a special certainty as self-evident findings of reason.

Golden Rule: The injunction widely considered at the heart of ethics to treat other people as one would wish to be treated oneself. (Famously articulated at *Analects* (15.24) and in the Bible (*Matthew* 7.12, *Luke* 6.31)).

Great Oxygenation Event: A catastrophic change to the Earth's climate about 2½ billion years ago when large amounts of the carbon dioxide in the atmosphere were converted into oxygen.

The Harming to Help Objection: The objection to utilitarianism that implies that in some cases (such as **Bridge, Sheriff,** and **Transplant**) you should harm some people to help others when you should not do so.

Hedonism: The word 'hedonism' comes from the Greek *hedonē*, meaning 'pleasure'. It is sometimes used as a name for the monistic understanding of *goodness* that identifies goodness with pleasure, and sometimes as a name for an understanding of *welfare* as pleasure.

Higher pleasures: Mill, in his utilitarian philosophy, thought some pleasures had far greater value than others, distinguishing higher from lower pleasures. He thought a test of which of two pleasures should count as higher would be to consult the preferences of competent judges, people acquainted with both pleasures.

Humean cost-benefit analysis: An imaginary exercise where we seek to "compute, estimate and compare" the value of everything that has ever existed or will exist that has a value in order to arrive at a valuation of the entire world.

Indifference postulate: A postulate applying the supposition that when we are confronted with a range of possible future outcomes about whose respective probabilities we have no information, we reasonably assign them equal probabilities.

Identity-affecting actions: Actions that make a difference to the identities of people who will subsequently come to exist.

Instrumental goodness: Something has instrumental goodness if it is good as a means to some other good thing or things.

Interval scale: An interval scale allows us not merely to order whatever we are counting or measuring, but to quantify and compare the intervals things lie apart on it. So we can say not only that my office is warmer than your office and your kitchen is warmer than my kitchen but also that the difference in temperature between our offices and our kitchens is the same. We may still not be able to say that, e.g., my office is twice as warm as your office is. For that we need a *ratio* scale where there is some fixed and determinate place to put zero.

Intuition: *See* **moral intuition**.

Intuitionism: A British school of moral philosophy with its roots in the writings of Richard Price (1723–91). Its best-known 20th-century representatives were G. E. Moore (1873–1958) and W. D. Ross (1877–1971). Intuitionists see moral properties as real properties known by intuition, whereby we apprehend certain moral propositions as self-evident. Twentieth-century intuitionists like Moore and Ross tend to understand moral properties as being non-natural properties. They are **robust realists**. (The great Victorian English utilitarian Henry Sidgwick (1838–1900) has an ambivalent relationship with intuitionism. On the one hand, having been unimpressed by the once influential ethical writings of intuitionist William Whewell (1794–1866), he was highly critical of what he calls 'intuitionism' (sometimes 'dogmatic intuitionism'), understood as an attempt to give philosophical expression to the morality of common sense, while at the same time characterizing his own position as a 'philosophical intuitionism' which grounds our moral knowledge in ethical *axioms*—self-evident "intuitive propositions of real clearness and certainty".)

Integrity Objection to Utilitarianism: The thought, classically aired by Williams (1973), that utilitarianism compels an agent, absurdly, to regard any cost or benefit to be gained from any of his or her projects, concerns and relationships simply as one cost or benefit among others. It is a version of the **Alienation Objection**.

Ks and rs: Human beings are Ks: we have a small number of offspring and take very good care of them till they are old enough to look after themselves, rather than doing what fish do, being rs, having thousands of offspring, most of which will be eaten in short order but whose sheer weight of numbers ensures a few will get lucky and survive long enough to reproduce in their turn.

Law of large numbers: The law of large numbers is a statistical law that says that if we grow the size of our sample of whatever it may be we are interested in, we will find the actual distribution of whatever variable may concern us will approach ever more closely to the underlying probability distribution.

Longtermism: a view notably championed by some leading adherents of effective altruism urging that we give immense priority to enhancing the likely beneficial consequences of what we do in the very long term, in particular by making it more likely that humanity—or some successor creatures, biological or otherwise—will survive into the very distant future in conditions conducive to flourishing. Sometimes the view is known as *strong longtermism* to distinguish it from *moderate longtermism*, which is the more commonplace thought that we should give due consideration to the long-term effects of our actions, though not on so grandiose a scale.

Meno's Paradox: AKA the Paradox of Inquiry. You cannot inquire into what x is if you know what x is because you already know what x is. And you cannot inquire into what x is if you do not know what x is because you do not know what it is you are supposed to be inquiring into. So you cannot inquire into what x is. On close examination, it is an example of a false dichotomy.

Mere Addition Paradox: If we move from world A to world A+ by adding some extra people who are happy enough but not as happy as the existing A people, we do not make things worse. But we make things better if we then move to world B where some redistribution has made the better off A people somewhat less well-off and raised the welfare of the people we added. B is more populous than A, but everyone in B is less happy than everyone in A. But people who reject total utilitarianism will be reluctant to accept that B is not worse than A. But it must be if A+ is no worse than A and B is better than A+. The argument requires many assumptions and has many variations. Parfit's original statement (1984) is greatly complicated by some big natural obstacle between the original A people and the extra people added at A+ that is supposed to tame concerns about distributive justice in the transition from A to A+, an obstacle that is then imagined to somehow disappear by natural causes. More recent variations like that discussed in Chapter 4 are generally simpler.

Metaethics: The part of moral philosophy that does not directly concern itself with what ethical claims are true but with what we are talking about when we make them. Metaethics is concerned with semantics—what ethical language means, metaphysics—what is the nature of moral properties and epistemology—can we have ethical knowledge, and if so, how? Emotivism and robust realism are examples of metaethical theories.

Modal realism: We sometimes unpack our talk of possibility and necessity in terms of how things might and might not have been. Moral realism, a view defended by Lewis, takes it that all the possible ways the world might have been, all *possible worlds* as these are sometimes called, are *real*, no less real than the actual world. So, for modal realism, being actual and being real are not the same. Many worlds are real, but only one is actual.

Moderate longtermism: *See* longtermism.

Moderate utilitarianism: *See* utilitarianism.

Modus ponens: Logic studies *logical forms*. Consider the following:

If George's parents are both lions, then George is a lion.
George's parents are both lions.
∴George is a lion.

If Jill is away then Angus is grumpy.
Jill is away.
∴Angus is grumpy.

These are both *valid* arguments. That is, if the premises are true, so, too, must the conclusion be. (It is another question whether the premises are true. If an argument ticks that box too, it is not only valid but *sound*.) The arguments are about very different subject matters, but they are the same in an important way. They are both valid for the same reason, which is that they both have the same structure.

If P, then Q. P. ∴Q.

And it is that structure that explains why they are valid. Such structural features of language that determine and explain logical validity are called *logical forms*. The valid logical form the previous arguments share is called *modus ponens*.

Another very common logical form is *modus tollens*:

If P, then Q. Not Q. So not P.

Modus tollens is also valid.

(P and Q here are sentential variables. Think of them as standing for *any (declarative) sentence you like*.)

Modus tollens: *See* **modus ponens.**

Monism: Monistic accounts of a given thing are accounts that regard it as basically a single thing or kind of thing (from Greek *monos* = alone). **Pluralist** accounts of a thing say it is a plurality—more than one—of things or kinds of things. So there are monist or pluralist accounts of *goodness*. The former say (final) goodness is just one kind of thing, say welfare if you are a welfarist. The latter says it can be any of a number of things, as did Ross who thought final goodness was realized by all of pleasure, virtue, knowledge and justice. There are also monist and pluralist accounts of *welfare*. Monists think it just one thing - the classical English utilitarians thought it was pleasure. Pluralists think it can be a number of things, perhaps, e.g., pleasure, relationships, achievements.

Moral intuition: In its most general sense, moral intuition is a state of mind of being more or less confident about some moral matter. Intuitionist moral philosophers have a particular understanding of intuitions as apprehensions of self-evident moral principles, but the term is used more widely by philosophers of different schools of thought with various ideas about what intuitions are.

Non-anti-egalitarianism: Non-anti-egalitarianism says this. Suppose one world has greater average welfare than the other. The first world also has greater total welfare. And it is more equal. In that case, non-anti-egalitarianism says the first world is better.

Non-identity Problem: The problem of explaining how one outcome can be better or worse than another if there is *no one for* *whom* the first outcome is better or worse. Some philosophers do not attempt to explain this but simply deny it is true.

Normal distribution: A kind of distributive pattern described in statistical theory. The precise definition is very technical, but normal distributions have, though not uniquely, the important features of being bell shaped and symmetrical around the mean.

No True Scotsman: "No true Scotsman puts ice in his whisky." "Excuse me, but my Uncle Hamish puts ice in his whisky." Exactly! I said no *true* Scotsman! Evidently, your uncle is not a *true* Scotsman." Where a generalization about what is a true or real or genuine K is understood in such a way as to rule out any putative counterexample in advance, it is difficult to refute at the cost of draining it of much interest.

Objective act utilitarianism: *See* utilitarianism.

The Order of Explanation Worry: A worry articulated by Susan Wolf and others. Utilitarians get things backward. We do not think, e.g., great works of art are good because they please or interest us. Rather, they please or interest us because they are good.

Outsmart: "Outsmart v. To embrace the conclusion of one's opponent's *reductio ad absurdum* argument. 'They thought they had me, but I outsmarted them. I agreed that it was sometimes just to hang an innocent man'" (Dennett, 1982).

Paradox of Inquiry: *See* Meno's paradox.

Person-affecting utilitarianism: *See* utilitarianism.

The 'Philosophy of Swine' Objection: Utilitarianism commends to us a world where we all live long lives consisting purely of intense bodily pleasures.

Pluralism: *See* monism.

Positive linear transformation: A positive linear transformation is a function of the form $F(x) = mx + n$ where $m > 0$. That is, multiply everything by some positive number and add a constant. So starting with a line on a graph, we shift it up or down and change its gradient, steeping or flattening it.

Rs: *See* Ks and rs.

Reasons utilitarianism: *See* utilitarianism.

Reductio: AKA reductio ad absurdum. Which is when we find something we are confident is false to follow from some supposition and infer that that supposition is false:

Reflective equilibrium: An ideal that gives its name to an understanding of moral inquiry as concerned with seeking to bring our more general and theoretical understandings of morality into coherence with our intuitions or, as Rawls calls them, *considered judgements* about particular cases culminating ideally in a coherent and intuitively appealing corpus of moral beliefs which will remain stable under reflective scrutiny. Of course, we would like our moral beliefs to cohere not merely with each other but with our beliefs about other matters - biology, economics, etc. This ideal state is known as **wide reflective equilibrium**.

Repugnant Conclusion: The proposition that a population living drab but OK lives is to be preferred to a much smaller population living wonderful lives. This proposition is widely taken following Parfit (1984) to follow from total utilitarianism and serve as a *reductio* argument against it.

Requirement utilitarianism: *See* utilitarianism.

Robust realism: A view of moral properties as non-natural properties of things that are constituted prior to and independently of human moral experience and that it is the business of ethics to investigate.

Rule consequentialism: *See* consequentialism.

Rule utilitarianism: *See* utilitarianism.

Sandboxing: The practice of considering examples under the pretence that the consequences spelled out in the examples are all the consequences there are. The term is pinched from computing, where it refers to a security precaution when a piece of software is tested in isolation from its effects on other stuff.

Satisfaction: (1) The psychological thing that is pleasure or enjoyment. (2) The semantic thing that is the proposition entertained by a thought being realized or made true.

Self-effacing theories: Theories that imply (perhaps in conjunction with some known or supposedly known facts) that we ought not to believe them.

Self-refuting theories: Theories that imply (perhaps in conjunction with some known or supposedly known facts) their own falsehood.

Separateness of Persons Objection: It is an old worry about utilitarianism that it fails to make good sense of the concern of distributive justice with how fairly utility is shared out between persons and not just how much of it (whether in total or on average) there is. Harm to one group of people cannot be compensated by some greater benefit to another. In this way Rawls urges (1971), utilitarianism fails to take the distinction between persons seriously.

Sheriff: A famous thought experiment due to McCloskey. You are the sheriff of a rough town in the Wild West. After the murder of a popular citizen, you arrested a suspect you now know is innocent but an angry crowd is hungry for the suspect's blood and greater bloodshed will ensue if you let them go.
Standby consequentialism: *See* consequentialism.
Strong longtermism: *See* longtermism.
Subjective Act Utilitarianism: *See* utilitarianism.
Sub specie aeternitatis: Under the aspect of eternity, i.e., from a cosmic, eternal perspective.
Total utilitarianism: *See* utilitarianism.
Transhumanists: Philosophers who advocate the use of technology to improve on human nature by engineering better, less limited, human, and, perhaps ultimately, posthuman creatures.
Transitivity: A relation is transitive if when A has it to B and B to C, A must have it to C. I am taller than you. You are taller than Brian. So I am taller than Brian because 'taller than' is transitive. I love you and you love Brian but maybe I do not love Brian. That is quite possible as 'love' is not transitive.
Transplant: A famous thought experiment of Thomson. In your hospital in a remote place are five people who are dying from organ failure. They could all be saved with transplants. The organs that are failing are different, so just one healthy, fresh corpse would do the job. As you are alone in the reception area, a healthy young person comes in to make some inquiries. You know who this person is. He has no family and no friends. No one will miss him or notice he has gone. No one will ever find out what you did. Do you kill him?
Two Wars: A famous thought experiment of Parfit. Parfit asks us to consider the following three scenarios: (1) peace, (2) a war that kills 99% of the world population, and (3) a war that kills 100% (resulting in human extinction). According to Parfit, while (2) is obviously much worse than (1), the difference in badness between (2) and (3) is far greater still. To fully account for the badness of (3), it is not enough to appeal to the additional harms caused to the final 1% of humanity. Intuitively, says Parfit, its badness has to do also with the *loss of all the happy people who would have come to exist had humanity kept going*.
Underlying probability distribution: the distribution of likelihood across a range of possible outcomes.

Universalizable/universalizability: Universalizability is the property of being universalizable that normative thought is often taken to have. The idea is that normative concepts must be applied with a certain generality. What is a good reason on Monday should still be a good reason on Tuesday. So for some reason of principle legitimately to guide my action in some circumstance, I must also endorse its similarly guiding action in any relevantly similar circumstance.

Utilitarianism: The view that the fundamental aim of ethics is the maximization of welfare or utility. Sometimes characterized as a conjunction of consequentialism and welfarism.

Total utilitarianism: The view that the fundamental aim of ethics is the maximization of total welfare.

Average utilitarianism: The view that the fundamental aim of ethics is the maximization of average welfare.

Person-affecting utilitarianism: The view that the fundamental aim of ethics is to maximally benefit sentient things such that a given state of affairs is better than another only to the extent that particular sentient things are better off in the former than they are in the latter.

Act utilitarianism: The view that any given action's rightness or moral value is to be understood in terms of the utility of its consequences. Philosophers sometimes distinguish **objective** forms of act utilitarianism, where it is the utility of consequences an act will in fact have that determine this, from **subjective** versions, where it is the **expected utility** of the act's consequences that determines it.

Rule utilitarianism: Rule utilitarianism claims, first, that what we should do is *obey the ideal moral code*. And secondly, it says that we should understand the ideal moral code as the code general acceptance of which would generate as much welfare as possible.

Moderate utilitarianism: Moderate utilitarianism is a form of act utilitarianism that says to do the thing with the best prospect of generating as much welfare as possible, but supposes the best strategy for doing that is to follow the familiar rules of common sense morality

Requirement utilitarianism: The view that we are required to do whatever would produce most utility.

Reasons utilitarianism: The view that whatever would produce most utility is what we have most reason to do.

Utility: (1) AKA **welfare, well-being, happiness:** These terms are used more or less interchangeably in the literature for the thing utilitarians (to which it gives its name) think we should maximize. There is much disagreement and discussion about how we may understand utility, but roughly, we might think of it as what a person has to the extent that that person's life goes well *for them*. (2) 'Utility' is sometimes used more narrowly as a technical term, widely used in economics, for, roughly speaking, desire-satisfaction where that is defined mathematically in terms of a ranking of states of the world with respect to the extent to which they satisfy a given person's preferences. Such a ranking can get mathematical expression in something called a **utility function**, provided that a person's preferences among alternatives satisfy certain formal properties.

Utility function: *See* utility.

Utility monster: A fanciful creature with a vast capacity for utility. Utilitarianism might be thought, alarmingly, to demand we incur astronomical costs to keep such a monster at its massively high potential utility.

Utopian extinction: An imaginary scenario where human beings someday choose to become extinct after many years of tremendous flourishing.

Veil of ignorance: Some people have thought we could model fair or otherwise morally desirable ways to distribute some good between people or types of people by thinking about what distribution rational agents would choose who did not know which persons, or which types of person, they themselves were. Thought experiments in which rational agents are imagined somehow stripped of this information are said to involve a veil of ignorance.

Welfare: *See* utility.

Welfarism: The monistic view that goodness is simply welfare or well-being.

Well-being: *See* utility.

Wide reflective equilibrium: *See* reflective equilibrium.

孝 (xiào): Filial respect: a core virtue in Chinese Confucian ethics.

Further Reading

Every student of moral philosophy should aim to read the great classics of utilitarianism, Bentham's *An Introduction to the Principles of Morals and Legislation* (1970), Mill's *Utilitarianism* (1998), and Sidgwick's *Methods of Ethics* (1981). Half a century ago R. M. Hare was a massively influential advocate of utilitarianism whose work is now very undeservedly somewhat forgotten. See especially his 1981. A rightly famous earlier debate book on the subject is Smart and Williams 1973.

Many of the central issues here are discussed in Kagan's brilliant 1991 and his magisterial 1997. The most celebrated contemporary utilitarian is Peter Singer who has written many very accessible books. His 2011 is perhaps the best way into his thinking. More recently the two books he has written with Katarzyna de Lazari-Radek - Lazari-Radek and Singer 2014 and 2017 – are clear and instructive. Excellent introductory works on utilitarianism are Crisp 1997 and Bykvist 2010. An excellent book on rule consequentialism is Hooker 2000. For two hugely important discussions of utilitarianism in more wide-ranging books, see Rawls 1999, sections 5 and 27–30 and Nozick 1974, chapter 3.

The vast literature concerning itself with runaway trolleys, bridges and transplants all begins with Thomson 1976. On acts and omissions, see Bennett 1995, Woollard 2013, Kagan 1991, esp. chapter 3. On demandingness, see Kagan 1991 especially chapter 7, Sobel 2007. For impartiality, alienation and integrity see Williams 1976, Williams in Smart and Williams 1973, Scheffler 1982, Railton 1984, Crisp 1997, chapter 6, Hurley 2010. On justice see Hare 1981, chapter 9, Crisp 1997, chapter 7, Rawls 1999, Hooker 2014.

Goodness: for Ross, see Ross 2002. Thomson's view of the good is developed across many writings, notably Thomson's bit of Harman and Thomson 1995, Thomson 1997, Thomson 2001, Thomson 2003, Thomson 2009. See also Foot 1983. Moore 2003 casts a very long shadow here. Scanlon 1998, chapter 2 has been influential. Anderson 1993 is a wonderful discussion of value. Also wonderful are the essays in Part 1 of Wolf 2014. Kraut 2011 is excellent.

Welfare: Griffin 1986 transformed discussion of this topic and is still the go-to book. For excellent introductions see Fletcher 2016 and Heathwood 2021. Lenman's discussion here owes much to Tiberius 2018. For a rich and important discussion see Scanlon 1998, Chapter 3. See also Bramble 2013 and Bramble 2016. Utility theory is the subject of a large, often very technical, literature in which the work of Amartya Sen and John Broome stands out for the pains these writers go to make their work accessible (and in other ways). See especially Sen 1970, Broome 2004. On the history of attempts to quantify and measure utility, Narens and Skyrms 2020 is clear and wonderfully learned.

On Nature: Mill 1904 is less well known than some of his other essays but remains a classic. For the original attempted reductio argument about wild animals see Williams, "The Human Prejudice" in Williams 2008 and Hills 2010. For the outsmarter literature see, e.g., Johannsen 2020, Bramble 2021b. Palmer 2022 is an excellent critical discussion of Johanssen. For the advocacy of human replacement, see Shiller 2017. A very nice critique of the bleak picture of wild animal happiness often aired here is Browning and Veit 2023. Hill 1983 is a wonderful essay. See also Nussbaum 2006, chapter 6, Palmer 2010, chapter 4, Donaldson and Kymlicka, 2011, chapter 6. On the "Promethean Ideal", see McPherson 2022, chapter 1.

On population, see Narveson 1967, 1973, Parfit 1984, part 4. Broome 2004 has an excellent, characteristically clear discussion of the central issues. Finneron-Burns 2024 is wide-ranging and excellent.

On intuitions, Hare 1971 is a lively classic discussion. Lazari-Radek and Singer 2014 is a very influential recent discussion. Sandberg and Juth 2011 discusses an earlier airing of Singer's views. Williams 1985, chapter 6 is a brilliant treatment of moral epistemology. So are Hare 1981 part 1 and Gibbard 1990, part 3. Lenman 2024, especially chapter 7 has much to say that is relevant. On reflective equilibrium see Rawls 1999, sections 9 and 87. See further Scanlon 2003.

Cluelessness

See Lenman 2000, Boyd 2003, Mason 2004, Lang 2008, Hare 2011, Dorsey 2012, Burch-Brown 2014, MacAskill and Mogensen 2021.

Climate Change

Excellent philosophical discussions of the problem of climate change are Gardiner 2011, Broome 2012.

Extinction

Human Extinction is discussed in e.g. Lenman 2002, Benatar 2006, chapter 6, Scheffler 2013. Finneron-Burns 2017, Ord 2020.

Non-identity

Kavka 1981, Parfit 1984, chapter 16, Kumar 2003, Gardner 2015, Finneron-Burns 2016, Bramble 2021a.

References

The Analects (Lúnyǔ 论语)
The Bible

* * *

Sara Algoe and Jonathan Haidt, "Witnessing Excellence in Action: The 'Other-Praising' Emotions of Elevation, Gratitude, and Admiration," *Journal of Positive Psychology*, 4 (2003): 105–127.
Elizabeth Anderson: *Value in Ethics and Economics* (Harvard University Press, 1993).
G. E. M. Anscombe: *Metaphysics and Philosophy of Mind* (University of Minnesota Press, 1981).
Aristotle: *Nicomachean Ethics*.
Nomy Arpaly: "It Ain't Necessarily So" in *Oxford Studies in Metaethics* 13 2018, 145–160.
Nomy Arpaly: Interview with Richard Marshall at https://www.3-16am.co.uk/articles/in-praise-of-desire-and-some, 2023
John Austin (1954). *The Province of Jurisprudence Determined and the Uses of the Study of Jurisprudence*. (Weidenfeld & Nicolson). Edited by John Austin.
Kurt Baier: *The Moral Point of View* (Cornell University Press, 1958).
Sigal G. Barsade, "The Ripple Effect: Emotional Contagion and Its Influence on Group Behavior", *Administrative Science Quarterly* 47 (2002): 644–675.
Nick Beckstead, Peter Singer, and Matt Wage, "Preventing Human Extinction", *Effective Altruism Forum* (2013), accessible here: https://forum.effectivealtruism.org/posts/tXoE6wrEQv7GoDivb/preventing-human-extinction.
Duncan Bell: *Reordering the World: Essays on Liberalism and Empire* (Princeton University Press, 2016).

David Benatar: *Better Never to Have Been: The Harm of Coming into Existence* (Oxford University Press, 2006).
Jonathan Bennett, "On Maximizing Happiness" R. I. Sikora and B. Barry (eds): *Obligations to Future Generations* (Temple University Press, 1978), 66.
Jonathan Bennett: *The Act Itself* (Oxford University Press, 1995).
Jeremy Bentham: *An Introduction to the Principles of Morals and Legislation*, J. H. Burns and H. L. A. Hart (eds.) (Oxford University Press, 1970) First published 1789).
Nick Bostrom: "The Future of Humanity" Jan-Kyrre Berg Olsen, Evan Selinger, & Soren Riis (eds): *New Waves in Philosophy of Technology* (Palgrave McMillan, 2009). Also here: https://nickbostrom.com/papers/future.pdf.
Nick Bostrom: *Superintelligence: Paths, Dangers, Strategies* (Oxford University Press, 2014).
Richard Boyd: "Finite Beings, Finite Goods: The Semantics, Metaphysics and Ethics of Naturalist Consequentialism, Part I," *Philosophy and Phenomenological Research*, 66 (2003): 505–553.
Ben Bramble. "The Distinctive Feeling Theory of Pleasure". *Philosophical Studies* 162 (2) (2013): 201–217.
Ben Bramble. "A New Defense of Hedonism about Well-Being". *Ergo: An Open Access Journal of Philosophy* 3 (2016): 85–112.
Ben Bramble: "The Defective Character Solution to the Non-Identity Problem" *Journal of Philosophy* 118 (2021a): 504–520.
Ben Bramble: "Painlessly Killing Predators" *Journal of Applied Philosophy*, 38 (2021b): 217–225.
R. B. Brandt: *A Theory of the Good and the Right* (Oxford University Press, 1979).
Skott Brill, "Does It Matter that Nothing We Do Will Matter in a Million Years?' *Dialogue*, 46(19) (2007), 3–25.
John Broome: *Ethics out of Economics* (Cambridge University Press, 1999).
John Broome: *Weighing Lives* (Oxford University Press, 2004).
John Broome: *Climate Matters: Ethics in a Warming World* (Norton 2012)
Heather Browning and Walter Veit: "Positive Wild Animal Welfare," *Biology and Philosophy*, 38 (2023), 1–19.
Joanna M. Burch-Brown: "Clues for Consequentialists," *Utilitas*, 26 (2014), 105–119.
Edmund Burke; *Reflections on the Revolution in France* (Penguin, 1982) First published 1790.
David Chalmers. *Reality+: Virtual Worlds and the Problems of Philosophy* (W. W. Norton, 2022).
Joseph Chancellor, Seth Margolis, Katherine Jacobs Bao, and Sonja Lyubomirsky, "Everyday Prosociality in the Workplace: The Reinforcing Benefits of Giving, Getting, and Glimpsing," *Emotion*, 18(4) (2018): 507–517.

Milan M. Ćirković: "Who's Really Afraid of AI?: Anthropocentric Bias and Postbiological Evolution" in *Belgrade Philosophical Annual*, 35 (2022), 17–29.
G. A. Cohen: *Finding Oneself in the Other* (Princeton University Press, 2013).
Tyler Cowen: "Policing Nature," *Environmental Ethics*, 25 (2003): 169–182.
Tyler Cowen: "The Epistemic Problem Does Not Refute Consequentialism," *Utilitas*, 18(04) (2006): 383–399.
Roger Crisp: *Mill on Utilitarianism* (Routledge, 1997).
Stephen Darwall: *Value and Rational Care* (Princeton University Press, 2002).
Charles Darwin: *The Descent of Man and Selection in Relation to Sex*, John Murray, 1871. Published Project Gutenberg https://www.gutenberg.org/ebooks/2300, 2000.
Daniel C. Dennett: The Philosophical Lexicon, first published 1987, at http://hdl.handle.net/10427/56709.
Charles Dickens: *David Copperfield*, many editions (first published 1850) Bradbury and Evans.
Sue Donaldson and Will Kymlicka: *Zoopolis: A Political Theory of Animal Rights* (Oxford Univerity Press, 2011).
Dale Dorsey: "Consequentialism, Metaphysical Realism and the Argument from Cluelessness," *Philosophical Quarterly*, 62 (2012): 48–70.
Julia Driver: *Uneasy Virtue* (Cambridge University Press, 2001).
Elizabeth Finneron-Burns:, "Contractualism and the Non-identity Problem," *Ethical Theory and Moral Practice*, 19, 2016, 1151–1163.
Elizabeth Finneron-Burns: "What's Wrong with Human Extinction?" *Canadian Journal of Philosophy*, 47 (2017): 327–343.
Elizabeth Finneron-Burns: *What We Owe to Future People: A Contractualist Account of Intergenerational Ethics* (Oxford University Press, 2024).
Jerry Fodor: *Psychosemantics* (MIT Press, 1989).
Philippa Foot: "Utilitarianism and the Virtues" in *Proceedings and Addresses of the American Philosophical Association* 57, 1983, pp. 273–283.
Philippa Foot: *Virtues and Vices and Other Essays in Moral Philosophy* (Oxford University Press, 2002).
James Fowler & Nicholas Christakis, "Cooperative Behavior Cascades in Human Social Networks", *Proceedings of the National Academy of Sciences of the United States of America*, 107(12) (2010): 5334–5338.
Harry Frankfurt, 1999, "Autonomy, Necessity, and Love" in his *Necessity, Volition, and Love*, (Cambridge University Press, 129–141.
Stephen M. Gardiner: *A Perfect Moral Storm: The Ethical Tragedy of Climate Change* (Oxford University Press, 2011).
Molly Gardner: "A Harm-Based Solution to the Non-Identity Problem," *Ergo* 2 (2015): 427–444.

Allan Gibbard: *Wise Choices, Apt Feelings* (Oxford University Press, 1990).

Jonathan Glover, *Causing Death and Saving Lives* (Penguin, 1977).

Joshua Greene: *Moral Tribes; Emotion, Reason and the Gap Between Us and Them* (Penguin, 2013).

Amy Gutmann and Dennis Thompson. *Democracy and Disagreement* (Harvard University Press, 1996).

Jonathan Haidt, "The Moral Emotions" R.J. Davidson, K.R. Scherer, & H.H. Goldsmith (eds.): *Handbook of Affective Sciences* (Oxford University Press): 852–870.

Jonathan Haidt, "Elevation and the Positive Psychology of Morality" C.L.M. Keyes & J. Haidt (eds): *Flourishing: Positive Psychology and the Life Well-Lived* (American Psychological Association, 2003).

Sven Ove Hansson: "Philosophical Problems in Cost-Benefit Analysis," *Economics and Philosophy*, 23 (2007): 163–183.

Caspar Hare: "Obligation and Regret When There is No Fact of the Matter About What Would Have Happened if You Had not Done What You Did," *Noûs*, 45 (2011): 190–206.

R. M. Hare: 'The Argument from Received Opinion', in his *Essays on Philosophical Method* (Macmillan, 1971), 117–135.

R. M. Hare: *Moral Thinking: Its Levels, Method and Point* (Oxford University Press, 1981).

Gilbert Harman and Judith Jarvis Thomson: *Morality and Objectivity* (Blackwell, 1996).

J.C. Harsanyi: "Cardinal Welfare, Individualistic Ethics, and Interpersonal Comparisons of Utility," *Journal of Political Economy*, 63 (1955), 309–321.

Chris Heathwood: "Preferentism and Self-Sacrifice," *Pacific Philosophical Quarterly*, 92 (2011): 18–38.

Thomas E. Hill Jr. "Ideals of Human Excellence and Preserving Natural Environments," *Environmental Ethics*, 5 (1983): 211–224.

Alison Hills, "Utilitarianism, Contractualism, and Demandingness," *Philosophical Quarterly*, 60 (2010): 225–242.

Brad Hooker: *Ideal Code, Real World: A Rule-Consequentialist Theory of Morality* (Oxford University Press, 2002).

Brad Hooker: "Utilitarianism and Fairness" Ben Eggleston and Dale Miller (eds): *The Cambridge Companion to Utilitarianism* (Cambridge University Press, 2014).

David Hume: *A Treatise of Human Nature*, many editions.

David Hume: *Dialogues Concerning Natural Religion*, many editions.

Paul Hurley, *Beyond Consequentialism* (Oxford University Press, 2010).

Susan Hurley: *Natural Reasons: Personality and Polity* (Oxford University Press, 1989).

Rosalind Hursthouse: *On Virtue Ethics* (Oxford University Press, 1999).

The Intergovernmental Panel on Climate Change *Climate Change 2022: Mitigation of Climate Change* 2022, https://www.ipcc.ch/report/ar6/wg3/.

IPBES (2019): "Global Assessment Report On Biodiversity and Ecosystem Services of the Intergovernmental Science-Policy Platform on Biodiversity and Ecosystem Services" E. S. Brondizio, J. Settele, S. Díaz, and H. T. Ngo (eds): *IPBES Secretariat*, 1148 pages. https://doi.org/10.5281/zenodo.3831673.

Frank Jackson: "Decision-Theoretic Consequentialism and the Nearest and Dearest Objection," *Ethics*, 101 (1991), 461–482.

Kyle Johannsen: *Wild Animal Ethics* (Routledge, 2020).

Gregory Kavka, "The Paradox of Future Individuals," *Philosophy & Public Affairs*, 11 (1981): 93–112.

Shelly Kagan: *The Limits of Morality* (Oxford University Press, 1991).

Shelly Kagan: *Normative Ethics* (Taylor and Francis 1997).

Toshika Kaneda and Karl Haub: "How Many People Have Ever Lived?" https://www.prb.org/articles/how-many-people-have-ever-lived-on-earth/, 2022.

Dacher Keltner & Jonathan Haidt, "Approaching Awe: A Moral, Spiritual, and Aesthetic Emotion," *Cognition & Emotion*, 17 (2003): 297–314.

Andrew, H. Knoll: *Life on a Young Planet: The First Three Billion Years of Evolution on Earth* (Princeton University Press, 2003).

Richard Kraut: *Against Absolute Goodness* (Oxford University Press, 2011).

Karin Kuhlemann: "Complexity, Creeping Normalcy and Conceit: Sexy and Unsexy Catastrophic Risks," *Foresight – The Journal of Future Studies, Strategic Thinking and Policy*, 21 (2019): 35–52.

Rahul Kumar: "Who Can Be Wronged?" *Philosophy and Public Affairs*, 31 (2003): 98–118.

Katarzyna de Lazari-Radek and Peter Singer: *The Point of View of the Universe: Sidgwick and Contemporary Ethics* (Oxford University Press, 2014).

Katarzyna de Lazari-Radek and Peter Singer: *Utilitarianism: A very Short Introduction* (Oxford University Press, 2017).

Gerald Lang: "Consequentialism, Cluelessness and Indifference," *Journal of Value Inquiry*, 42 (2008): 477–485.

James Lenman: "Consequentialism and Cluelessness," *Philosophy and Public Affairs*, 29 (2000): 342–370.

James Lenman: "On Becoming Extinct," *Pacific Philosophical Quarterly*, 83 (2002): 253–269.

James Lenman: "Contractualism and Risk-Imposition," *Politics, Philosophy and Economics*, 7 (2008): 99–122.

James Lenman: "Thomson on Goodness," *Metafísica y Persona*, 19 (2018), 181–188.

James Lenman: "How Effective Altruism Lost the Plot," *IAI News*, 1st November 2022. https://iai.tv/articles/how-effective-altruism-lost-the-plot-auid-2284

James Lenman: *The Possibility of Moral Community* (Oxford University Press, 2024).

C. S. Lewis: *That Hideous Strength: A Modern Fairy Tale for Grown-Ups.* (Scribner, 1996, first published 1943).

David Lewis: *Counterfactuals* (Harvard University Press, 1973).

William MacAskill: *Doing Good Better: Effective Altruism and How You Can Make a Difference* (Random House, 2015).

William MacAskill: "The Definition of Effective Altruism", Hilary Greaves, and Theron Pummer (eds): *Effective Altruism: Philosophical Issues, Engaging Philosophy* (Oxford University Press, 2019), 10–28.

William MacAskill and Andreas Mogensen "The Paralysis Argument," *Philosophers' Imprint*, 21 (2021): 1–17.

William MacAskill, *What We Owe the Future* (Basic Books, 2022).

H. J. McCloskey, "An Examination of Restricted Utilitarianism," *Philosophical Review*, 66 (1957): 466–485.

Brian McElwee. "The Rights and Wrongs of Consequentialism." *Philosophical Studies: An International Journal for Philosophy in the Analytic Tradition*, 151(3) (2010): 393–412.

J. L. Mackie: *Persons and Values: Selected Papers, Volume II* (Oxford University Press, 1985).

Jeff McMahan: "The Moral Problem of Predation," Chignell et al. *Philosophy Comes to Dinner* (2015): 268–293.

Jeff McMahan, "Causing People to Exist and Saving People's Lives", *Journal of Ethics*, 26 (2013): 5–35.

David McPherson: *The Virtues of Limits* (Oxford University Press, 2022).

Elinor Mason: "Consequentialism and the Principle of Indifference," *Utilitas*, 16 (2004): 16–21.

John Stuart Mill: *Three Essays* (Oxford University Press, 1975).

John Stuart Mill: *On Nature* (The Rationalist Press, 1904), first published 1874. and available here: https://www.lancaster.ac.uk/users/philosophy/texts/mill_on.htm

John Stuart Mill: *Utilitarianism*. Ed. Roger Crisp (Oxford University Press, 1998) First published 1861.

G. E. Moore: *Principia Ethica* (Cambridge University Press, 1903).

Louis Narens and Brian Skyrms: *The Pursuit of Happiness: Philosophical and Psychological Foundations of Utility* (Oxford University Press, 2020).

Jan Narveson (1973). "Moral problems of population," *The Monist*, 57, 62–86.

Jan Narveson. "Utilitarianism and New Generations," *Mind*, 76(301) 1967: 62–72.

Jill North: "An Empirical Approach to Symmetry and Probability," *Studies in History and Philosophy of Science Part B: Studies in History and Philosophy of Modern Physics*, 41 (2010): 27–40.

Robert Nozick: *Anarchy, State, and Utopia* (Basic Books, 1974).

Robert Nozick: *Examined Life: Philosophical Meditations*. (Simon & Schuster, 1990).

Martha Nussbaum: *Frontiers of Justice* (Harvard University Press, 2006).

Amy Olberding: *Moral Exemplars in the Analects: The Good Person is That* (Routledge, 2012).

Amy Olberding: *The Wrong of Rudeness: Learning Modern Civility from Ancient Chinese Philosophy* (Oxford University Press, 2019).

Toby Ord, *The Precipice* (Bloomsbury, 2020).

Thomas Paine: *Common Sense* (Robert Bell, 1776).

Clare Palmer: *Animal Ethics in Context* (Columbia University Press, 2010).

Clare Palmer: "The Value of Wild Nature: Comments on Kyle Johannsen's *Wild Animal Ethics*," *Philosophia*, 50 (2022).

Derek Parfit: *Reasons and Persons* (Oxford University Press 1984).

Philip Pettit: "The Inescapability of Consequentialism" Ulrike Heuer & Gerald R. Lang (eds): *Luck, Value, and Commitment: Themes from the Ethics of Bernard Williams* (Oxford University Press USA, 2012.

Plato: *Gorgias*.

Plato: *Meno*.

Plato: *Republic*.

Plato: *Theaetetus*.

Douglas W. Portmore: "Consequentializing" in *Philosophical Compass*, 4 (2009): 329–347.

Peter Railton, "Alienation, Consequentialism, and the Demands of Morality," *Philosophy & Public Affairs*, 13(2) (1984): 134–171.

Susan Ratcliffe (ed.): *Oxford Essential Quotations*, Online version (Oxford University Press, 2016) "Zhou Enlai".

John Rawls: *A Theory of Justice* (Harvard UP, 1971).

W. D. Ross: *The Right and the Good* (OUP, 2002) (originally published 1930).

Mark Sagoff: *The Economy of the Earth* (Cambridge University Press, 1988).

T. M. Scanlon: *What We Owe to Each Other* (Harvard University Press): 1998).

T. M. Scanlon: "Rawls on Justification in Samuel Freeman" Samuel Freeman (eds): *The Cambridge Companion to Rawls* (Cambridge University Press, 2003), 139–167.

Samuel Scheffler: *The Rejection of Consequentialism* (Oxford University Press, 1982).

Samuel Scheffler: *Death and the Afterlife* (Oxford University Press, 2013).

Simone Schnall, Jean Roper, and Daniel M.T. Fessler, "Elevation Leads to Altruistic Behavior," *Psychological Science* 21(3) (2010): 315–320.

A. K. Sen: *Collective Choice and Social Welfare* (Holden Day, 1970).
A. K. Sen and Bernard Williams: "Introduction: Utilitarianism and Beyond" in their edited volume, *Utilitarianism and Beyond* (Cambridge University Press/Editions de la Maison des Sciences de l'Homme, 1982), 1–21.
Nicholas Shakel: "Bertrand's Paradox and the Principle of Indifference," *Philosophy of Science*, 74 (2007): 150–175.
George Bernard Shaw: Maxims for Revolutionists https://www.gutenberg.org/cache/epub/26107/pg26107-images.html
Derek Shiller: "In Defense of Artificial Replacement," *Bioethics*, 31 (2017): 393–399.
Henry Sidgwick: *The Methods of Ethics* (Hackett, 1981) (originally published 1874).
Peter Singer: *Practical Ethics* (3rd ed.) (Cambridge University Press, 2011).
Peter Singer: *The Most Good You Can Do* (Yale, 2015).
Edward Sligerland (translation and commentary): *Confucian Analects with Selections from Traditional Commentarie*s (Hackett, 2003).
Jack Smart: "An Ourtline of a System of Utilitarian Ethics in Bernard Williams. A Critique of Utilitarianism" J. J. C. Smart and Williams Bernard (eds): *Utilitarianism For and Against* (Cambridge University Press, 1973), 1–74.
Jack Smart and Bernard Williams: *Utilitarianism: For and Against* (Cambridge University Press, 1973).
David Sobel: "The Impotence of the Demandingness Objection," *Philosophers' Imprint*, 7 (2007): 1–17.
Robert Stalnaker: *Inquiry* (MIT Press, 1987).
C. L. Stevenson: *Ethics and Language* (Yale University Press, 1944).
Michael Stocker. "The Schizophrenia of Modern Ethical Theories," *The Journal of Philosophy*, 73(14) (1976): 453–466.
Michael Stocker: "How Emotions Reveal Value and Help Cure the Schizophrenia of Modern" Roger Crisp (ed): *How should One Live: Essays on the Virtues* (Oxford University Press, 1998), 173–190.
Sharon Street: "A Darwinian Dilemma for Realist Theories of Value," *Philosophia Studies*, 127 (2006), 109–166.
Eileen P. Sullivan: "Liberalism and Imperialism: J. S. Mill's Defense of the British Empire," *Journal of the History of Ideas*, 44 (1983): 599–617.
Charles Taylor: *Sources of the Self: The Making of the Modern Identity* (Cambridge University Press, 1989).
Larry Temkin, *Rethinking the Good* (Oxford University, 2012).
Judith Jarvis Thomson: "Killing, Letting Die, and the Trolley Problem," *The Monist*, 59 (1976): 204–217.
Judith Jarvis Thomson: "The Right and the Good", *Journal of Philosophy*, 94 (1997) 273–298.
Thomson, Judith Jarvis, *Goodness and Advice* (Princeton University Press, 2003).

Judith Jarvis Thomson: *Normativity* (Open Court, 2008).
Valerie Tiberius: *The Reflective Life Living Wisely Within Our Limits* (Oxford University Press, 2008).
Valerie Tiberius: *Well-Being as Value Fulfillment: How We Can Help Each Other to Live Well* (Oxford University Press, 2018).
Brian Tomasik: "Habitat Loss, Not Preservation, Generally Reduces Wild-Animal Suffering" at https://reducing-suffering.org/habitat-loss-not-preservation-generally-reduces-wild-animal-suffering/, 2017.
David Velleman: "Love as a Moral Emotion", *Ethics*, 109 (1999): 338–374.
Tatjana Višak: "Do Utilitarians Need to Accept the Replaceability Argument?" Tatjana Višak, and Robert Garner (eds): *The Ethics of Killing Animals* (online edn, Oxford University Press, 22 Oct. 2015).
Michael Walzer: *Interpretation and Social Criticism* (Harvard University Press, 1993).
Bernard Williams: *Morality: An Introduction to Ethics* (Cambridge University Press 1976a) (first published 1972).
Bernard Williams. "A Critique of Utilitarianism" J. J. C. Smart and Bernard Williams (eds): *Utilitarianism for and Against*. (Cambridge University Press, 1973), 77–150.
Bernard Williams (1976b). "Persons, Character, and Morality." in Williams *Moral Luck* (Cambridge University Press, 1981), 1–19.
Bernard Williams: *Ethics and the Limits of Philosophy* (Fontana, 1985).
Bernard Williams: *Philosophy as a Humanistic Discipline* (Princeton University Press, 2006).
Susan Wolf: "Good-for-nothings," *Proceedings and Addresses of the American Philosophical Association*, 85(2) (2010): 47–64.
Susan Wolf: "Moral Saints," *The Journal of Philosophy*, 79(8) (1982): 419–439.
Susan Wolf, *The Variety of Values: Essays on Morality, Meaning, and Love* (2015; Oxford University Press).
Fiona Woollard: "If This Is My Body …: A Defence of the Doctrine of Doing and Allowing," *Pacific Philosophical Quarterly*, 94 (2013): 315–341.
WWF: (2022) *Living Planet Report 2022 – Building a nature- positive society*. Almond, R.E.A., Grooten, M., Juffe Bignoli, D. & Petersen, T. (Eds). (WWF).
Linda Zagzebski: *Exemplarist Moral Theory* (Oxford University Press 2017).

Index

Alienation 12, 146–154, 176–178
Animals 38–44, 186, 192–193
Anscombe, G. E. M. 24, 36
Aristotle 29, 31
Austin, John 148, 152–153, 174–175

Beckstead, Nick 107
Bennett, Jonathan 109–110
Bentham, Jeremy 28, 105
Boyd, Richard 62–63
Brandt, Richard 53
Bridge/Footbridge case 10, 52, 57, 60–64, 157–158, 167
Brill, Skott 132
Burch-Brown, Joanna 69–72
Burke, Edmund 54, 56

Chancellor, Joseph 131
Christakis, Nicholas 103–131
Circumstances of Virtue 26
Climate change 74–82
Cluelessness 60–93, 127–133, 136, 157, 164–167
Cohen, Jerry 44
Confucius 164, 172, 175
Consequentialism: relation to utilitarianism 5–6; *see also* utilitarianism
Cowen, Tyler 128

Darwall, Stephen 31
Darwin, Charles 55
David Copperfield (Dickens) 174
Debunking 56–58, 185–186; *see also* evolution

Demandingness 10–11, 138–145, 153–154
Dennett, Daniel 51
Desire-satisfaction 33–35
Driver, Julia 24

Effective altruism 105, 138, 143–144
Emotivism 19–20, 23
Evolution 40, 57–58, 66, 77, 184–185, 187–188, 193; *see also* debunking
Experience Machine 33, 120–124
Extinction 44, 89–90, 105–110, 120; *see also* longtermism

Fowler, James 130–131
Frege, Gottlob 29
Friendship 114, 116, 122–123, 152; *see also* love

Glover, Jonathan 106
Golden Rule 35
Goodness 16–26, 99
Great Oxygenation Event 74–82

Haidt, Jonathan 131
Hare, R. M 34–35, 53–54, 56
Harming to Help Objection 9–10, 156–158
Harsanyi, John 43
Hill Jr., Thomas 43, 119–120
Hills, Alison 39
Hume, David 35, 75–76
Humean Cost-Benefit Analysis 75–76, 79–80

Index

Humility 43, 60–63, 91, 120

Identity-Affecting actions 65–66, 127–130, 166–167
Integrity Objection 12–15, 153–154
Intuitions 51–59, 187–189
It's A Wonderful Life 131–133, 144, 146

Kagan, Shelly 11, 129
Kant, Immanuel 158
Kindness 131–133, 140
Kuhlemann, Karin 45

Lazari-Radek, Katarzyna 56–58, 185–187
Les Miserables (Hugo) 131
Lewis, C. S. 38
Lewis, David 77
Longtermism 45, 81, 100; *see also* extinction
Love 144, 146, 150, 152–153, 169–176; *see also* friendship

MacAskill, William 41–42, 46–50, 81, 84–89, 107
Mackie, J. L. 60–62
McMahan, Jeff 107
McPherson, David 43–44
Meno's Paradox 29–31
Mere Addition Paradox 47
Mill, John Stuart 28, 40–41, 62, 105, 112, 114
Mogenson, Andreas 84–89
Monism versus pluralism 17
Moore, G. E. 5, 18

Narveson, Jan 109–110
Nature 38–44, 117–120, 192–193
Non-identity problem 164–167
Nozick, Robert 8, 120

Ord, Toby 107

Paine, Thomas 56
Palmer, Clare 43
Paralysis Problem 84–94
Parfit, Derek 7–8, 46–48, 92, 104, 106

Pettit, Philip 147–148, 152–153, 178
Philosophy of swine 112–124
Plato 29, 31
Pleasure: higher versus lower 114; nature of 33, 113–117
Probst, Christoph 52–53

Railton, Peter 147, 178
Rawls, John 8–9, 52–53, 56
Reflective equilibrium 53–58, 193
Repugnant Conclusion 7, 44–50, 104
Robust realism 18–20, 58, 185–186
Ross, W. D. 17–19, 24, 26, 28, 32, 58

Sad versus bad 108–110, 124
Scholl, Sophie 52–53, 55
Scholl, Hans 52–53
Self interest 31–32, 139, 141, 145, 152
Separateness of persons 8–9
Shaw, George Bernard 35
Sheriff Case 10, 167
Sidgwick, Henry 20, 57, 147
Singer, Peter 56–58, 107, 185–187
Smart, J. J. C. 19, 51
Stalnaker, Robert 77–78
Standby consequentialism 148, 153, 172
Stocker, Michael 148–149, 178

Temkin, Larry 106–109
Terrestrial Ethics 25, 58
Thomson, Judith Jarvis 10, 20–24, 31
Tiberius, Valerie 31–32, 35–36
Transhumanism 38–44
Transplant case 10, 60, 158, 167
Trolley cases 10, 64, 157
Two Wars 106

Universalizablity 34–35
Utilitarianism: motivation for 104–105; objective versus subjective utilitarianism 67–72, 138–154; reasons versus requirement utilitarianism 100,

135–136, 138; rule versus act utilitarianism 13, 61; total versus average utilitarianism 8, 44–50; total versus person-affecting utilitarianism 100–101, 103–104, 110, 129–130, 133, 159, 164–168
Utility Monster 8
Utility: as a technical term 33; *see also* Wellbeing
Utopian Extinction 107

Veil of Ignorance 34

Velleman, David 150–151
Virtue 16, 24–26, 91–93, 113, 132, 137
Višak, Tatjana 104

Wage, Matt 107
Welfare *see* Wellbeing
Well-being: nature of 6, 28–37, 113–124, 189–192
Williams, Bernard 12, 14, 39, 54, 146, 153–154, 173
Wolf, Susan 113, 117, 139, 142
Wollstonecraft, Mary 56

Printed in the United States
by Baker & Taylor Publisher Services